11th edition

A Legal Guide for
Lesbian and Gay Couples

**by Attorneys Hayden Curry, Denis Clifford
and Frederick Hertz**

Keeping Up-to-Date

To keep its books up-to-date, Nolo issues new printings and new editions periodically. New printings reflect minor legal changes and technical corrections. New editions contain major legal changes, major text additions or major reorganizations. To find out if a later printing or edition of any Nolo book is available, call Nolo at 510-549-1976 or check our website at http://www.nolo.com.

To stay current, follow the "Update" service at our website at http://www.nolo.com/lawstore/update/list.cfm. In another effort to help you use Nolo's latest materials, we offer a 35% discount off the purchase of the new edition of your Nolo book when you turn in the cover of an earlier edition. (See the "Special Upgrade Offer" in the back of the book.) This book was last revised in: **March 2002**

Eleventh Edition	MARCH 2002
Editor	BETH MCKENNA
Illustrations	LINDA ALLISON
Cover Design	TONI IHARA
Production	SARAH HINMAN
Book Design	TERRI HEARSH
Proofreading	ROBERT WELLS
Index	THÉRÈSE SHERE
Printing	BERTELSMANN SERVICES, INC.

Curry, Hayden
   A legal guide for lesbian and gay couples / by Hayden Curry, Denis Clifford, and Frederick Hertz. -- 11th ed.
      p. cm.
   Rev. ed. of: A legal guide for lesbian and gay couples / by Hayden Curry ...[et al.].
10th ed. 1999.
   Includes index.
   ISBN 0-87337-790-7
    1. Gay couples--Legal status, laws, etc.--United States. 2. Lesbian couples--Legal status, laws, etc.--United States. 3. Same-sex marriage--Law and legislation--United States. I. Clifford, Denis. II. Hertz, Frederick. III. A legal guide for lesbian and gay couples. IV. Title.

KF539.L44 2002
346.7301'6--dc21
                                            2001051210

Acknowledgments

We thank all those friends, new and old, who worked with us on this book; their assistance has been truly invaluable and working with them was fun. Special thanks to those people who read and critiqued the original manuscript back in 1980: Roberta Achtenberg, Gloria Bosque, Kay Clifford (Mom), Jim Duerr, Patrick Ferruccio, Michael Fuchs, Linda Graham, Pamela Gray, Linda Gryczan, Linda Guthrie, Donna J. Hitchens, Floyd S. Irvin, Keith Kelgman, Phyllis Lyon, Terri Lyons, Mary Morgan, Joseph Nieberding, Zona Sage, Sue Saperstein, Kim Storch and Michael Thistel.

For keeping the book up-to-date in the 1990s and beyond, thanks go to Nolo editors Shae Irving, Barbara Kate Repa and Beth McKenna, Nolo editorial assistant Stan Jacobsen for his cite checking and other research, and Oakland, California, lawyer Rachel Ginsburg, for her help with the parenting information.

Special thanks to Emily Doskow of Oakland, California, and Kate Kendell, Executive Director of the National Center for Lesbian Rights, for their insights and assistance regarding the recent developments involving the children of lesbian and gay parents.

We would also like to thank Stefen Johnson of Lambda Legal Defense and Education Fund, Los Angeles.

Table of Contents

About the Authors

Introduction

1 Creating Family: Marriage, Domestic Partners and More

2 Living Together and the Real World

3 I'm Mom, She's Mommy (Or I'm Dad, He's Papa)

4 Medical and Financial Matters: Delegating Authority

5 Looking Ahead: Estate Planning

6 Living Together Contracts for Lesbian and Gay Couples

About the Authors

(A little bit of history)

First Edition

A Legal Guide for Lesbian and Gay Couples was first published in 1980. At that time, Hayden Curry and Denis Clifford were partners in the Oakland, California, law firm of Clifford, Curry and Cherrin. They had met in 1967, in a special training program for recent law school graduates going into poverty law, and later worked together for several years in a neighborhood legal services office in East Oakland.

They proudly introduced themselves in the first edition of the book with the following personal statement:

> *"We've been close personal friends for almost two decades. Hayden is gay and has lived with his lover for many years. Denis is straight. We mention this because people are curious and we want to get it out and out of the way. For those of you who are interested, we speak a little more about who we are—and our friendship—in the About the Authors section at the beginning of this book.*
>
> *"Because this book is designed for lesbians as well as gay men, we felt a special responsibility to seek out the advice, experience and resources of the lesbian community, especially the lesbian legal community. We didn't want to presume knowledge of their experiences. Obviously, there are many similar experiences in being a lesbian and being a gay man (calling a lesbian a 'Dyke' and calling a gay man a 'Faggot' hurt in much the same way). The law, too, treats the two com-*

> *munities as one. But aside from the anatomical, there are many differences between lesbians and gay men. One major difference is economic. As Phyllis Lyon, a lesbian activist in San Francisco, pointed out to us, gay men, on the average, make considerably more money than lesbians, who, as women, make between 65 and 70 cents (nationwide) for every $1.00 men make. Where appropriate, we discuss other important differences in the text. We want to thank the many lesbian women who helped us to assemble these materials. They provided information and encouragement, assisted with defining issues and problems, and helped scrutinize the manuscript from its initial draft to the finished product. And beyond all that, we made new friends."*

In the About the Author section they referred to in their personal statement, Hayden and Denis described how they came to write this book:

> *"We feel this book has evolved from our earlier work with the civil rights movement and poverty law. One of the strongest conclusions we drew from our years of bringing 'test cases' for the rights of poor people was that the established (or establishment) legal system was cumbersome, and generally unsympathetic to minorities. We came to believe that preventative law—people creating their own legal arrangements and avoiding courts and lawyers—was both eminently sensible and long overdue.*

"It's ironic, but true, that while laboring in South Florida for the rights of the economically oppressed and racial minorities, Hayden was simultaneously suppressing his own awareness of himself as an oppressed minority—a gay man. It was necessary for him to reach the healthier and more supportive climate in Northern California before he could begin the process of publicly coming to terms with his identity, and be able to work overtly for his own minority group. Denis has been an observer and supporter of Hayden's coming-out process (and he hasn't exactly been standing still the last twenty-some years either).

"After leaving legal services, we set up our private law practice, which has served many lesbian and gay clients. Our belief that litigation and courts should be the last resort for problem-solving was reaffirmed by our clients' experiences; we began helping them devise ways to solve their problems outside traditional (and expensive) legal remedies.

"Writing this book has been a shared experience. We've both learned a lot. We don't believe people are confined to understanding only those who have the same sexual identity as they do. One of the beauties of being free is that people can learn, as we have, that our differences can bring us closer. We hope this book will do that for many lesbian/gay couples, and it was in this spirit of optimism that we worked and wrote together."

Fifth Edition

As Hayden and Denis revised and updated this book for the fifth edition in early 1989, they contemplated the changes in the lesbian and gay community over the previous nine years. In describing themselves, they wrote: "Hayden has a great many more wrinkles than he had nine years ago; he got them the old-fashioned way, he earned them. And Denis has worry lines too. Although, we must say, growing older seems like a rather fine alternative these days."

Hayden, unaware that the AIDS virus lived inside him, wrote about the disease's effect on the lesbian and gay community in the special introduction to the fifth edition.

"The tragedy of AIDS continues. In February, we buried our good friend Dan Bradley. Dan's story is similar to many of ours. When we worked with him in legal services in the late '60s and early '70s we didn't know the torments he was going through discovering his homosexuality. By the late '70s, when the cultural and political climate had become positive, Dan, in true Bradley fashion, burst out of his closet with an announcement in the New York Times— *'High Government Official Announces He Is Gay.' In the early and hopeful '80s, Dan became a national gay rights leader. But his true heroism came after he was diagnosed with AIDS. Rather than retreat into his illness, he used the small energy he had to fight for the rights of people with AIDS and ARC. Now Hayden has made Dan's quilt for the Names Project; Hayden's mother did the needlepointing.*

"We've lost many wonderful friends and many more are ill. The political right has used AIDS to fan hatred and discrimination against us. Much of our time is spent caring for our brothers, and our political energies are sapped by health care and survival issues.

"There's another side to this tragedy. We've matured as a group. We've coalesced as a community. We're vastly proud of the compassion we, men and women, have shown each other, and the organizations we've built.

"We've set up many programs to care for our community. And the lesbian community has shown deep concern, caring and commitment. We've created our own memorial: the Names Project, where the friends of someone who died due to the virus stitch a 3' x 6' quilt for that person. The individual quilts are woven together into a beautiful and powerful expression of love and grief.

"We've proven ourselves a proud, caring and dedicated clan. We're exhausted. We're sad. We'll do what's needed of us."

Sixth Edition

Hayden Curry died on September 30, 1991, from AIDS. Denis Clifford wrote the following memorial to Hayden, which first appeared in the sixth edition of *A Legal Guide for Lesbian and Gay Couples*:

> *"I first met Hayden in 1967, when we were both in a special training program for poverty lawyers. Right away, I was taken with his flair and zest for life. After two years working with migrant workers in rural Florida, Hayden moved to California in 1969. For five years we worked together in a legal services office in East Oakland, California. We were both East Coast refugees—he'd gone to Yale, then University of Virginia law school. We became best friends. After we left legal services, we were law partners for several years. We remained very close until his death.*
>
> *"Hayden and I shared many wonderful adventures. He was a seeker, adventurer, philosopher and bon vivant. He was a good friend of many in the Nolo family, in whose hearts he will always be smiling.*
>
> *"The following is from Hayden's obituary:*
> *'Hayden was a proud participant in gay life in the Bay Area. Living in what he termed the 'supportive climate' of Northern California, he publicly presented himself as gay in the early 1970s. Fully accepting himself, he opened his loving heart and flamboyant spirit to his many, many friends.... Hayden became seriously ill in March of 1991. He bore his afflictions with such grace and courage that he truly transcended his disease, becoming increasingly luminous in spirit until his death.'*
>
> *"His premature death is a tragedy. He will be missed."*

Seventh Edition

With the publication of the seventh edition of *A Legal Guide for Lesbian and Gay Couples* in 1993, Robin Leonard was added as an author. Robin has been an active member of whatever lesbian and gay community she's lived in since the late 1970s. She came to Nolo in 1985 after practicing law in San Francisco, and was the editor of the fifth and sixth editions of this book.

Robin and Denis worked together updating the material to reflect the new direction in which the lesbian and gay community was going. Although AIDS continued to take its tragic toll, the 1990s began the era in which lesbians and gay men got married (even though the law didn't recognize it), registered as domestic partners, challenged traditional limits on the definition of family and continued to have a lot of kids.

Robin and Denis made a commitment to making Hayden's voice and spirit come through in their words. And, beginning with the seventh edition, they dedicated *A Legal Guide for Lesbian and Gay Couples* to Hayden's memory.

Tenth Edition

For the tenth edition, Oakland, California, attorney Frederick Hertz joined the effort.

Fred's practice includes counseling and representing unmarried partners about their legal rights in their relationships, as well as serving as mediator and arbitrator in non-marital dissolutions. Fred co-founded the San Francisco AIDS Legal Referral Panel and is the author of *Legal Affairs: Essential Advice for Same-Sex Couples* (Owl Books). Fred lives in the Bay Area with his partner, and has been active in the lesbian and gay legal community for more than 15 years. Fred was a friend and colleague of Hayden's, which does much to ensure that Hayden's spirit lives on in the book. You can contact Fred through his website, at http://www.samesexlaw.com. ∎

Introduction

This book is designed to help lesbian and gay couples understand the laws that affect them and take charge of the legal aspects of their lives. Much of the material covered can also be very useful for lesbians and gays who aren't in a couple.

Many of the legal consequences of "coupling" are immediately apparent, but many others don't surface until times of stress—misunderstandings, separation or death. Married couples' relationships are closely regulated by each state's family law rules; lesbian and gay couples can't legally marry, so except under Vermont's civil union statute, our relationships are structured under the far looser—and less appropriate—rules of contract law. This discrimination can mean, among other things, higher estate tax rates and insurance payments, the unavailability of marriage discount prices or memberships and significant obstacles in adopting. But it also allows lesbian and gay couples the freedom to create their own legal relationships.

This is an optimistic book. Our purpose is to explain your legal alternatives and show you how to use them to contribute to a harmonious and productive life together. We feel strongly that discussing and planning the financial, practical and legal aspects of a relationship leads to greater understanding and trust. It's possible to use the law in a positive, conflict-avoiding way. Unfortunately, however, there's also a less happy theme to this book—failure to work out your legal relationship with each other can lead to surprising, and dire, consequences. We've heard too many horror stories not to warn you.

This is also a practical book. We supply sample form legal documents such as living together agreements, wills, parenting agreements and the like so you can design and prepare your own documents. We focus on the nitty-gritty of daily life; we spend little time discussing broader political concerns, such as the essential struggle of lesbians and gays to remove prejudice from the laws and culture of America. One of the happiest results of this struggle is that it is now matter-of-fact that many thousands of lesbians and gay men live together as couples in pursuit of life, liberty and happiness.

This doesn't mean that the political work is over—it obviously isn't—but that our focus is on the personal and not the political. Certainly you'll find evidence of our anger toward, and frustration with, a society that has made being lesbian or gay so difficult. The AIDS crisis has led to increased oppression and the increased need for prudence. And the information we provide is especially essential if you haven't told your family, friends or the world about your relationship and sexual orientation.

A. Lesbians, Gay Men and "The Law"

Most lesbian and gay people we know are wary of "the law," even if they're lawyers themselves, and for good reason. For eons, the law has been a force for oppression. The litany of codified homophobia includes sodomy laws, loitering laws, exclusion from the military, prohibitions against child custody—the list goes on and on. In addition, the law has permitted—and in some cases even encouraged—many other types of oppression, such as job and housing discrimination and police entrapment. Obviously, a legal system that makes people criminals because of sexual orientation doesn't engender trust.

In 1986, the U.S. Supreme Court upheld the constitutionality of enforcing Georgia's sodomy statute against gay men (*Bowers v. Hardwick*, 478 U.S. 186 (1986)). But states are free to offer their citizens more protection than is given by the federal constitution, and in fact, the Georgia Supreme Court has since ruled that state's sodomy law illegal under the Georgia constitution. This means that whether or not it's legal for you to have sex with your lover depends on where you live. Sixteen states still have enforceable laws against private, consensual sodomy—sometimes heterosexual and homosexual, sometimes just homosexual. And though states with sodomy laws on the books don't necessarily prosecute people for having sex, those laws can potentially used to negate contracts between sexual partners because the relationship is an "illegal" one.

Below is a summary of state sodomy laws—to find out about any changes, check the website of the National Gay and Lesbian Task Force, at http://www.ngltf.org, or the ACLU's website, at http://www.aclu.org.

State	Status of sodomy law	Maximum sentence
Alabama	Heterosexual and homosexual sodomy illegal, except for married couples	1 year
Alaska	No sodomy law	
Arizona	No sodomy law	
Arkansas	Sodomy law invalidated by lower court (currently on appeal)	
California	No sodomy law	
Colorado	No sodomy law	
Connecticut	No sodomy law	
Delaware	No sodomy law	
District of Columbia	No sodomy law	
Florida	Heterosexual and homosexual sodomy illegal	60 days
Georgia	No sodomy law	
Hawaii	No sodomy law	
Idaho	Heterosexual and homosexual sodomy illegal	Life
Illinois	No sodomy law	
Indiana	No sodomy law	
Iowa	No sodomy law	
Kansas	Homosexual sodomy illegal	6 months
Kentucky	No sodomy law	
Louisiana	Heterosexual and homosexual sodomy illegal	5 years
Maine	No sodomy law	
Maryland	No sodomy law	
Massachusetts	Heterosexual and homosexual sodomy illegal	20 years
Michigan	Heterosexual and homosexual sodomy illegal	15 years
Minnesota	Heterosexual and homosexual sodomy illegal	1 year
Mississippi	Heterosexual and homosexual sodomy illegal	10 years
Missouri	Homosexual sodomy illegal	1 year
Montana	No sodomy law	
Nebraska	No sodomy law	
Nevada	No sodomy law	
New Hampshire	No sodomy law	
New Jersey	No sodomy law	

State	Status of sodomy law	Maximum sentence
New Mexico	No sodomy law	
New York	No sodomy law	
North Carolina	Heterosexual and homosexual sodomy illegal	10 years
North Dakota	No sodomy law	
Ohio	No sodomy law	
Oklahoma	Homosexual sodomy illegal	10 years
Oregon	No sodomy law	
Pennsylvania	No sodomy law	
Rhode Island	No sodomy law	
South Carolina	Heterosexual and homosexual sodomy illegal	5 years
South Dakota	No sodomy law	
Tennessee	No sodomy law	
Texas	Homosexual sodomy illegal	$500 fine
Utah	Heterosexual and homosexual sodomy illegal	6 months
Vermont	No sodomy law	
Virginia	Heterosexual and homosexual sodomy illegal	5 years
Washington	No sodomy law	
West Virginia	No sodomy law	
Wisconsin	No sodomy law	
Wyoming	No sodomy law	

Sodomy laws aren't the only manifestation of a legal system that continues to discriminate against lesbians and gay men. Although our legal system generally does a good job of protecting certain freedoms, like freedom of speech, even here the rights of lesbians and gay men have taken a back seat to judicial homophobia. In 1987, the U.S. Supreme Court ruled that Congress and the U.S. Olympic Committee can control the use of the word "Olympics" by denying San Francisco Arts and Athletics, Inc., the use of the phrase "Gay Olympics" to describe their every-four-years international athletic competition.

Entering a new century gives us pause to reflect on the many gains, losses and near misses celebrated and suffered by the lesbian and gay community. Former President Clinton appointed more than 100 lesbians and gay men to top administrative positions, but supported the ban on gays in the military. Television shows and movies now feature openly gay characters. And the United States Supreme Court has recognized our basic civil rights by invalidating the homophobic Amendment 2 in Colorado. At the same time, however, anti-gay legislation is repeatedly proposed—and enacted—across the country. Furthermore, violence against lesbians and gays—most vividly demonstrated in the murder of Matthew Shepard of Wyoming—continues to flourish.

For those fighting to protect the rights of same-sex couples, the new century brings great cause for celebration, because the state of Vermont has passed legislation allowing same-sex couples to be accorded the same rights, privileges and responsibilities as straight married couples. After the Vermont Supreme Court found that denying gay and lesbian couples the right to marry was unconstitutional, the state passed a law allowing same-sex couples to register as a "civil union." Once registered, a couple is subject to the same laws that govern married couples, including laws relating to public benefits, inheritance, child custody and support, medical decisions and division of property when a couple splits up.

For more information about Vermont civil unions, and the status of same sex marriage in America, see Chapter One, Section A.

One of the consequences of our homophobic laws is that lesbian and gay couples in America cannot legally marry, no matter how deep their love and how firm their commitment. Lesbian and gay couples are also denied the many legal rights that come with marriage. (Vermont couples who have registered as a "civil union" have most of the state law marriage protections, but none of the federal ones.) These rights include the rights to:

- file joint income tax returns
- claim estate tax marital deduction
- claim family partnership tax income
- recover damages based on injury to your lover
- receive survivor's benefits
- enter hospitals, jails and other places restricted to "immediate family"
- obtain health insurance, dental insurance, bereavement leave and other employment benefits

- collect unemployment benefits if you quit your job to move with your lover to a new location because he or she has obtained a new job
- get residency status for a noncitizen spouse to avoid deportation
- automatically make medical decisions in the event your lover is injured or incapacitated (otherwise, parents, adult children or siblings are given the right), and
- automatically inherit your lover's property in the event he or she dies without a will (otherwise, it goes to parents, children and siblings).

We are mistrustful of our legal system for another reason. The law tends to be cumbersome, time-consuming, expensive and incredibly picky. As you'll see throughout this book, we urge you to avoid courts and litigation if at all possible. But avoiding lawsuits doesn't mean you can avoid the legal system altogether. The fact that lesbian and gay couples are no longer in the closet and live together openly necessarily brings them into contact with the law. This is especially true if the couple, or one or both individually, have children or significant amounts of money or property.

We're often asked such questions as, "Is it possible for a court to remove my child from my home because I live with my lover?" "If I die, can my lover inherit my car and my house?" "Can a hospital legally prevent me from visiting my lover in intensive care?" We answer these specific questions later in the book. What we can tell you generally, however, is that the opportunities for legal hassles to intrude into a couple's life are endless, and the best way to avoid entanglements with the law is to take matters into your own hands. In this book, we give you the information necessary to create legal documents to give yourselves many of the rights which accompany marriage.

B. Some Words About Words

Wouldn't it be great if there were a genie who created words for such realities as "a man who loves men" or "a woman who loves women" or "comrades through life who share sexual intimacies" that meant exactly what we wished them to mean, neither more nor less? These words would be free of latent sexual prejudice and orientation, and their meaning and political acceptability wouldn't erode over time. Unfortunately, the opposite has been more the case, as words have been part of the perpetuation of homophobia. "Faggot," for instance, is derived from the French word for the bundles of sticks used to burn homosexuals at the stake, and its use should serve as a reminder of that oppression. As Truman Capote said, "A fag is a homosexual gentleman who has left the room."

Words free of ugly overtones, which accurately (to say nothing of poetically) describe the realities we discuss in this book aren't easy to find. What do you call the person you live with? "Co-vivant" does have a delightful French ring to it, but seems more than slightly pretentious. "Living in bedlock without benefit of wedlock" is silly, but at least it rhymes. How about "consort" or "URAW," a welfare department term for a person living with an "unrelated adult woman" (URAM, for men).

"Lover" and "partner" are the words we use. They are accurate and succinct. We also use the words "lesbian" and "gay" because those are the words used most often in our own particular culture (San Francisco Bay Area) by women and men to identify themselves. As for general pronouns, sometimes we use "she," sometimes "he" and sometimes the awkward "he or she."

Transgendered people often find themselves in particularly complex legal situations. Oftentimes their birth certificates, driver's licenses and other identification documents create confusion and uncertainty. Their legal rights and duties with respect to their unmarried partners, however, are the same as those who are lesbian, gay or bisexual. For this reason, the issues raised by this book for the most part apply to the transgendered members of our community, and we certainly mean to include transgendered persons in our audience.

We know that creating and using words untainted by the prejudices of the past and reflective of pride and self-worth is important, so we've tried to be sensitive to the power and implication of words. But finally, words are just that—words; they won't break our bones, and we're all free to use the ones we like best. When Christopher Isherwood was asked what he liked to be called, he answered, "I don't really like the word 'gay' for it makes us seem like silly ninnies. I rather like the karate chop sound of 'faggot.' The word 'homosexual' is too much of a mouthful. Frankly, when alone and with friends, I say 'queer.'"

C. Using the Forms in This Book

Sprinkled throughout this book are sample agreements, covering such topics such as living together, raising children, buying a home together and (sadly) splitting up. As you will see, each of these agreements is personalized to the individualized circumstances of the actors involved. We encourage you to use our sample agreements as starting points for your own documents. We suggest that you type up your agreements on your computer, and use the language and structure from the agreements included in this book as they fit your needs. If it would make you more comfortable to have a lawyer draft your documents, by all means do so. As a cheaper alternative, you can instead have a lawyer review the documents that you write yourselves (although not every lawyer will be willing to perform this service).

D. Icons Used in This Book

 A caution icon warns you of a potential problem.

 This icon refers you to other books or resources for further information.

 The tip icon gives you hints on dealing with special situations.

 The briefcase lets you know when you need the advice of an attorney.

 Related topics covered in this book.

Creating Family:
Marriage, Domestic Partners and More

According to *Webster's New Collegiate Dictionary*, a family is "the basic unit in society having as its nucleus two or more adults living together and cooperating in the care and rearing of their own or adopted children." Despite this all-inclusive definition, a lesbian or gay couple—with or without children—is hardly the image conjured up when most people picture a family.

Nevertheless, lesbian and gay couples consider themselves to be families. And over the past several decades, same-sex couples have sought societal recognition of their families. It began in the early 1970s, when lesbian and gay couples applied for marriage licenses, asked courts to allow one partner to adopt the other and took other steps to legally cement their relationship. Most of these efforts failed.

By the mid-1980s, the emphasis changed to seeking "domestic partnership" recognition for same-sex couples from both municipalities and private companies. This effort continued, with increasing strength, in the 1990s. And the desire to marry has again emerged. Some couples are applying to the state for marriage licenses and suing their states when their requests are denied. Others (*many* others) are participating in their own ceremonies, sanctioned by their friends, families and spiritual communities. And in Vermont, same-sex couples can register as a civil union, and be subject to the same state laws that govern married couples.

In this chapter, we discuss:
- gay and lesbian marriages
- domestic partnerships
- states granting benefits (such as unemployment insurance) to partners in lesbian and gay couples where previously only married spouses were given those benefits
- case law expanding the definition of "family," and
- adult adoptions.

The debate over same-sex marriage has profoundly transformed the lesbian and gay community. For many, the right to marry is a basic civil right—as long as lesbians and gay men are denied the right to marry their lovers, they will be considered second-class citizens. And as long as society offers benefits based on the status of marriage, then lesbian and gay couples want their fair share. The battle to bestow greater legitimacy on our relationship is also changing the way each of us thinks of our relationship with our partner. More and more couples are pooling their assets and formalizing their interdependency on each other, living more and more how married couples do. And an increasing number of partners are seeking post-dissolution financial support or a share of joint assets from their exes upon the termination of their relationships.

To others—especially many lesbian feminists—marriage is a sexist and patriarchal institution that lesbians and gay men should not seek to be a part of.

We find this debate to be intellectually and politically fascinating (and we certainly have our opinions about lesbians and gay men seeking the right to marry), but we have decided to keep our own opinions out of print. We include information on lesbian and gay marriages because any "Legal Guide for Lesbian and Gay Couples" should include it, and because many readers have asked for it.

A. Same-Sex Marriage

In 1978, the United States Supreme Court declared marriage to be "of fundamental importance to all individuals" (*Zablocki v. Redhail*). The court described marriage as "one of the 'basic civil rights of man'" and "the most important relation in life." The court also noted that "the right to marry is part of the fundamental 'right to privacy'" in the U.S. Constitution.

Although marriage has been declared a fundamental right, no state yet recognizes same-sex marriages. Some states have passed laws specifically barring same-sex marriages, and the number of states with such laws are increasing. And even states without an explicit "no-same-sex-marriage" law on the books do not allow same-sex couples to enter into legal marriage.

Despite all this, however, there is some good news to report.

1. The Ongoing Fight for Same-Sex Marriage

Gay and lesbian couples have been fighting for legal marriage in this country for decades. As early as 1971, a gay male Minnesota couple filed a court case claiming that they were entitled to legally marry under the state's marriage statute. That case was unsuccessful, but the fight continued through the 1980s and 1990s, culminating in two landmark cases: the Hawaii case of *Baehr v. Miike*, and the Vermont case of *Baker v. State*.

In the Hawaii case, three same-sex couples sued the state, arguing that its failure to issue marriage licenses to them violated the Equal Rights Amendment to the state constitution. The Hawaii Supreme Court—while not explicitly finding in favor of same-sex marriage—ruled that the couples' lawsuit raised legitimate gender-discrimination concerns under the state constitution, and sent the case back to lower court. After a trial in the lower court, that judge ruled that same-sex marriage ban was invalid. The state appealed. While that appeal was pending, Hawaii voters passed a constitutional amendment banning same sex marriage. This new law effectively ended the case.

Although in the end Hawaii did not permit same-sex marriage, when the case was pending the "threat" of legalized gay marriage was in the air. The furor unleashed by the Hawaii case caused many state legislators to pass laws banning same-sex marriage. The federal government also got caught up in the hysteria, passing the "Defense of Marriage Act" (DOMA) in 1996. The DOMA prohibits the federal government from recognizing same-sex marriages or denies federal benefits (such as income tax, immigration and Social Security) to spouses in same-sex marriages. Furthermore, in anticipation of a time when some forward-thinking state might allow full legal marriage for a same-sex couple, The DOMA permits states to ignore a same-sex marriage entered into in another state.

Hawaii's Compromise: The Reciprocal Beneficiaries Law

In an effort to prevent Hawaii courts from allowing same-sex marriage, the state legislature passed the Reciprocal Beneficiaries Law of 1997. Couples who sign up as reciprocal beneficiaries gain many of the rights and benefits granted by the state to married couples. Although not quite the victory that the same-sex marriage movement had hoped for, it was still groundbreaking because it was the first state-wide domestic partnership law passed in the United States. (For more on domestic partnerships, see Section B.)

Any two individuals over the age of 18 who are not permitted to marry under Hawaii law are eligible to register with the state as reciprocal beneficiaries. Rights and benefits extended to reciprocal beneficiaries include hospital visitation rights, the ability to sue for wrongful death and property and inheritance rights similar to those enjoyed by married couples. Unlike couples registered under Vermont's civil union law (see below), reciprocal beneficiaries in Hawaii are not granted access to family court—which governs issues like divorce, alimony and child support for married couples.

The website of Hawaii's Vital Records Office has information about how to register as reciprocal beneficiaries, at http://www.state.hi.us/doh/records/rbrfaq.htm.

Across the county in Vermont, the state supreme court issued a landmark decision in *Baker v. State* (1999). The Vermont Supreme Court ruled that prohibiting same-sex marriage violated the Vermont constitution because it denied same-sex couples the rights granted straight couples. But instead of ordering the government to issue marriage licenses to gay and lesbian couples, the court left it up to the state legislature to remedy the situation.

In response to the court's order in *Baker v. State,* the legislature passed a law creating the civil union registration system. Under this system, same-sex couples can register their civil union, and they are then subject to all state laws applying to married couples. (For more details, see the box "The Vermont Civil Union Law" below.)

It is too soon to tell what effect of the Vermont civil union statute will have on the nation. The statute allows couples who aren't Vermont residents to register their civil union, but it is doubtful that other states will recognize their status. Although the federal constitution requires each state to give "full faith and credit" to the laws of other states—such that a heterosexual marriage or divorce in one state is recognized in another—the federal Defense of Marriage Act (DOMA) was passed with the express purpose of undercutting that guarantee in the case of same-sex marriages. At the same time, because the DOMA abridges the rights guaranteed under the full faith and credit clause it seems ripe for a constitutional challenge.

The recent years have been marked by a rapid succession of victories and disappointments in the fight to legalize same-sex marriage. The best we can tell you at this point is: "Stay tuned." And you can always check the website of the Lambda Legal Defense and Education Fund's Marriage Project for the latest news, at http://www.lambdalegal.org.

The Vermont Civil Union Law

In 1999, the Vermont legislature passed the Vermont Civil Union law, which went into effect on July 1, 2000. While this law doesn't legalize same-sex marriages, it does provide gay and lesbian couples with many of the same advantages including:

- use of family laws such as annulment, divorce, child custody, child support, alimony, domestic violence, adoption and property division
- the right to sue for wrongful death, loss of consortium and any other tort or law related to spousal relationships
- medical rights such as hospital visitation, notification and durable power of attorney
- family leave benefits
- joint state tax filing, and
- property inheritance without a will.

These rights apply only to couples residing in Vermont. Even for Vermont residents, this new civil union law does not provide same-sex couples with rights and benefits provided by federal law; for example, same-sex couples cannot take advantage of Social Security benefits, immigration privileges and the marriage exemption to federal estate tax. Couples from outside Vermont can come to Vermont and be joined in civil union, but it appears unlikely that any other state will recognize the union.

To read Vermont's official state guide on the new law, visit http://www.sec.state.vt.us/pubs/civilunions.htm.

Same-Sex Marriage Around the Globe

Americans aren't the only ones wrestling with the issue of providing legal rights for same-sex couples. A number of European countries now provide recognition of gay and lesbian couples.

Belgium. A nationwide law gives same-sex couples inheritance rights.

Canada. The Canadian Supreme Court has ruled that where protections are offered to "spouses" they must also be offered to same-sex couples. While the right to marry was left undecided, a poll taken after the decision showed that the majority of Canadians support the right of same-sex couples to have legally recognized marriages.

Denmark. Denmark was the first country, in 1989, to allow same-sex couples to form "registered partnerships," giving them a status and benefits similar to marriage. Registered couples in Denmark are not permitted to adopt children, however.

Finland. In 2001, Finland passed a same-sex partnership law similar to Denmark's.

France. Registered partnerships are available, including tax benefits, public insurance and pension benefits, inheritance and lease protections and even the right to demand concurrent vacation schedules. In addition, property acquired together is considered jointly owned unless an agreement states otherwise.

Germany. Gay and lesbian couples may register same-sex partnerships. Registered partners have the same inheritance rights as married couples, and may adopt the same last name, but they do not have the same tax advantages and rights to adopt that married couples have.

Greenland. The Danish law extends to same-sex couples in Greenland. (Greenland is a terri-

tory of Denmark.)

Hungary. Same-sex couples are covered by the nation's common-law marriage rules, which carry some of the same rights—particularly regarding inheritance rights. Same-sex couples do not, however, have the right to register under Hungary's marriage law.

Iceland. Iceland's law is similar to Denmark's, allowing same-sex couples to register their partnerships in order to receive many of the rights of marriage, but registered couples cannot adopt children.

Italy. Pisa and Florence allow same-sex couples to register as domestic partners.

Netherlands. The Netherlands has become the first and only country to offer full legal marriage to same-sex couples. Under a law that went into effect in 2001, couples who registered as domestic partners under Dutch law will have the option to convert that partnership into a marriage, and will be subject to the same laws that govern straight married couples. The law applies only to citizens and legal residents of the Netherlands.

Norway. Registered partnerships similar to those in Denmark are available to same-sex couples.

Spain. Many cities allow same-sex couples to register as domestic partners. Also, a nationwide law allows a widowed partner to remain in rental housing when only the deceased signed the lease.

Sweden. Sweden's law is similar to Denmark's, allowing same-sex couples to register their partnerships in order to receive many of the rights of marriage, but registered couples cannot adopt children.

2. If You Could Marry, How Would It Affect You?

If same-sex marriage ever is legalized, you and your partner will need to decide whether marriage is right for you. Some couples are also now faced with deciding whether to register their civil union in the state of Vermont. Here are some tips for deciding whether you are ready to pop the question:

- If you have children or hope to raise a family, marriage is probably the right option. Married couples by law have equal rights to raise their children, as well as equal obligations of support. In a dissolution, both parents can seek visitation and custody, and if one parent dies the other one steps right in as the primary legal parent. It is nearly impossible to make these sorts of arrangements absent a legal marriage.

- Marriage isn't a prerequisite for owning property together, but if you get married, in most situations in most states your property will be jointly owned regardless of who pays for it. This is the reverse of the presumption that applies to unmarried couples. Getting married may be the most efficient way of establishing a property merger—though if keeping things separate is more to your taste, you will have to sign a prenuptial agreement to avoid the joint ownership presumptions of a legal marriage.

- In most states, each married spouse's earnings are owned by the two of you, and if the marriage breaks up—regardless of who's at fault—you each generally get half of everything you've accumulated. By contrast, if you are unmarried, your property is co-owned only if you have an agreement to make it so; and likewise for debts and obligations. Divorcing spouses are also entitled to demand alimony if the marriage doesn't last, without the need for any explicit contract providing for post-separation support.

- Every marriage requires a formal ceremony and every marital separation requires some kind of formal court action—quite often the help of a lawyer. Unmarried couples can break up informally, on their own terms.

- Absent a legal marriage, a couple needs to sign several agreements to create even a partial framework of protection in the event of death, and certain tax benefits are forever denied to unmarried couples. If you are married, however, the surviving spouse generally inherits all the property if the partner dies without a will. At death, a bequest from one spouse to another is tax free, regardless of its size.

- Transfers of property upon dissolution of the relationship are also tax free for legally married couples, but not for unmarrieds.

- Marriage can bestow a bevy of important benefits, including military or Social Security benefits, healthcare and nursing home coverage. Marriage may also qualify you for unpaid leave from your job under the Family Leave Act. But watch out—a married person's income could disqualify a spouse from receiving Social Security, welfare or medical benefits she'd receive if she was unmarried.

- A legal marriage is the only reliable method of providing a foreign lover with the privileges of immigration to this country, when he doesn't qualify under work or other provisions of the Immigration Act.

If you are ever allowed to make this difficult decision, first decide whether you fall into one of the got-to-marry or better-not-marry situations. Raising kids, courting a foreign lover or facing a serious illness, for example, generally favors a marriage (unless it disqualifies you for Medicaid), whereas getting saddled with your partner's debts or losing Social Security benefits probably favors a no vote.

If you don't fall into either extreme, take a close look at the marital property rules for your particular state, evaluate the benefits given your personal situation and get a good sense of what being married would do for you financially. Then, consider whether being married feels right for both of you emotionally. If the answers come back positive for both of you, then proceed, but consider creating a prenuptial agreement if any aspect of the traditional marriage structure doesn't meet your needs. If the impact of marriage feels unduly negative for one or both of you, however, hold off. If and when same-sex marriage becomes legal, it isn't likely to be mandatory.

B. Domestic Partnerships

Despite the fact that an estimated mere 10% of American families are made up of a working husband, a stay-at-home wife and children, our legal and social systems still provide benefits and protections based on that model. Having been left out, lesbian and gay activists in the early 1980s sought recognition of their relationships and new definitions of family. And so, domestic partnerships were born. Domestic partners are unmarried couples—same sex or opposite sex—who live together and seek economic and noneconomic benefits granted their married counterparts. These benefits may include:

- health, dental and vision insurance
- sick and bereavement leave
- accident and life insurance
- death benefits
- parental leave (for a child you co-parent)
- housing rights and tuition reduction (at universities), and
- use of recreational facilities.

When a state, municipality, county, organization, private company or university or college considers providing domestic partnership benefits, it must address several important issues: Who qualifies as a domestic partner—should heterosexual couples be covered as well as gay and lesbian couples? How will an employer identify the employee's domestic partner—by registration? Must the couple be together a minimum number of years? Must the couple live together? Must they share expenses? Must they be financially responsible for each other? How does a couple terminate their domestic partnership?

Note that even though most domestic partnership applications ask you to state that you are financially responsible for each other's needs, these applications are generally not considered binding contracts of support. In other words, your partner can't sue you for failing to provide for him, as promised.

If you are interested in working with your employer toward obtaining domestic partnership benefits, we recommend that you get a copy of *The Domestic Partnership Organizing Manual for Employee Benefits*, published by the Policy Institute of the National Gay and Lesbian Task Force. You can download it from the NGLTF website at http://www.ngltf.org/pubs.

In 1982, the *Village Voice* newspaper became the first private company to offer its employees domestic partnership benefits. The city of Berkeley was the first municipality to do so in 1984. In 1995, Vermont became the first state to extend domestic partnership benefits to its public employees. In 1997, Hawaii became the first state to extend domestic partnership benefits to all same-sex couples throughout the state. (See Section A for more on Hawaii's reciprocal beneficiaries law.)

Today, hundreds of municipalities, counties, private companies, organizations, colleges and universities offer domestic partnership benefits. The complete list of institutions is extensive; the benefits offered by each is not, however. In some cases, all that is offered is bereavement or sick leave. In other situations, the benefits offered are extensive—and expensive. Often, either the employee foots the bill for his or her partner, or the company pays (when it also pays for spouses), but the employee must pay taxes on the benefits. This is because the IRS considers benefits awarded to an umarried partner as taxable compensation.

For a list of states, municipalities and other entities offering domestic partnership benefits, as well as updates on litigation on this issue, go the domestic partnership section of the Lambda Legal Defense and Education Fund's website, at http://www.lambdalegal.org. Another excellent source of information on domestic partnership benefits is the Human Rights Campaign's WorkNet website, at http://www.hrc.org/worknet.

Local governments. A handful of state agencies and many municipalities and counties offer domestic partnership benefits for their employees. A few also allow city residents to register as domestic partners, even though they obtain no tangible benefits by doing so. The requirements for domestic partnerships vary a lot from city to city, but essentially the partners must live together in an exclusive relationship and share the basic necessities of life.

Cities and counties offering sick leave, bereavement leave and parental leave have had few problems implementing their programs. After all, by offering these domestic partner benefits, the institution has made the commitment to absorb these costs. Providing health, dental or vision insurance, however, has not been as easy. A commitment on paper does not translate into a tangible benefit if the city or county's insurance carrier refuses to extend coverage to the domestic partner of a city employee. In Ann Arbor, for example, the city has been unable to find an insurance carrier willing to cover the domestic partners of its nonunionized employees; the union that represents 80% of the city's employees won't support domestic partner benefits out of fear of losing other benefits in exchange. And in Minneapolis, a Court of Appeals has held that the city charter does not permit the extension of health insurance benefits to the same-sex partners of city employees.

Berkeley allows its employees to choose among several different health insurance companies. When Berkeley began offering domestic partnership coverage, one company refused to participate and the city dropped the carrier.

Private employers. For a long time, the *Village Voice* newspaper looked as if it would be the first and last private employer to offer domestic partner benefits. By the year 2001, however, many other companies joined in—there are now hundreds of private sector employers who provide domestic partner benefits to their employees.

The Alternatives to Marriage website (at http://www.unmarried.org) has links to information on domestic partnership benefits, including a list of major companies that provide domestic partnership benefits and a guide to getting your employer to offer domestic partner benefits. You can find a list of the Fortune 500 companies that offer domestic partnership benefits by visiting the Insure.com website at http://www.insure.com/health/domesticemployers700.html.

Private organizations. Even if your employer doesn't have domestic partner benefits, other organizations with which you do business might. For example, airlines which used to let frequent flyer members use their accumulated miles only for their spouses now usually let you bring anyone. Some airlines have extended bereavement discount fares to domestic partners. Several other institutions, such as museums, health clubs and public television stations, which used to offer membership discounts only to married couples, now offer them to any household, regardless of marital status or sexuality.

Colleges and universities. Over 100 colleges and universities offer some type of domestic partnership benefits to students or staff, or both.

California's New Domestic Partnership Law

A comprehensive new domestic partnership law took effect in California in January 2002. With this new law, California, along with Hawaii and Vermont, is in the forefront of states offering legal protections to same-sex couples.

Under the California law, a registered domestic partner may now:

- adopt a partner's child using the stepparent adoption process—a faster and less expensive process than second-parent adoption
- sue for wrongful death of a partner
- make healthcare decisions for a partner who becomes incapacitated
- use sick leave to care for an ill domestic partner or the child of a domestic partner
- relocate with a partner without losing eligibility for unemployment benefits
- apply for disability benefits on behalf of an injured or incapacitated partner, and
- deduct the cost of a domestic partner's health insurance or other benefit from state income taxes.

Same-sex partners must register with the California Secretary of State's Office (http://www.ssa.ca.gov) to be eligible for the rights and benefits extended under this law.

C. Other Gains for Gay and Lesbian Families

One tragedy of society's failure to recognize lesbian and gay relationships is that government benefits traditionally awarded to married spouses—such as unemployment insurance and workers' compensation—are denied to same-sex partners. Similarly, lovers of lesbians and gay men have been denied the right to sue for emotional distress or to stay in an apartment after their lover dies when their name isn't on the lease, because they were not considered "immediate family." Slowly, however, things are changing.

Although we report on the victories achieved by lesbian and gay couples, these cases are not the norm. Most lesbian and gay partners are denied unemployment, workers' compensation and emotional distress recoveries on the grounds that they are not spouses or members of each other's immediate family.

1. Government Benefits

Several years ago, a gay man in California was awarded unemployment insurance from the state when he left his job to care for his lover who had AIDS. Married partners have for years received benefits if they quit their jobs to care for terminally ill spouses. In extending the benefits to gay couples, the Unemployment Appeals Board declared that gay relationships are often as serious, loving and committed as marriages.

Another Californian (Susan) quit her job to accompany her lover who was beginning a medical residency in Pennsylvania. Susan was awarded unemployment insurance. The Unemployment Appeals Board judge who decided the case simply stated that benefits are available when a person leaves his or her employment to accompany a spouse to a place from which it is impractical to commute and that the applicant's "spouse was accepted into residency and this certainly provided good cause for the couple to move." The judge knew the couple was lesbian, but clearly chose to refer to them as spouses, without regard to their sex or sexual orientation.

In another California case (yes, there are reasons gay men and lesbians flock to the Golden State), a gay man was awarded workers' compensation death benefits when his lover, a county district attorney, committed suicide because of job-related stress. The Workers' Compensation Appeals Board found that the lover was dependent on the employee for support, and said that the homosexual relationship of the two men shouldn't preclude the lover's rights to benefits.

2. Defining "Family"

New York City has a rental vacancy rate of approximately 0%; this means that affordable and decent housing is virtually impossible to find for those without it. When a lover dies and the survivor's name was not on the lease or named as the successor in interest to a co-op or condominium, lesbians and gay men dealing with the death of their mate have suffered the added injustice of losing their homes. In addition, when a tenant's lover moves into an apartment, the tenant risks violating the standard lease clause limiting occupancy to the named tenant and the tenant's "immediate family."

Between 1979 and 1983, several cases were litigated in New York addressing these problems. The essential issue in each case was the definition of "immediate family." The cases seesawed back and forth. In the first case, the court denied the surviving lover a place to live, stating "[no] authority… holds [that] homosexuals living together constitute a family unit." Two years later, the same court upheld the eviction of a lesbian whose lover had moved in with her, stating that "[two] lesbians living together do not constitute a…family."

But less than a year later, another court refused to let a landlord evict a man and his female lover simply because her name was not on the lease. The court held that the eviction violated New York City's Human Rights Law barring discrimination on the basis of marital status.

In the same year, another court refused to allow the eviction of a gay male couple, holding that the traditional nuclear family is no longer the reality for many people, and that the tenant did not breach the "immediate family" clause in his lease. But just a year later, a court upheld the eviction of a different gay man for violating the "immediate family" clause. And in 1983, New York's highest court upheld an eviction of a woman for breaching the "immediate family" clause of her lease when her male lover moved in. *Whether or not he (her lover) could by marriage or otherwise become part of her immediate family is not an issue…. Were the additional tenant a female unrelated to the tenant, the lease would still be violated without reference to marriage.*

But this decision lasted only six years. In 1989, New York's highest court reversed itself. After Leslie Blanchard died, his lover, Miguel Braschi, sought to stay in the rent-stabilized apartment the two men shared for over 11 years, despite the fact that only Blanchard's name was on the lease. The landlord instituted eviction proceedings against Braschi, who fought back. The court ruled:

> *In the context of eviction, a more realistic, and certainly equally valid view of a family includes two adult lifetime partners whose relationship is long-term and characterized by an emotional and financial commitment and interdependence.*

The litigation in New York City should be at an end. In 1998, New York's mayor signed into law a comprehensive domestic partnership bill, which includes the right to rental succession.

Courts have been called upon to define "family" in other contexts. In Denver, for example, a city worker who took three days off to care for her seriously injured lover was granted sick leave by a hearing officer who declared the sick leave policy to care for family members applicable to all city employees, regardless of sexual orientation. In Washington, D.C., a woman was allowed to file a claim under the District's Wrongful Death Act after her lover died from injuries sustained when a tree branch broke through the windshield of the car she was driving. A court found that the surviving partner qualified as

her deceased lover's "next of kin." And in California, a surviving lover of a man who died from AIDS was awarded $175,000 by a court for emotional distress experienced after a funeral company mishandled the deceased man's ashes in breach of the contract the deceased man signed with the company. This expanded the definition of family, as previously such recoveries were limited to spouses.

D. Adult Adoption—Another Way to Cement a Relationship

One of the legally recognized relationships that a handful of couples unable to marry have entered into is that of adoptive relatives.

Three New York City men have sought to adopt their lovers. In *In re Adoption of Adult Anonymous*, the judge allowed the adoption because:

- sodomy is not illegal in New York
- New York's incest law only prohibits sexual relations between *blood* relatives, and
- the men claimed legitimate economic reasons—facilitating inheritance, handling insurance policies and pension plans and acquiring suitable housing.

A similar adoption was permitted in *In re Adult Anonymous II* one year later. In *In re Adoption of Robert Paul P.*, however, the New York court denied a same-sex adult adoption application, holding that "the evasion of existing inheritance laws" was a main purpose of the adoption.

Nearly a decade later, the Delaware Supreme Court in 1993 approved a same-sex adult adoption. The court specifically stated that the couple's desire to formalize their close emotional relationship and facilitate estate planning were permissible reasons to allow the adoption.

A few states, including Florida, have passed laws barring gays and lesbians from adopting. Florida's ban was upheld by a federal judge in August 2001 in the case of a proposed adoption of a child. And in the recent case of *Rickard v. McKesson*, the niece of a deceased Florida man, Donald Blackwell, successfully challenged her Uncle Donald's adult adoption of his friend Gordon McKesson under the law banning gay adoption. Naturally, the niece sued because she was due to inherit her uncle's estate if the adoption of Gordon was found invalid.

These cases aptly demonstrate the reasons lesbian and gay couples want their relationships legally recognized—to benefit from housing, inheritance, investment and other laws. But there are barriers you will likely face if you try to adopt your lover. First, a court may prove reluctant to grant a same-sex adult adoption when it is clear that the relationship is a sexual one. Adoption connotes parent and child; to allow lovers to use it to confer legal status upon themselves is repugnant to many people.

Same-sex lovers planning to adopt face additional potential barriers:

- state laws barring adult adoptions—Alabama, Arizona, Hawaii, Michigan, Nebraska and Ohio all have such laws
- state laws barring gays and lesbians from adopting—currently, Florida, Utah and Mississippi have such laws
- sodomy statutes
- incest statutes, and
- laws specifying a minimum age difference between the adoptive parent and child.

Only a handful of states prohibit adult adoptions. Sodomy, however, is still illegal in many states. And in most states, incest laws prohibit sexual relations between an adoptive parent and child.

These are the outside forces that keep lesbians and gay men from adopting their lovers. But many other factors give lesbians and gay men reason to pause. First, as lesbians and gay men seek the right to raise children, adopting a lover seems inappropriate. Second, adoption is permanent—most same-sex lovers want the option of ending their relationship. Finally, adoption necessarily means that the court must terminate the parent-child relationship between the person to be adopted and his legal parents. For a lesbian or gay man with a positive relationship with her or his parents, this could be both destructive and insulting.

Other Ways to Create a Family

Marriage, domestic partnerships and adoption aren't the only ways to cement a relationship with your lover. You can also write a living together contract. We cover general living together agreements in Chapter 6, and agreements for buying a house together in Chapter 7. And of course, you can make an estate plan together—that is, draft a will, living trust or other documents—leaving your property to one another. We cover estate planning in Chapter 5.

E. The Sad Side of "Marriage"

Wouldn't it be wonderful if lesbians and gay men fell in love, moved in together and lived happily (or mostly happily) ever after? It does happen, on occasion. But, human beings and human nature being what they are, relationships can turn sour.

1. Breaking Up

Ending a relationship can be harder than starting one. If you have kids, we suggest you read Chapter 3 and the pertinent sections of Chapter 9. For help on dividing your property, take a close look at Chapter 9. Here, we just want to talk about ending your "family" status.

If you went through some kind of union, commitment or marriage ceremony, you are not required to take any legal steps to end the relationship—remember, you are not legally married. (Vermont couples who register their civil unions in that state must seek a dissolution in the same family courts that married couples use.) Many people go back to whomever officiated at their ceremony and seek help in splitting up. Sometimes, a couple will stand before friends and community to assert their new status as single people and to commit to working toward a healthy end of the relationship. Certain religious traditions require that you get a religious divorce decree. Of course, if this "touchy-feely" stuff seems strange to you, you can simply pack your bags and move out. (As Paul Simon said, there are "50 ways to leave your lover.")

If you registered as domestic partners, be sure to de-register. If one of you adopted the other, you may want to have a lawyer look at your state's adoption statute to see if there are grounds to rescind the adoption decree.

2. When Relationships Turn Violent

Of course we'd prefer if there were no need for this section. But domestic violence and abuse are a very real part of the gay and lesbian community. The good news is that the community has become much more responsive to these issues, with many more resources now available to those in crisis.

If you are the victim of domestic violence, your number one concern is your own safety. You may be ashamed, embarrassed or feeling guilty, and all of those feelings are understandable. But it's most important that you get out of your living arrangement and into a safe environment. If you are a lesbian, contact a battered women's shelter. If you're concerned about the homophobia you may encounter—or if you're a gay man with no shelter to turn to—then go to a friend or supportive relative.

A few states, including California, Massachusetts and Ohio, cover same-sex relationships in their domestic violence statutes. This means that you can get a restraining order to keep the abuser away from you. You will probably need the help of a lawyer or women's clinic.

Here is a list of some resources and contacts on the issue of gay and lesbian domestic violence.

- Go to this site, http://www.rainbowdomesticviolence.itgo.com, for research and links on domestic violence in the gay and lesbian community.
- The National Domestic Violence Hotline, at 800-799-SAFE, is a national toll-free number that provides information to callers (gay and straight) about shelters and assistance programs in their area. You can also check out the hotline's website at http://www.ndvh.org.
- The Lambda Gay & Lesbian Anti-Violence Project (AVP), has a website at http://www.lambda.org, and their address is P.O. Box 31321, El Paso, TX 79931-0321. The telephone number for the Lambda Anti-Violence Project is 916-562-GAYS.
- The New York City Gay & Lesbian Anti-Violence Project maintains a website at http://www.avp.org, and their 24-hour hotline number is 212-714-1141.
- San Francisco's Community United Against Violence has a hotline at 415-333-HELP, and their website address is http://www.cuav.org.
- Massachusetts residents can contact the Gay Men's Domestic Violence Project at 800-832-1901. Their website is located at http://www.gmdvp.org. ■

Living Together and the Real World

When you and your lover decide to live together, you are probably (or hopefully) acting on romantic impulses. Unfortunately, practical problems inevitably tag along in the wake of romance. Most of these problems aren't legal and don't involve lawyers. All the barristers in the world can't help you when you and your lover discuss where to vacation, what to play on the stereo and what to hang on the living room wall.

Many day-to-day hassles, however, are connected with law. Some, such as employment discrimination, aren't addressed here because they aren't specifically related to living together as a lesbian or gay couple. In this chapter, we focus on the legal situations lesbian and gay couples face, living in the world. Our goal is to be specific enough to be helpful without being overly technical. If you need more information on a subject, see Chapter 10, *Help Beyond the Book*.

Although lesbian and gay couples lack the benefits and protections of marriage, many of the practical problems arising from this reality can be managed through careful planning. For example, even though your partner has no statutory right to your property at your death, by preparing a will you can leave your partner any property you want to. And while no spousal support rules govern what happens if you split up (unless you are Vermont residents who have registered as a civil union), you can draw up a legally binding agreement defining what happens financially if you separate.

Frustratingly, though, you'll face some real problems concerning how the government treats you as a same-sex couple. You'll probably pay more taxes at some point in your relationship. Further, no federal law prohibits discrimination against lesbian and gay people or couples in areas such as employment, housing, public accommodations or credit. Some type of protection exists in 17 states (California, Connecticut, Colorado, Hawaii, Illinois, Massachusetts, Minnesota, Montana, Nevada, New Hampshire, New Jersey, New Mexico, Pennsylvania, Rhode Island, Vermont, Washington and Wisconsin), the District of Columbia and over 150 cities and towns, but often places that pass anti-discrimination ordinances are the very localities that largely accepted gays and lesbians before they passed the law.

We mean no criticism of antidiscrimination ordinances when we say that in many cities these laws are more symbolic of lesbian and gay political acceptance than they are devices to bring about change. We support and applaud lesbian and gay political activists while, at the same time, we've written a book about living together, not fighting political struggles. It is important to remember, however, that because of many pioneering political battles, lesbian and gay couples can live openly in several parts of the world.

⚠ **The law can be unpredictable when applied to gays and lesbians.** *The laws regarding the practical matters we discuss in this chapter can vary from state to state, and—perhaps worse—can be unclear. Moreover, these laws as they are applied can be distressingly different from how they are written. Lesbian and gay couples must, unfortunately, still live with substantial legal uncertainty. Your goal, as we urge throughout this book, is to avoid uncertain outcomes by staying out of court to the extent possible and to instead arrange your legal and financial affairs so you stay far away from lawsuits.*

A. Can I Take My Lover's Last Name?

When Reverend Jim Dykes and his lover affirmed their commitment, they decided to symbolize that commitment by sharing the same last name. They agreed that hyphenated names were ungainly; Jim chose to take his lover's last name. "We decided I would change my name to Dykes," he told us, "because my lover comes from a wonderful Southern family with a proud and historic name."

Lots of lesbians and gay men change their names. Some women who changed their name in a heterosexual marriage want to return to their premarital name. Gay and lesbian partners in a couple sometimes hyphenate their names or choose a name that's the combination of the two. (Audrey Berman and Sheila Gander become Audrey and Sheila Bergan.) And then there are people like Jim Dykes, who simply take their lover's last name.

Changing your name is perfectly legal and usually easy. Bear in mind that you cannot change your name to defraud creditors, for any illegal purpose or to benefit economically by the use of another person's name—that is, you probably can't become Bette Midler or Gore Vidal. Otherwise, you can change your name for any reason and assume any name you wish.

You can change your name in one of two ways—usage or court order.

1. Change of Name by Usage

One way to change your name is simply to use a new one. Last week you were Steve Nurd; this week you're Steve Savage. If you use Savage consistently and insist it's your name, it is. The obvious example of usage name change is marriage. There's no legal proceeding (aside from the marriage itself) when one spouse changes her name to the other's. She simply does it—and it's perfectly legal. Any adult can accomplish a similar name change, although you must obtain a court order to change a child's name.

The keys to changing your name by usage are consistency and stubbornness. You must use your new name in all aspects of your life—socially, professionally and on identity cards and personal documents such as credit cards, driver's license and your Social Security card. Getting most documents with your new name shouldn't be too much trouble. Clerks are familiar with changing forms for women after marriage and quite agreeably change a woman's name on request. More men are changing their name after marriage—often by hyphenating their name with their wife's—so few clerks will hassle a man requesting a new document to reflect a name change. Many organizations and agencies have a specific form to request a name change. Others will accept an official-looking form declaring your name change.

⚠ **Changing your name via the usage method has become more difficult in California.** *California judges have consistently affirmed an adult's traditional (common law) right to change his or her name without going to court. But as the world gets more bureaucratic and pressure increases to stop unscrupulous people from stealing another person's name (identity theft) getting your name accepted via the usage method has become* *more difficult. In particular, the California Department of Motor Vehicles (DMV) has adopted regulations which make it difficult to change the name on your driver's license without showing a court order of your name change. Obviously, a driver's license is one of the most essential pieces of identification a person can have.*

For information on changing your name in the Golden State, including strategies for using the usage method despite the DMV's obstacles, see How to Change Your Name in California, *by Lisa Sedano (Nolo).*

2. Change of Name by Court Order

The second way to change your name is by court order. Getting a court order is usually pretty simple: You fill out and file at the courthouse a short petition, publish legal notice of your intention to change your name in a local legal newspaper (which no one reads) and attend a routine court hearing.

Unfortunately, a few courts, including one in Delaware and more recently in Ohio, have refused to allow a lesbian or gay to change names. In contrast, a New Jersey appeals court recently upheld the statutory right of a lesbian to change her last name where she was taking on the name of her lover. In that case, the New Jersey court reversed the lower court judge who had refused to approve the name change based on the theory that granting the name change would (somehow) show approval for same-sex marriage. The appellate court declared that a judge had no authority to deny a name change based on his "personal view of what is or should be the public policy of this state."

If you live in a state where you must give a reason for the change and you'd rather not tell the judge that you're changing your name to your partner's, you don't have to. You can state that your new name will make it more convenient for business or simply state that you like the new name better.

Once you obtain the court order changing your name, you must still change your records, identity cards and documents. All you need to do is show the various bureaucrats the judge's order.

B. Renting an Apartment or House Together

One first and favorite act of togetherness for many couples is living together. Here, we discuss rentals. Sometimes, a couple rents a new apartment or house, making a fresh start, so they can live without hovering ghosts of relationships past or established territorial rights. But perhaps more commonly (especially in areas with tight rental markets) one person moves into a place already occupied by the partner. Maybe it's a beautiful place, maybe it's a bargain, maybe it's too much hassle to seek a new place, maybe it's all of the above. How you go about living together in a rental place, as well as sexual orientation discrimination in housing, are covered in this section.

For information on buying a home together or moving into your lover's purchased home, see Chapter 7.

1. Sexual Orientation Discrimination

If you live in a state or municipality with a law prohibiting sexual orientation discrimination in housing and you believe you're being discriminated against because you are gay or lesbian, call the local city attorney's office and find out what agency is responsible for enforcing the gay rights ordinance. Even if you're protected by a nondiscrimination ordinance and have filed a complaint under the law, some landlords may go out on a limb to try to prove that they don't have to rent to you. One possible argument is that being forced to rent to a certain type of person—gay men or lesbians or unmarried heterosexual couples—violates their protected religious beliefs. While some state supreme courts have ruled that a nondiscrimination law takes precedence, a federal court has ruled otherwise, saying religious convictions prevail.

If you live in a place with no antidiscrimination ordinance and a landlord discriminates against you, there's usually not much you can do. So the question becomes whether or not to inform a prospective landlord that you're gay. It's far from automatic that a landlord will discriminate against you because of your sexual orientation. There are all sorts of landlords. Some "love their gay boys because they do know how to keep an apartment." Most are concerned with money and responsible tenants, not your private life. Still, your sexual orientation is not the landlord's business, and nothing legally requires you to volunteer the information. This is a tactical, not a legal, decision. If the landlord lives downstairs and is almost sure to figure it out, it may make sense to be candid. If the landlord lives halfway across the country, why bother?

Once you're living in your new place, you might be concerned about being evicted if the landlord discovers your relationship. If you rent under a month-to-month tenancy, not in a rent control area, your landlord can simply give you a 30-day notice to get out. It can be for any reason or no reason at all, and you have no protection.

If you have a lease or live in a "just cause" rent control area, the landlord must show that you broke a term of the lease or rental agreement, such as you failed to pay the rent, made too much noise (disturbing the "quiet enjoyment" of your neighbors), damaged the apartment and refused to pay for repairs, got a pet in violation of a "no pets" clause or something else. Being gay or lesbian is not a "just cause" for eviction.

But most leases prohibit illegal activity on the premises, and a landlord might threaten to evict you in a state where sodomy is illegal. (See *Introduction.*) And a conservative judge (who decides if the landlord can evict you) or a conservative sheriff (who does the physical evicting) may require the landlord to present little proof that you're gay. But if the landlord encounters an open-minded judge,

this sort of eviction will be extremely difficult. To prove that illegal activities transpired on the property, the landlord would have to present evidence, not just vague suspicions. If you keep your mouth shut, such proof would be difficult, if not impossible, to get.

⚠ Read your lease or rental agreement carefully. *Some leases and rental agreements contain illegal provisions, such as one giving the landlord the right to evict you with no court action if you're late with the rent. Before signing a lease or rental agreement, ask the landlord to cross off any clause that rubs you the wrong way. Watch especially for clauses prohibiting "immoral behavior" or "association with undesirable people." In the states with sodomy laws, an "immoral behavior" clause can be a problem if the landlord wants to evict you. If your landlord agrees, cross out the offending language and have your landlord add his or her initials.*

If you are seriously concerned about discrimination, consider having just one of you sign the lease to minimize calling attention to yourselves as a couple. But if you do this, be sure the lease doesn't limit the number of occupants to one. Also, be sure to sign a private agreement between the two of you confirming your agreement to both pay rent, or whatever other arrangement you make.

A friend experienced the following nasty situation many years ago:

One night, my landlady, who lived downstairs, telephoned and shouted, "It's illegal, you two living together. Get out or I will call the cops." To be honest, even though I was a lawyer, the call was so incredibly jarring and frightening that my first response was to do just that—to get out. But after talking it over with my lover, we decided that we had to stay and fight. And then, after staying long enough to establish the fact that we weren't being driven out, we realized that we wanted to move. Right or wrong, legal or illegal, wasn't the question. We simply didn't want to live above someone who was so hostile. We learned one valuable lesson from the experience, though: Never rent from someone who lives in the same building, unless you know she's okay.

If your landlord evicts or otherwise harasses you because you're gay, and you want to fight it, you'll have to file a written response to the eviction papers and raise the defense that you're being illegally discriminated against. Keep in mind, however, that even if an ordinance prohibits sexual orientation discrimination in housing, you could have a problem. A smart landlord will give a nondiscriminatory (phony) reason for evicting you.

Books to help you. *All the information you need to know on your rights as a tenant can be found in* Every Tenant's Legal Guide, *by Janet Portman and Marcia Stewart (Nolo). Californians should take a look at* Tenants' Rights, *by Myron Moskovitz and Ralph Warner (Nolo).*

2. Making an Agreement About Sharing a Rental

To repeat something you already know, it's vital that you and your partner agree on the basics of how you'll share your place. What that means in real life varies greatly from couple to couple. Some say no more than, "We both promise to be fair." Others get far more definite about what each wants and doesn't want. And some, once they've hashed out their understanding, put it in writing. Except for the financial aspects, this may not be a legally enforceable contract. Usually, its primary purpose is to provide clarity that hopes or memory alone might not. Whatever relationship you establish with your landlord, the crux of living together will be the understandings you two work out between yourselves. Don't underestimate the need to be clear. Renting a place to live isn't only a monetary investment; it

also provides you with a special haven of relaxation and refuge. Obviously, it's worth a little effort to ensure that you both will feel secure and protected.

Below is an example of an agreement covering moving into a newly (jointly) rented living space.

Renting Together Contract

Audrey Rabinowitz and Candice Dunk just rented Apartment 6B at 1500 Avenue B, New York, New York, and agree as follows:

1. We will each pay one-half of the rent and one-half of the gas, electricity, water and fixed telephone charge. Each person will pay for her long-distance calls. Our rent will be paid on time and the electricity, gas, water and telephone bills will be paid within ten days of receipt.

2. If either wants to leave, she will give the other and the landlord at least 30 days' written notice. The person moving agrees to pay her rent (before she moves) for the entire 30-day period, even if she leaves sooner.

3. We intend to live as a couple and neither of us wants a large number of house guests. Therefore, no third person will be invited to stay overnight without the permission of both of us.

4. If we want to stop living together but both want to remain at this address, a third party will flip a coin to decide who stays. The loser of the coin flip will move out within 30 days and will pay all her obligations for rent, utilities and any damage to the apartment.

1/13/xx	
Date	Audrey Rabinowitz
1/13/xx	
Date	Candice Dunk

Some people adopt an approach more rational than flipping a coin to decide who gets to stay in the event there is a conflict. They have an "objective" third person decide, who will base her decision on proximity to work, needs of any children, relative financial status and other relevant facts. This approach can work well, but don't pick a close friend. If she's ever called upon to make a decision, she's likely to end up a friend of only one of you.

3. Moving Into Your Lover's Rented Home

What happens when one of you moves into a house or apartment rented by the other? Is the move legal? Is the original tenant required to tell the landlord that someone has moved in?

Legally, you must notify your landlord that you are living with someone only if your lease or rental agreement specifically requires you to or limits the number of people who can occupy your unit. But even without a requirement, it's normally wise to notify your landlord. He will almost surely figure it out, and it's especially important to avoid looking sneaky if you have a month-to-month tenancy in a non-rent control area where the landlord can evict for any reason. Whether you tell the landlord that you're lovers or merely roommates is entirely up to you.

Often, the landlord will want more rent for the additional person. Unless the amount is exorbitant, it's probably better to accept the rent raise than start apartment hunting.

If your lease doesn't cover someone else moving in, you can probably bargain with your landlord. For your landlord to get you out before the lease expires, he would have to establish that you have violated one or more lease terms.

Even if your lease prohibits someone else from moving in, once your landlord accepts rent knowing that you live with someone, many courts will refuse to let him enforce the lease prohibition. If your lease states that the premises shall not be used for "immoral or illegal purposes," it is highly unlikely your landlord can terminate the lease simply

because you live with someone, unless your state has a sodomy law. Even then, the landlord's case would be difficult to prove.

a. Is There a Legal Relationship Between the New Tenant and the Landlord?

If Renee moves into Jane's apartment does Renee have a legal relationship with Jane's landlord? More specifically, does Renee have a legal duty to pay rent if Jane fails to? If Jane moves out, does Renee have the right to stay? If Jane damages the formica or lets her dog scratch the wall, does Renee have a legal obligation to pay the landlord for the damages?

There are no simple answers to these questions. If Renee just spends a few nights, she'd have no rights as a tenant and no obligation to pay rent. The same would be true during the first weeks of her tenancy, if she moves in. Jane, not Renee, entered into a contract with the landlord. But just as Renee has no legal obligations at this early stage, she has no rights either. If Jane moves out, Renee can't stay unless the landlord consents.

Renee can easily turn into a tenant with all the legal rights and responsibilities that go with tenant status by doing any of the following:

- Having the landlord prepare a new lease that includes both Jane and Renee as tenants.
- Talking to the landlord and agreeing orally to a tenant-landlord relationship. Renee must be careful of two things, however. First, an oral agreement is difficult to prove—if the landlord reneges, Renee may have a hard time proving she made an agreement. Second, an oral agreement can be easily implied from a casual conversation. Suppose Renee meets the landlord in the laundry room, introduces herself, explains that she's moved into Jane's apartment and agrees to pay rent. The landlord says "Okay." A valid agreement has been formed. Renee can be evicted only in a formal court action, but is liable for all rent and

damage to the apartment. If you're not sure you want to become a tenant, be careful of casual conversations with the landlord.

• Paying rent directly to the landlord or property manager. If Renee does this, especially repeatedly, an "implied contract," as it is known in legalese, is formed. Nothing formal has been said or written down, but the conduct of both Renee and the landlord clearly creates a landlord-tenant relationship.

b. Putting Your Agreement in Writing

When one lover moves into an apartment or house already rented by the other, turning it into a shared home requires sensitivity and openness, especially by the person who was there first. Sometimes, a party to rechristen the home your shared home provides a valuable symbolic "rite of passage."

However you manage the exciting emotional change, it's a good idea to write down your economic and legal understanding. If you fall into tough times, a question like, "Whose apartment is this?" can come up and cause pain, even paranoia. If you write down your understanding when you begin living together, you are forced to clarify the issues while you're both loving, not combative. Below is a sample that may help.

Moving-In Contract

Roger Rappan and Peter Majors agree as follows:

1. Roger will move into the apartment that Peter has been renting at 111 Prairie Street, Chicago, Illinois, on August 1, 20XX, and will pay Peter one-half of the $1,200 monthly rent on the first of each month. Because Peter has been renting under a lease, he will continue to pay the landlord on the first of each month for the remainder of the lease term (six months).

2. Roger and Peter will each pay one-half of the electric, gas, water, garbage and monthly telephone service charge. Peter will collect the payments, because the accounts are in his name.

3. For the first six months, Peter retains the first right to stay in the apartment should he and Roger decide to separate. If either person decides that Roger should move out during this period, he shall give (or be given) 30 days' written notice and shall be responsible for his share of the rent and utilities during the 30 days.

4. After the initial six-month period, if Peter and Roger decide to continue living together, they shall jointly lease the apartment and change half of the utilities into Roger's name. From this point forward, they have equal rights to stay in the apartment, should they break up. If both want to retain the apartment, but either or both wants to end the relationship, a third party will flip a coin to determine who gets to stay.

_____ _____
Date   Roger Rappan

_____ _____
Date   Peter Majors

4. Legal Relationship of Tenants to Each Other

Although many tenants have problems with their landlords, the truth is that people sharing a home get into far more hassles with one another than they do with their landlord. One reason is that we deal with landlords at arm's length and take steps to protect ourselves. We aren't usually businesslike with those we love. But whatever the reason, we've learned that paying reasonable attention to business details helps to preserve romance.

Let's assume you find that wonderful little affordable house next to the park and you and your lover happily sign a lease, or reach a rental agreement with your landlord. Are you each obligated to pay one-half of the rent? No. You've made a contract obligating each one of you to pay all the rent and be financially responsible for all damage done.

EXAMPLE: John and Alfonso verbally agree to a month-to-month tenancy in a brown-shingle bungalow. After three months, John becomes unhappy with the relationship. One day, he refuses to pay his share of the rent and attacks the house. The result is two broken windows, a badly dented radiator and a refrigerator without a door. Not surprisingly, Alfonso asks John to move out, which he does. Alfonso also asks John to pay for the damage and for his half of the rent. John laughs. Alfonso is legally responsible for all the rent and damage, and the landlord can sue him if he doesn't pay. Alfonso can sue John for reimbursement, but good luck collecting.

EXAMPLE: Louise and Arlene sign a one-year lease. After six months of amicably living together, Arlene quits her job and leaves. The parting isn't so amicable after Arlene informs Louise that she knows Louise is a responsible person and will take care of the rent. Louise is liable for it all for the remaining six months. Louise, however, does have a partial out. If she

doesn't want to stay, she can try to find someone to take over the remainder of the lease. Even if the lease prohibits subletting and the landlord insists on enforcing it, Louise can legally move out with no financial obligation as long as she finds a suitable new tenant who will pay at least the same rent. This is because the law requires the landlord to do whatever possible to re-rent the apartment ("mitigate damages," in legalese), and not just sit back and insist on the lease payments.

Even though you have a particular legal relationship with the landlord, you will be best off if you come to a complete understanding between yourselves—who pays what portion of the rent, who gets the place if you split up and the like—and write it down. (Use the examples above.) This isn't binding on your landlord; the main purpose is to record your understandings for one another in the event a dispute later arises.

5. Moving On

What do you do if you decide to go separate ways, but never made a written living together agreement specifying who gets the place? All you can do is make the best effort to compromise, remembering that, in most good compromises, each person believes he gave at least 60%.

Here are a few suggestions when both people want to stay, but not with each other, and haven't written anything down.

- If one person occupied first, pays the rent *and* is the only one who signed the lease or rental agreement, she has a superior claim to the apartment. But she must give the other person, with whom she has a sort of tenant-subtenant relationship, reasonable time—at least 30 days—to find another place.
- If the partners have an equal relationship with the landlord—both pay rent or both signed a lease or rental agreement—they probably have equal rights to stay. This is

true even if one occupied first. Flip a coin or have a third person mediate or arbitrate to settle the dispute. Avoid court action if you can. (See Chapter 9, Section B, on gay and lesbian dispute resolution services.)

- If the rent is a bargain or protected from dramatic increases by a local rent control ordinance, the partner who stays should consider compensating the partner who moves for the higher rent the moving partner will have to pay in her new place.

C. Will I Lose My Public Benefits If My Lover Moves in With Me?

Lesbians and gay men who receive public benefits sometimes worry that they will lose the benefits if their lover moves in. The rules vary from state to state, but in many places, having a lover move in can cause problems. If you receive benefits based on your financial condition and a physical or mental condition—aid to the aged, blind or disabled, for example—you don't risk any loss. These programs function like Social Security—once you qualify, you're left alone, other than when the agency does routine reviews of recipients.

Welfare and food stamp programs, however, are based on your financial condition only. They are large and expensive programs, often the subject of political attack. As a result you may be scrutinized in an effort to weed out "welfare cheats."

A welfare recipient is legally required to tell the welfare department of all changes in her circumstances that could affect her grant. This includes living with a lover who may be paying some bills. If the recipient doesn't report her lover's presence and the department discovers it, the recipient can be penalized, or even have her grant terminated, on the ground of "noncooperation" with the department. If the recipient reports that she's living with her lover, she'll face other problems.

If the welfare department determines that the lover is contributing money to the recipient, her grant will be reduced, normally by the amount contributed. A person is considered to be "contributing" whether she gives $100 a month cash, pays $100 of the rent, pays for food or buys the kids $100 worth of clothing. Moreover, some state regulations presume that a live-in lover contributes a set amount per month to the recipient's family, whether or not she actually does. And if the lover moves in with a recipient and doesn't contribute toward rent and utilities (or claims she doesn't), she's committing a crime of living off a welfare grant for which she doesn't qualify.

The best advice is to treat your lover as a roommate. Under welfare rules, a roommate is not presumed to contribute anything to a welfare recipient. In some counties, welfare officials may require a sworn statement by the "roommate" that she does not contribute to the recipient's support. And if your total rent exceeds the maximum amount allowed by welfare officials, be sure to tell the welfare officials that your "roommate" pays more. (Make sure the bigger room is "hers.")

Also, keep all finances separate. Avoid letting the recipient have any access or control over any of her lover's money or the welfare department will conclude the lover is "contributing" to the family. Avoid letting the lover have access to the recipient's money or the welfare department will conclude the lover is living off the recipient's grant.

Don't hide financial facts. *If one of you is receiving public assistance or benefits, be very careful how you take title to property or hold your financial assets. It can seem tempting to put or buy all property in the name of the partner who is not receiving public aid. But doing so can cause two serious problems. First, you may be exposing yourselves to claims of welfare fraud. Second, if you separate, the person whose name is "off title" will have a very hard time convincing any judge or jury that she was really a (secret) co-owner of the property. In sum, even though we frequently question what passes for the "morality" of government policy, it's bad karma, as well as a bad idea, to lie in order to obtain or preserve receipt of public funds.*

Keep food separate, at least in theory; be able to show the welfare department that you buy and store food separately. Keep cupboards marked with each woman's name in case of a home visit by the social worker. Tell the social worker that you prepare and eat all meals separately. Keep a receipt book or ledger showing that your lover pays her share, and only her share, of household expenses, such as rent and utilities. These shares are calculated on a welfare department schedule. Your lover should keep the car registered in her name only, and state that you don't have permission to use it. Yes, all this is quite a hassle, but worth it. Welfare crackdowns come unpredictably and can lead to jail sentences, not just the termination of benefits.

Having a Child by Artificial Insemination

If you have a child by artificial insemination and apply for welfare, be aware of the following: If your state doesn't automatically terminate the donor's parental rights and obligations, the welfare department might look for the donor, bring a paternity action to have him declared the father and request that he support the child. Before applying for welfare, consult a legal aid attorney who can help you keep the donor's identity private. For more on donor insemination, see Chapter 3, Section C.

These precautions sound technical as well as burdensome, we know. But technical or not, we want to stress that it is very important. If possible, try to discuss your situation with a sympathetic case worker before you set up housekeeping or apply for benefits. Most welfare departments can be a bit easier to deal with if you use a little advance planning.

D. Cash and Credit

As most of us eventually learn, often to our chagrin or regret, money is funny stuff and can do strange things to people. While most of us aspire to rise above crass money concerns, it doesn't require a big dose of realism to see that any couple must clearly agree who pays for the rent, car installments or groceries. If one partner feels she is being monetarily exploited, she is almost guaranteed to be resentful, and perhaps even enraged. We urge you to create a written agreement regarding your finances. (See Chapter 6.) But we also know that a written agreement is no substitute for trust and communication. Contracts won't enable two people to continue loving one another or prevent them from splitting up, but if times get hard, a written agreement can do wonders to reduce paranoia and confusion, and help people deal with one another fairly.

1. Joint Accounts—Dos and Don'ts

As soon as a couple moves in together, questions come up about pooling money and the property obtained with that money, or keeping it all separate. Just because you live with someone doesn't mean your financial lives need to become one. If you want to combine finances, be sure you really know and trust your partner. Don't feel pressured to combine everything when you're just starting out simply because the lesbian couple upstairs—who have been together 32 years—have only one bank account.

If you combine bank or credit accounts—that is, put both names on the accounts—both partners are responsible for all activity that takes place with the account. You're equally liable for bounced checks, overdrafts, charges over the limit and all the rest. If, on the other hand, you keep your property and debts separate, you'll have no financial obligation if your lover lives beyond his financial means. This means your paycheck cannot be garnished and your property cannot be taken to satisfy your lover's overdue bills. If your lover declares bankruptcy, your property cannot be taken, as long as you have kept it separate.

Most lesbian and gay couples choose to handle their finances according to one of the following models.

Marriage Model. Property owned prior to the relationship remains the owner's separate property. Property acquired during the relationship is jointly owned, no matter who earns the money to pay for it or who actually acquires it. You put most or all accounts—bank, credit and the like—in both names. If you split up, the property acquired during the relationship is divided fairly or equally.

Socialist Model. You open joint accounts and pay the joint bills out of joint accounts to which you have contributed according to your abilities, such as three-fourths and one-fourth.

Business Partnership Model. You open joint accounts for limited purposes, such as paying household expenses or to fund a distinct project—for example, renovating a house, saving for a vacation or making a joint investment. For all other purposes, you keep your income and expenses separate. If you open a joint account for a specific purpose, identify it as such. Ask the bank if you can name the account—"The Anderson-Henry Vacation Account." You can supplement your accounts with a living together contract specifying the percentage ownership in all property accumulated together. We use partnership-style agreements in many of the sample contracts in this book. (See Chapters 6 and 7.)

Splitsies Model. Each partner agrees to be absolutely responsible for his or her own support. Like college roommates, each buys separate food, clothes, entertainment and everything else. This couple has no joint accounts. This arrangement can be taken to extremes or can be worked out in a fairly easygoing, commonsense, "I-paid-for-breakfast, you-pay-for-lunch" way.

a. Joint Bank Accounts

In general, joint bank accounts are sensible if you limit their purpose and keep adequate records. That said, let us add that we know many lesbian and gay couples who have peacefully maintained joint bank accounts for years. But still, a joint account is a risk; each person has the right to spend all the money, unless you require both signatures on checks and withdrawals—a requirement that can be cumbersome. Another problem is recordkeeping. It's hard to know how much money is in an account if you both write checks and make withdrawals. How many of us dutifully write down withdrawals every time we visit the ATM? Can (should) we expect our lovers to do any better?

Obtaining a joint account isn't a problem. Financial institutions are happy to have your money under any name or names. You'll have to decide how many signatures will be necessary to write a check or make a withdrawal. It's easier to require only one signature, but it's riskier, too.

b. Joint Credit Accounts

Joint credit card accounts are even riskier than joint bank accounts—if your lover goes nuts, the most damage he can do with a joint bank account is for the amount you have deposited (or up to your overdraft protection). But with a joint credit card, he can charge to the credit limit and potentially do damage to your credit rating. Each of you is individually liable for the entire amount owed on a joint credit account. Here's an area where banks treat you as "family" whether you want that or not. If you want to be generous, you are better off being generous with cash, not credit. Nevertheless, many lesbian and gay couples open joint credit card accounts—some for broad purposes and some for limited purposes.

It's fairly easy to put two names on a credit card. You fill out a joint credit card application. Many companies have changed the blanks formerly labeled "spouse" to "co-applicant" or "co-applicant/

spouse." If the application form hasn't, cross off the word "spouse" and write in "co-applicant." Don't present yourself as spouses—those terms have specific legal meanings (having to do with liability and responsibility) and lying on the application is fraud.

As long as one of you has sufficient income or savings to be considered a good credit risk—that is, you'll pay the bills—you'll probably get the credit card. Creditors will generally open joint credit accounts—and why shouldn't they? A joint account means more people are responsible for a debt. Thus, if Roger and James have a joint credit card, and Roger lets his sister Fiona charge $2,500 on it, Roger and James are both legally obligated to pay the bill, even if James didn't know about it, or knew about it and opposed it. Similarly, if James retaliates by leaving Roger and going on a buying binge, Roger is legally responsible for all the charges James makes.

If one of you has a poor credit history, you may be denied a joint card, even if the other's credit is A1. The partner with better credit may have to reapply in his name only. (See Section D1d, below.)

 It's not smart to open a joint credit account with someone who has money troubles. *If your lover owes money, her creditors can cause you difficulties if you've mixed your money and property. Indeed, when living with someone who has debt problems, you should sign a contract keeping everything separate to avoid possible confusion.*

 If you break up, immediately close all joint accounts. *All too often, one person feels depressed during the break-up and tries to pamper himself or herself with "retail therapy." Don't just allot the accounts so that each of you keeps some of them. You're both still liable for all accounts—and you could get stuck paying his or her "therapy" bill.*

c. Credit Discrimination

Discrimination against lesbians and gays in credit is no longer common. Ability to pay seems to be the criterion used—not sexual orientation. If you believe you were discriminated against when requesting credit, check to see if your state or local municipality has a law barring sexual orientation discrimination. Then see if it covers credit transactions. If it does, report the creditor to the agency that oversees the law.

Beyond this, there is probably little you can do. A federal law called the Equal Credit Opportunity Act bars creditors from discriminating on account of race, color, religion, national origin, sex, marital status or age, or because all or part of a person's income derives from public assistance. Court interpretations of this law have declined to extend coverage to include sexual orientation.

d. Checking Your Credit

If you've lived together for a long period of time, or have had joint credit cards or bank accounts, it's possible that your credit histories have become intertwined, or even erroneously attributed to each other. This is usually not to your advantage, especially if one of you has bad credit. What can you do, aside from getting angry when your credit application is denied? Simple. Check your credit rating.

Credit bureaus are companies that specialize in keeping credit histories on almost everyone. When a bank, department store, landlord or collection agency wants information about a person, they can get it by paying a small fee to a credit bureau. The federal Fair Credit Reporting Act gives you the right to examine your credit file. If the file contains false or outdated information, the credit bureau is required to correct it, or, if it disputes your claim that it's false or outdated, to include your version of the dispute in your file.

How (and Why) to Check Your Credit Report

If you've lived together for a long time or have had joint credit card or bank accounts, it's possible that your credit report has become intertwined with that of your partner or has information on it that belongs only to her, and not to you. This is usually not to your advantage, especially if your partner has bad credit.

Your credit report contains your credit history. Credit reports are maintained by credit bureaus—companies that collect information related to your creditworthiness, including your bank and credit card accounts, loans (such as mortgages, car loans or student loans), payment history on those loans and accounts, delinquencies on accounts, bankruptcy filings, criminal arrests and convictions, current and previous employers, lawsuits and judgments against you and tax or other liens. Creditors, landlords, employers, banks and collection agencies can request and review your credit report.

Unfortunately, many credit reports contain inaccurate or outdated information. If you have some joint accounts with your partner or have been living together for a long time, the credit bureaus may have included information on your credit record about your partner's separate accounts. Information about separate accounts should only appear on the report of the partner responsible for that account. Information about joint accounts should appear on both reports.

Each partner should request a copy of his or her credit report and review it for errors or outdated information. It's a good idea to do this every year. Contact one of the three major national credit bureaus to get your report. You'll have to pay a small fee (about $8.50; less in some states). In some circumstances, the report is free—for example, if you are unemployed and looking for work, are on public assistance, have been denied credit or believe someone stole your identity or opened up accounts in your name without your authorization.

The three major national credit bureaus are:

- Equifax, P.O. Box 740241, Atlanta, GA 30374; 800-685-1111; http://www.equifax.com
- Experian, National Consumers Assistance Center, P.O. Box 2002, Allen, TX 75013; 888-397-3742; http://www.experian.com
- Trans Union, Consumer Disclosure Center, P.O. Box 1000, Chester, PA 19022, 800-888-4213; http://www.tuc.com.

If you find errors on your report (for example, a car loan for which your partner is the only signatory on the promissory note) or outdated information, notify the credit bureau in writing. The bureau is required by law to correct your report. If the bureau investigates the item and disagrees with you, at the very least you can include a brief explanation on your report about the disputed item.

For more information on what information can appear on your credit report and for how long, how to correct errors and how rebuild credit after a financial setback, see *Credit Repair*, by Robin Leonard and Deanne Loonin (Nolo).

2. Buying and Investing Together

Many couples make purchases and investments together, such as houses and cars. Shared home ownership is covered in Chapter 7. Here we cover shared ownership of and investment in other assets.

It's not difficult to make any joint purchase or investment. Salespeople are used to seeing all combinations of people buying and investing together. In major urban areas, you may be able to find gay or lesbian investment brokers, car brokers, loan brokers and the like. Take a look at the classified section of your local gay or feminist newspaper.

If you make a shared purchase or investment, you should prepare an agreement reflecting your joint ownership or investment percentages. Samples are in Chapter 6. If your purchase or investment comes with an ownership document (car title slip, for example), be sure to complete the document thoroughly. Even if only one of you takes out a loan to finance the purchase or uses separate money to invest or buy, you can both be legal owners, if that's what you want.

Certain property items come with title documents—common examples are motor vehicles and stock certificates. Stock certificates and other documents showing how investments are held are prepared by investment brokers or the company in which you invest. Title documents for motor vehicles are prepared by your state motor vehicle department.

The purpose of a title document is to show the type of ownership you have. In most states, there are two possible ways to share ownership and register property with title certificates. (This information is general. Different states have different procedures. For motor vehicle purchases, check with the local department of motor vehicles for details.)

- **Tenants in Common.** With this type of ownership, each owner owns a specific portion of the property, and can do with it whatever she likes. Ownership of tenancy-in-common property may be divided however the owners choose. There can be two owners with equal shares or one owner with 90% and the other with 10%. Or there can be several different owners all with different percentages (adding up to 100%).
- **Joint Tenancy.** With this form of ownership, by definition there are two owners, each of whom owns an equal share of property. When one owner dies, the surviving owner automatically inherits the deceased owner's share.

Joint tenancy ownership must be spelled out in the ownership document. Generally, if no type of ownership is specified on a title document of jointly owned property, it is owned as a tenancy in common. For further explanation on the types of joint property ownership, see Chapter 7, Section D.

3. Can We File Joint Income Tax Returns?

Only legally married couples who are married on December 31 of the tax year can file joint income tax returns. Until same-sex couples win the right to legally marry in the U.S., gay and lesbian couples can't file joint tax returns. (See Chapter 1 for more information on lesbian and gay marriage.)

If one partner supports the other, however, the supporter can file a tax return as a single person and claim the other as a dependent. This is possible if you meet the five following tests:

Unmarried person. If the supported person is married and files a joint tax return with his spouse —this will be unusual in your situation—the supporting partner in this relationship cannot claim him as a dependent. There's one exception—if the married couple did not earn enough to have to file a tax return, and did so only to get a refund, the supporting partner can claim the dependent.

Citizen or resident. The supported person must be a U.S. citizen, resident alien or citizen of Canada or Mexico.

Income. The supported person's gross income cannot exceed $2,900. Nontaxable money, such as gifts, welfare benefits and nontaxable Social Security benefits don't count toward gross income.

Support. The supporting partner must provide at least 50% of the other partner's total support for the year. Support includes food, shelter, clothing, medical and dental care, education, entertainment and just about anything you can think of.

Relationship. Under IRS regulations, a person who lived in your home for the entire year can be considered a dependent as long as the relationship does not violate local law. Three calls to the IRS asking what that sentence meant led to "It says what it says."

The California Franchise Tax Board has ruled that a lesbian supporting her partner and their child can file her state income tax return as head-of-household. She was previously denied head-of-household filing status because she is not legally or biologically related to the child, who was born to her partner through artificial insemination during their relationship. It remains to be seen whether this decision will be appealed or whether it will be followed in other states.

Help in Dealing With the IRS. *If you claim your lover as a dependent, the IRS objects and you want to fight it, we recommend that you get a copy of* Stand Up to the IRS, *by Frederick W. Daily (Nolo).*

E. Insurance

Ambrose Bierce observed that insurance is "an ingenious modern game of chance in which the player is permitted to enjoy the comfortable conviction that he is beating the man who keeps the table." Like Bierce, we're no great fans of insurance. Sure, insurance can be necessary or prudent, but it often seems that a giant corporation makes a lot of money by pandering to people's fears or taking advantage of their most basic needs and desires, like making sure their children will be provided for if they die.

Aside from our mistrust of large organizations and their advertising, we're frankly bothered by that contemporary killjoy, the notion that you shouldn't breathe unless you're insured against all possible disasters. Every time a fence closes off a field or an owner blocks off a swimming hole or some child care center closes down because people can't afford insurance and won't proceed without it, we all lose. You've heard it at least a dozen times. "Our insurance company says we won't be covered if we let you..." Or "We're very sorry, but our lawyer won't let us take the risk."

But sure, there may be times when you do need insurance—your home burns down, a child runs in front of your car, someone steals your color TV and VCR or you suffer an injury. Certainly, those so inclined can have lots of fun imagining possible catastrophes. We do believe that everyone should have automobile (liability) insurance and health insurance. And sadly, people with HIV or another life-threatening illness probably should have disability insurance in the event a time comes that they are unable to work.

Beyond that, it is our opinion that most Americans are overinsured. But rather than gripe about insurance, our concern is with the problems lesbian and gay couples face in getting insurance—any kind of insurance. We will let you decide whether or not you need it. If you have a problem obtaining the kind of insurance you want, try to find a gay or lesbian insurance agent. Ask your friends or check the ads in your local gay paper.

1. Health Insurance

It's a great mistake not to have health insurance—assuming you qualify for it and can afford it. Of course, you will want to get insurance before any illness or injury occurs. Some insurance companies will cover you after you suffer an ailment—such as a back injury—but won't pay any coverage for your back. As they put it, they exclude "preexisting conditions."

Many people obtain health insurance through employment; far more do not, and either have no insurance or purchase it on their own. Group health plans, usually available only through employment, are frequently less expensive and/or provide better coverage than individual plans. In addition, group plans rarely require medical examinations or questionnaires before covering employees. For information on obtaining insurance coverage for your lover or your lover's child through domestic partner benefits, see Chapter 1, Section B.

Affordable healthcare and healthcare in general for people with HIV and other life-threatening illnesses continue to be highly charged political issues. We don't have the space to write about them here. Suffice it to say, however, that the lesbian and gay community has gained "healthcare savvy" over the past decade or so. We support all efforts to make affordable healthcare a right, not a privilege, in this country.

2. Disability Insurance

Disability insurance pays you a certain sum of money, depending on how much insurance you have, each month while you are unable to work. You may have a state disability plan through your job. Don't assume your employer contributes to the state program—if your employer is self-insured, your coverage will be very different. If you do have state disability insurance, be aware that some states pay out only for a year or two, which is little help if your disability is chronic or long-lasting. In addition, anyone who has had Social Security deducted from his or her pay may qualify for Social Security Disability Insurance (SSI). AIDS qualifies for SSI; cancer may not.

Even if you're covered by state or federal disability plans, the maximum benefits payable in the event of disability may be inadequate. To determine if you need private disability insurance, find out if you're covered by other plans and, if so, how much you'll receive if you're disabled. Also check how many days must lapse between the disability and the coverage—some plans don't take effect for six months. Private disability insurance can help and can literally be a life-prolonger for people with AIDS or cancer. Most insurance agents will be delighted to tell you more about disability insurance than you ever thought you'd want to know.

3. Life Insurance

Many lesbian and gay people we know don't have life insurance, and, with a few exceptions, we don't see any compelling reason for them to get it. Of course, many people get life insurance as a benefit of employment. Life insurance makes sense primarily if any of the following is true:

- You have minor children and there would be insufficient money for them to live on—remember to consider any Social Security they'll receive—if you die without insurance.
- You include life insurance in your overall estate plan. This especially makes sense if your lover is dependent on you or you rely heavily on each other's incomes—for example, you need both paychecks to make your mortgage payments. (See Chapter 5.)
- You are facing retirement soon, and insurance can be a special kind of savings to help out the partner who will outlive the other.

If you have a life insurance policy, you can name your lover as the beneficiary. When asked the nature of the relationship, you may have to state "business partners," which is true if you own any property—even a set of dishes—together. You cannot, however, buy a policy on your lover's life and name yourself as the beneficiary unless you own property together. Insurance companies don't believe that nonmarried partners have an "insurable interest" in each other, and limit buying insurance on another person to married spouses, business partners and joint homeowners.

4. Homeowner's or Renter's Insurance

Homeowner's (or hazard) insurance is sold to homeowners when they buy a house. It insures the house against fire, flood and other acts of destruction. Any lesbian or gay couple that buys a house together will be required to have homeowner's insurance. You shouldn't have any trouble getting a joint policy. If only one of you owns the house, be sure the other has renter's insurance, because her personal belongings won't be covered under the homeowner's policy. (See Chapter 7 for more information on buying a house together.)

Renter's insurance protects tenants against the loss of their property due to theft or some act of destruction. A landlord's homeowner's policy covers only the building structure, not your possessions. Although we know one gay couple that was refused a joint renters' policy, most lesbian and gay couples have no trouble getting joint renters' insurance. The couple denied the insurance was told by the company that it didn't insure gay couples because if the couple broke up and one person moved out, taking the other's possessions, the remaining person could claim "theft" of the missing property. (That is indeed what the insurance agent said—we checked.) Of course, this characterization of gay relationships is nonsense, but so is all discrimination that lesbian and gay couples face in their lives.

Our friends wound up with two policies, but most people we know get one policy. Insurance companies, for the most part, insure property—not people—and are willing to issue one policy for a given address. They don't care who lives in the place or what the relationship is. If you do have to buy two policies, it's usually more expensive than covering everything with one policy. But on the whole, renter's insurance is pretty cheap. In addition, we've been told by a gay insurance agent that if you buy two policies, you should use the same insurance company. Two giant companies asked to settle a claim may try to shift responsibility to the other, rather than write you a check and let you replace the lost, stolen or damaged property.

5. Automobile Insurance

Being the registered owner of a car carries with it possible liability. In most states, a registered owner is financially responsible for any accident caused by his car, even if someone else is driving. The owner, or his insurance company, can pursue the driver for the money paid to the injured person, but the owner is liable even if the driver takes the first boat to Tahiti. The reason for this is simple and sound: It encourages car owners to carry insurance, and to carefully select who can drive their cars. As a practical matter, it means that you don't let just anyone, even your lover, drive your car unless you have ample insurance.

We strongly urge car owners to carry auto insurance—and in most states it is legally required. The automobile is the only lethal weapon most people use regularly. The statistical risk of an accident is all too high, and, if an accident occurs, there's a good chance that the damage will be serious. If you don't carry insurance, you may be wiped out economically, and even worse, an injured person may go without compensation because of your irresponsibility.

If you and your lover each own a car separately, you will have trouble getting one insurance policy. Insurers won't insure you and your cars as if you were married, but rather, will write you each a separate policy, and name the other as secondary driver. Of course, this costs more, which is probably one reason companies do it. If you really want one policy, change your title slips (you have to call the motor vehicles department), putting both cars in one person's name. The insurance will list the owner as the primary driver, and the other as a secondary driver. Of course, you'll need a separate written agreement stating clearly who really owns which car.

Even if you and your lover jointly own a car, you may have some trouble securing the policy you want. You shouldn't have too much trouble getting a joint policy, as long as your household looks stable and your driving records are good. But you may run into some other snags.

Some insurance companies refuse any secondary coverage to unrelated people who co-own a car. This means that you and your lover would be insured for accidents that occur when you're driving or riding in the car you own, but not while driving or riding in other cars, such as a rental car, or while you are a pedestrian. And other companies require that you designate just one person the "primary owner"—the company then provides secondary insurance for that person only. You may have to talk with a number of insurance agents before you find a policy that will provide complete coverage for both you and your lover.

If you have significant assets, you should also buy an umbrella policy, which provides additional coverage if you get into a major accident. As an unmarried couple, you'll each have to purchase your own umbrella policy.

F. Can My Foreign Lover Come Visit or Live With Me?

Suppose a fantasy comes true: You take a trip abroad and meet the person of your dreams, who just happens to be a citizen of that distant land. You come home and go back to work to earn money to take your next vacation. In the meantime, your new lover wants to know if any laws will stop him from visiting you in America. More optimistically, he wants to know that if he arrives here and you find that the sparks still fly, he can stay here with you.

1. Visiting the United States

Until the 1990s, lesbians and gay men coming to the United States for any reason at all could be denied entry if immigration authorities learned of their sexual orientation. This is because the former immigration law barred the admission of "sexual deviants" to the U.S. Now, however, no law restricts gay men and lesbians from entering the U.S. for a visit.

HIV, however, is still on the list of contagious diseases that denies entry to this country. This means that any person known to have HIV cannot come to the U.S., even for a short visit, unless the Justice Department issues a waiver.

2. Moving to the United States

Our friend Janet was traveling in Venice, and sent the following letter:

I met a woman named Sophie near the Bridge of Sighs whose hair smells of apples. She dresses in feathers and taffeta; her eyes are filled with magic and her heart with tenderness. She knows strange songs. I think I'm in love.

Janet was determined that theirs was a travel romance that wouldn't die after a few letters. Several months after Janet returned from her trip, Sophie came to the U.S. on a six-month tourist visa. As the six-month period was coming to an end, Janet and Sophie struggled to figure out a way for Sophie to stay. Finding a solution in this situation is not easy.

There are thousands of Sophies in the world—lesbians or gay men who are not U.S. citizens or permanent residents who want to move to the U.S. Most Sophies want to move here for one of the following reasons:

- Like our Sophie, she or he gets involved with a U.S. citizen or permanent resident, and the couple wants to live together in the U.S. A heterosexual U.S. citizen/resident can simply marry the non-citizen/resident and petition the government for residency rights for his or her spouse. Similarly, a U.S. citizen/resident can petition the government for residency rights for a parent, child over age 21 or sibling. Janet and Sophie considered adoption—that is, Janet would adopt Sophie—but an adopted child must be under age 14 to qualify for U.S. residency following a foreign adoption.

- Some Sophies aren't involved with Americans, but with a person from his or her own country who gets a temporary visa to work, study or do business in the U.S. The heterosexual spouse of Sophie is entitled to bring Sophie to the U.S. for the duration of the visa. A gay or lesbian Sophie won't automatically qualify for a "derivative" visa—but can apply for a separate tourist visa based on the relationship. See *Student and Tourist Visas: How to Come to the U.S.*, by Ilona Bray and Richard Boswell (Nolo).

- Sophie resides in a country that persecutes lesbians and/or gay men, and seeks refugee asylum in the U.S. (Our Sophie, who is from Italy, would not qualify for refugee status.) To qualify, the person must convince the INS that he or she has a well-founded fear of persecution based on his or her sexual orientation or HIV status. Several cases have been filed in the U.S., and more and more are succeeding. For example, lesbians and gay men from Cuba, Nicaragua, Pakistan, Brazil, El Salvador, Syria and Mexico have been granted asylum.

Anyone seriously considering applying for refugee status in the U.S. should contact a gay-sensitive immigration attorney, one of the gay legal organizations listed in Chapter 10, Section C, and the Lesbian and Gay Immigration Rights Task Force, which has offices in Los Angeles, New York, San Francisco, Seattle and Washington, D.C. You can visit LGIRTF's website at http://www.lgirtf.org. An attorney will want to gather evidence such as the text of antigay laws from the country of origin and documented persecutions of other gay people. (LGIRTF may have this information.)

Countries With Residency Rights for Same-Sex Partners

The rest of the world is moving much faster than the United States in offering immigration rights to same-sex partners. A number of countries, predominantly in Europe, now allow the non-citizen or non-resident partner to apply for permanent residency based on the relationship. Typically the couple must have first entered into a civil union, or lived together for a set period of time (usually two years). Some countries have more formal processes than others—in Canada for instance, the non-citizen must request an act of "administrative discretion" from the immigration authorities, based on humanitarian and compassionate grounds.

Here are the countries that currently allow permanent residency through a same-sex partner. However, this is a rapidly changing legal area, so for details on a particular country, or to see whether a country has joined the list, contact a local gay rights organization.

Australia
Belgium
Canada
Denmark
Finland
France
Germany
Netherlands
New Zealand
Norway
Spain
Sweden
South Africa
United Kingdom.

When Janet and Sophie talked to us, we told them that legally, their future together in the U.S. looked bleak. We suggested that if Sophie had worked in a senior-level position with a multinational corporation or had any special skills and had worked for at least two years in that field using her skills, she might qualify for an immigrant visa as a special worker or skilled worker. Sophie looked distraught, however, knowing she didn't possess any special skills. That was the last we saw of them for over a year. When we met again, they were arm-in-arm, and all smiles. Janet told us that they proceeded on a course that would have been illegal for us, as attorneys, to suggest, but which worked.

She and Sophie met Jacob, a gay American man who needed to marry for professional reasons. They arranged a marriage, along with a tidy prenuptial agreement keeping all their property separate. Sophie moved some clothing and a toothbrush to Jacob's apartment and even lived with him until they passed the grueling INS postmarriage interview, where the INS tries to weed out fraudulent marriages. After the interview, she moved in with Janet. We mentioned that we knew other couples forced to adopt the same subterfuge, but that we also knew the INS's high priority on discovering these fraudulent marriages. Janet responded that they were familiar with the INS practices and in consequence had been scrupulously discreet, telling absolutely no one about the arrangement who didn't need to know. We wished them good luck. ■

I'm Mom, She's Mommy (Or I'm Dad, He's Papa)

The desire to be a parent and raise a child is perhaps as prevalent among lesbians and gay men as it is among nongays, and the reasons are just as complex. Many feel the basic human desire to parent and nurture. Some believe that having a child ensures their immortality; still others wish to meet their parents' insistence on grandchildren. Indeed, for many lesbians and gay men, the only undesired consequence of their sexual orientation is the inability to conceive a child with the person they love.

Lesbians and gay men who wish to raise a child often face serious social and legal obstacles. As painful as these can be, those barriers were far greater ten or 20 years ago than they are today. Laws relating to lesbian and gay couples having and raising children are changing with compelling rapidity, and by the time you read this, the law will have no doubt changed again in some states. But, after centuries in which it was impossible for a person to be openly gay and raise a child, a growing number of segments of American society have begun to understand that a person's (or couple's) sexual orientation has no bearing on the ability to love and parent.

Although we provide the most up-to-date information we have, let us again emphasize that this area of law changes so quickly there may be new legal developments by the time you read these words. This is one arena in which obtaining up-to-date advice (and perhaps even assistance) from an experienced local attorney is crucial. For these reasons, don't rely on the general survey of legal issues we provide here as being definitive. Treat this as a place to start your own exploration of the process of bringing a child into your home.

Besides the obvious opportunities to become a "Big Brother" or the loving "aunt" to the little girl down the street, there are several ways to structure a legal relationship with a child. Women, obviously, can bear children, and these "single mothers" are perfectly legal parents. Men may be able to arrange to have a child with a surrogate mother and then adopt the child. Gay men and women can become adoptive parents, foster parents or guardians.

As you explore the difficult legal issues, don't underestimate the power of a child. The entry of a small being into your lives will change you drastically—and permanently. The mother of one of the authors, who raised seven children, wrote:

Most people take on the job, whether it's their own biological child or an adopted one, with unreasonable expectations as to the amount of pleasure versus the amount of frustration and resentment. Maybe children should come labeled "Warning, the Surgeon General advises that child raising may be dangerous to your health, way of life, and peace of mind."

Still, children offer fulfillment and fun, and most parents we know (including the author's mom, above) are pretty pleased with their lot, all things considered. But because child bearing will never occur "naturally" for a same-sex couple, you must decide up front the practical issues in raising a child:

- Will both of you be legal parents?
- Who will make the day-to-day decisions?
- How open will you be with neighbors, school officials and doctors?
- Will one of you stay home with the baby?
- If not, how will you handle child care—and illnesses, emergency calls from schools and the like once your child starts school?

These are only some of the issues, and we don't pretend to be authorities on child raising. We know many, many gay men and lesbians who are raising children, and are cheered by what we see. Love, commitment and understanding are clearly what matter most.

A. Becoming a Legal Parent

There are all kinds of parents in this world—loving, compassionate, youthful, open-minded, distant, stern—the adjectives go on and on. But when we describe parents—ours or any others we know—the last term we'd use is "legal." Yet for gay and lesbian couples wanting to raise a child, the question of legal parentage is of utmost importance. So before we explain how this concept applies to lesbian and gay parents, bear with us as we explain a little about the law of heterosexual parentage.

A legal parent is a person who has the right to be with a child and make decisions about the child's health, education and well-being. A legal parent is also a person who is financially obligated to support that child. When a married couple has or adopts a child, both partners are automatically considered legal parents. As a result, even if they split up and the court awards custody to one parent and orders the other to pay child support, they both remain legal parents unless a court terminates either the mom's or the dad's parental rights. Indeed, this rarely happens, unless a parent abandons a child or consents to the adoption of the child by the other parent's new spouse. A child and his legal parents have clearly spelled-out rights, even after divorce.

If the parent does not consent to adoption by the other parent's new spouse, also known as the stepparent, then the stepparent is not a legal parent. As much as the stepparent may be involved in raising and supporting the child, if the couple splits up, the stepparent won't be entitled to custody or obligated to pay child support. In a few states, a stepparent may be granted visitation with the child if a close psychological bond has developed between the stepparent and the child and it would be in the child's best interest to continue the contact.

So what does this have to do with you? A lot. The great gay and lesbian baby boom of the 1980s and 1990s (tens of thousands of lesbians and gay men have had or adopted children during those 20 years) did not, in most states, resolve the predicament of how to apply heterosexist parentage laws to the realities of same-sex parenting. Until recently, in most families, only one partner was recognized as the legal parent. And why was this? Historically, only one of you could be a biological parent; now, with ovum donation, two moms can be biological parents, but only one would be the genetic parent. Most state laws were written in a way to make adoption and foster parenting available only to married couples or single people. And so if a "single" person (such as the partner of the biological parent) sought to adopt, the rights of the biological parent (the other partner in the same-sex couple) would first have to be terminated—hardly a result a lesbian or gay couple wanted.

But then gay and lesbian lawyers got smart. They began reading the text of state adoption statutes. Most laws, they realized, authorized adoptions by married couples and single people, but didn't expressly exclude unmarried couples. Similarly, they read the stepparent adoption statutes. While all these statutes expressly authorized adoptions by the new spouse of a legal parent if the other legal parent was dead, had his parental rights terminated, abandoned the child or consented to the adoption, most statutes did not actually forbid an unmarried partner from becoming a second parent while the other parent retained her parental rights.

And now the good news: Joint adoptions by lesbian and gay couples (where both of you adopt the child born to someone other than the two of you) or second-parent (the equivalent of stepparent) adoptions by the legal parent's partner have been granted in many states. Alaska was the first state to grant a joint adoption—it did so in 1985. Since then, joint adoptions and second-parent adoptions have been granted in many states, including California, Connecticut, the District of Columbia, Illinois, Indiana, Massachusetts, Michigan, Minnesota, New Jersey, New York, Oregon, Texas, Vermont and Washington. Some have been allowed by statute, some by appellate courts and some by local judges acting in the absence of any higher court ruling. In California, parentage decrees are not always limited to egg donation situations, but can also be used in lieu of second-parent adoption—even when the second parent has no biological connection to the child.

At the same time, courts and legislatures in other states blocked joint adoptions by lesbian and gay couples—and in some states, what is allowed one year or in one particular county may not be okay in a different time or place. Because it is essential that you know your local law before you decide to raise a child together, this is one area where we strongly recommend that you seek legal advice first. Search out gay and lesbian parenting groups in your state, and others will surely point the way towards the information you need. If you don't know where to start, try the Web. The Queer Resources Directory (http://www.qrd.org) includes links to a number of parenting sites.

Adoption procedures vary widely from state to state. In Minnesota, for example, the court typically terminates the parental rights of the biological parent and then grants a joint adoption. In Washington, on the other hand, joint adoptions are handled like stepparent adoptions, which are simplified and don't require a social worker. California recently enacted a sweeping expansion of its domestic partner law. Beginning in January 2002, gay and lesbian couples registered as domestic partners can use the stepparent adoption process. This is vastly simpler (and cheaper) than using the second-parent adoption process, and is far more standardized in courts throughout the state.

From a legal perspective, the process for second-parent adoptions is similar to a conventional adoption, except that the birth parents' rights are not terminated. The adoptive parent is evaluated by an independent social worker, the judge must approve the adoption and the adoptive parent becomes a permanent, legal parent, even if she and her partner break up. Most of these cases are done as quietly as possible, with little press and hoopla.

Alternatively, some courts in California and Massachusetts have been willing to enter a parentage decree ruling that both co-parents are legal parents before the child is born, thus allowing both parents'

names to go on the birth certificate at the outset. This procedure eliminates the need for a second-parent adoption altogether. These rulings have been made in cases where one mother donated an egg to be fertilized and the other carried the baby, so that both parents had a biological connection to the child. It remains to be seen whether other states will adopt this procedure, or if it will be used where there isn't a joint biological connection.

Lawyers who represent gay and lesbian parents have developed excellent relationships with county social workers and judges who grant adoptions. Most cases end at the trial court level—this means no one appeals the case—because it's very rare that anyone opposes an adoption. The judge usually doesn't have to make a decision about placing a child in a gay household—the child will be raised there no matter what the judge decides. And judges love to grant adoptions—an adoption gives a judge a chance to put a family together, rather than to watch one fall apart.

Because of the legal complexities and political controversies, if you want to petition a court for a joint or second-parent adoption—whether or not your state is listed above—you will probably need the help of a lawyer. If you know people who have been granted a joint or second-parent adoption, call them and find out who they used. If you don't know anyone to call, contact the National Center for Lesbian Rights, Lambda Legal Defense and Education Fund or Gay and Lesbian Advocates and Defenders—the three national lesbian and gay legal organizations. Their addresses and phone numbers are in Chapter 10, Section C. They should be able to help you find a lawyer in your area.

And if your lawyer needs assistance in preparing materials for court, let him or her know that the National Center for Lesbian Rights has available a trial brief (the argument your lawyer must submit to the court) about why a joint and second-parent adoption is in your child's best interest.

Can Your Child Have More Than Two Legal Parents?

The gay and lesbian community has created all kinds of families over the past 10–15 years. As gay men and lesbians gain the rights to jointly parent, they must ask another logical question: Can a child have more than two legal parents?

We know of lesbians and gay men who marry each other and have children. In these situations, what legal role with the children, if any, do the lovers of the parents have? Or what about lesbian and gay couples who raise a child together—that is, four parents to one child (perhaps a ratio more families ought to try)?

And even more common is for a lesbian couple to have a child using the semen of a gay male friend. Often, the man is merely a donor—neither he nor the moms want him involved with raising the child. But sometimes, the man is actively involved in raising the child. Can the child have three legal parents? The answer is "possibly." In Alaska and Oregon, and in some counties in California, courts have declared both partners in a lesbian couple and the gay man who fathered the child all to be the legal parents of the child.

B. Protections for "Unrecognized" Co-Parents

Joint or second-parent adoptions may not be available in your state, or one of you may not wish to undertake this difficult process. If only one of you is (or will be) the legal parent of your child, you need to acknowledge from the outset that if conflicts arise your legal situation can be very dicey. Regardless of what the law is in your state, however, you will need to outline, in writing, your understanding about your legal relationships with the child. The purpose of the agreement is to give the nonlegal parent as much protection as possible vis-à-vis the child, in the event the legal parent is absent or the couple splits up.

As part of your preliminary education, it is imperative that you understand whether such an agreement is enforceable. In general, when parents split up and fight over custody or child support, they can go before a judge to resolve their disputes in one of two ways: as part of a divorce or as part of a paternity (proof of fatherhood) case.

Until recently, when a legal parent and his or her same-sex partner split up, there has been virtually no way for the nonlegal parent to assert her rights in court. Even now, in some cases lesbian co-parents, while receiving sympathy from the judge, have been unable to obtain visitation rights with the child they raised with the legal parent. But in many states the situation is changing. Courts in some states have granted lesbian co-parents visitation rights or even custody. Because the law on this issue is changing rapidly, and because so much depends on the state—or even the city—in which you live, we recommend that you consult a lawyer.

Because of the lack of access to second-parent adoptions for many couples, we recommend that you take two steps if only one of you is to be the legal parent of your child: First, write up an agreement specifying that although only one of you is the legal parent, both of you consider yourselves parents, with all the rights and responsibilities that come with parenting. Include a mandatory mediation (non-adversarial dispute resolution) and arbitration clause in your agreement in the event you do break up. Second, if you should split up, honor the agreement, regardless of whether or not a judge orders you to do so. It will only hurt your child if you don't.

Even though many courts may be reluctant to enforce an agreement between two adults regulating the fate of a third person—and that's what a child really is, legally speaking—having an agreement is still important. It encourages you to think more clearly about your plans, and it surely will be looked at closely by any court if disputes arise later on. Most importantly, it provides the occasion for talking out your concerns and reaching agreement on the key issues, which by itself will probably reduce the chances of a conflict later on. So while it is essential that you become aware of how the courts in your state will handle a co-parenting agreement and whether such an agreement will be strictly enforceable, writing a co-parenting agreement between the two of you will always be beneficial regardless of its enforceability.

Unlike married couples who don't have the choice of having only one partner be the legal parent, same-sex couples do have this option—and in many states, it's their only option. And, it's not surprising that in the event of a dissolution of the parents' relationship, there will be disputes about how to raise the children. Unfortunately, the legal barriers to joint parentage for lesbian and gay families can have devastating impacts in such situations.

We provide more detailed information about this situation in Chapter 9, the break-up chapter, but it's important to realize from the outset that the legal arrangements you make about your children while you are together can have a powerful impact on what happens to your family if there is a dissolution. Deciding to forgo a second-parent adoption or a joint adoption can leave the non-legal parent in a very weak position, legally speaking, and so both of you should be cognizant of this risk when you are evaluating your legal parentage options.

We also recommend that you nominate your co-parent as the guardian of your child in your will and in a guardian nomination form. The nomination form states your wishes as to who should care for your child in the event that you become unable, due to physical or mental incapacity, to raise your child. And by nominating a guardian in your will you are stating your wishes for who should take care of your child after your death. Neither form is binding on the court, but these documents can be highly persuasive and courts usually follow them.

Two sample co-parenting agreements and a sample guardian nomination form are below. For more on making your will, see Chapter 5.

Agreement to Jointly Raise Our Child

We, Erica Lang and Maria Ramos, make this agreement to set out our rights and obligations regarding our child, Chloe, who was born to us by Erica. We realize that our power to contract, as far as a child is concerned, is limited by state law. We also understand that the law will recognize Erica as the only mother of the child. With this knowledge, and in a spirit of cooperation and mutual respect, we state the following as our agreement:

1. It's our intention to jointly and equally parent, with both of us providing support and guidance to our child. We will do our best to jointly share the responsibilities involved in feeding, clothing, loving, raising and disciplining Chloe.

2. Erica has signed a consent for medical authorization giving Maria equal power to make medical decisions she thinks are necessary for Chloe.

3. We both agree to be responsible for Chloe's financial support until she reaches the age of majority (or finishes college). We each agree to contribute to Chloe's support equally. This agreement to provide support is binding, whether or not we live together.

4. Our child has been given the last name "Ramos-Lang."

5. Erica agrees to nominate Maria as executor of Erica's estate and as guardian of Chloe in her will and in a guardianship nomination form. We understand that designating Maria as the legal guardian of the child will not be legally effective until affirmed by the appropriate court. Erica is making this nomination because Maria is Erica's co-parent, and because of Maria's long-standing, close relationship with Chloe.

6. Because of the possible trauma our separation might cause Chloe, we agree to participate in a jointly agreed-upon program of counseling if either of us considers separating from the other.

7. If we separate, we will both do our best to see that Chloe grows up in a good and healthy environment. Specifically, we agree that:

   a. We will do our best to see that Chloe maintains a close and loving relationship with each of us.

   b. We will share in Chloe's upbringing, and will share in her support, depending on our needs, Chloe's needs and on our respective abilities to pay.

   c. We will make a good-faith effort to jointly make all major decisions affecting Chloe's health and welfare.

   d. We will base all decisions upon the best interests of Chloe.

   e. Should Chloe spend a greater portion of the year living with one of us, the person who has actual physical custody will take all steps necessary to maximize the other's visitation, and help make visitation as easy as possible.

   f. If either of us dies, Chloe will be cared for and raised by the other, whether or not we were living together at the time of the death. We will each state this in our wills.

8. Should any dispute arise between us regarding this agreement, we agree to submit the dispute first to mediation. If mediation is not successful, we agree to submit to binding arbitration, sharing the cost equally. In the event of such dispute, the arbitrator will be _____ . [See Chapter 9, Section B, for more detailed information on arbitration and mediation.]

9. We agree that if any court finds any portion of this contract illegal or otherwise unenforceable, the rest of the contract is still valid and in full force.

_____   _____

Date   Erica Lang

_____   _____

Date   Maria Ramos

Here is a more formal version of a parenting agreement.

Parenting Agreement

This Agreement is made on August 1, 20__, between Janice Borne (referred to herein as "Janice") and Joanne Amore (referred to herein as "Joanne") of St. Paul, Minnesota, regarding the parenting of the minor child Nina Christine Borne (referred to herein as "Nina").

The parties agree as follows:

1. This Agreement concerns the parenting of Nina, who was born to Janice on May 1, 20__. Nina is being raised in the home of Janice and Joanne and is equally bonded to both women in mother-child relationships. Janice is the sole legal parent of Nina. The parties intend, however, that Nina shall continue to be raised by both Janice and Joanne.

2. The parties agree that the residence of Janice and Joanne shall continue to be the primary residence of Nina, and that it is in both their interests that Nina be raised by both of them.

3. Even though Joanne is not the biological parent of Nina, she has participated in her upbringing since her birth and she was involved in the initial decision by Janice to have Nina. Nina has become bonded to Joanne just as much as to Nina, and Joanne has attained the status of psychological or "de facto" parent to Nina. Accordingly, both parties agree that Joanne shall have the same rights and obligations to Nina as if she were her biological parent. Should any dispute arise between the parties, Janice may not at any time assert that Joanne is not a parent of Nina or that she has any lesser parental status than any other party, by virtue of the lack of legal parentage by Joanne. Moreover, the parties hereby affirm that it is in Nina's best interests for her to maintain a parent-child relationship with both of the parties.

4. The financial support for Nina shall be borne equally by Joanne and Janice. The parties may agree from time to time as to the financial contributions by Joanne, but such modifications to this agreement shall only be voluntary by the parties.

5. If Janice and Joanne separate their residence and no longer reside together, their separation shall not alter their relationships to Nina. Each party shall continue to have the same parenting relationship to Nina, which is a primary custody relationship. The parties shall work cooperatively to make arrangements for the physical custody and/or visitation by each party, but each shall continue to share equally in the financial responsibilities for Nina.

6. In the event of any dispute between the parties regarding the custody, care, financial support or upbringing of Nina, all parties hereby agree that they shall attend mediation sessions in good faith to resolve the dispute. Each party shall willingly participate in at least four mediation sessions to be held once weekly, with the cost of the mediation to be shared equally by the parties.

7. The parties agree that the District Court of the State of Minnesota shall have jurisdiction to resolve all matters regarding the custody, visitation and support of Nina. Both parties agree that they will willingly allow the participation of the other party in any proceeding to determine the parentage, custody, visitation and/or support of Nina, without any jurisdictional objection.

8. If any attorneys' fees or costs are incurred by either party in a court proceeding regarding the custody or visitation or child support of Nina, then the Court shall have jurisdiction to award attorneys' fees and costs as provided by the relevant sections of this state's family code, even though the proceedings may be in a parentage or other action rather than in a dissolution or separation proceeding.

9. Joanne is hereby nominated by Janice as the guardian for the person and estate of Nina, in the event that Janice becomes unable to care for Nina, to serve without bond. If Joanne cannot serve as Nina's guardian, then Janice's mother Hermine Borne shall be nominated to serve as guardian.

10. This agreement is the only agreement between the parties with respect to Nina. It may be waived, altered or modified only with the written consent of both parties. In the event that any part of this agreement is held to be invalid, the remainder of the agreement shall be in full force and effect.

IN WITNESS THEREOF, the parties to this agreement have executed this agreement on the date and year written below.

_____   _____

Date   Janice Borne

_____   _____

Date   Joanne Amore

Nomination of Guardian for a Minor

1. I, Sara Wilson, the natural mother of the minor child Jacob Fong-Wilson, who was born on July 15, 20__, hereby declare my wishes as to the individuals to be appointed the legal guardian of the person and property of my son in the event that I am unable, physically or mentally, to care for my child.

2. I nominate Andrea Fong, currently residing at 220 Main Street, Springfield, California, to be the legal guardian of the person and property of my minor child Jacob Fong-Wilson. This nomination is based on the fact that a loving and parental relationship exists between Andrea and Jacob. Furthermore, my son has lived with this adult and looks to her for guidance, support and affection. It would be detrimental to my son to deprive him of this established relationship at a time when I am unable to provide the security and care necessary to my child's healthy development.

3. In the event that Andrea Fong is unable to serve as a guardian or is disqualified by a court of law from serving, I nominate Mona Wasserman to serve as the guardian of the person and property of the minor child Jacob Fong-Wilson.

4. Both the identity and whereabouts of the minor child's natural father are unknown to me. [*Or* The minor child was conceived through alternative insemination by donor and has no natural father.] [*Or* The minor child was conceived through alternative insemination by donor, and said donor has waived, in writing, any and all rights he may have to object to my nomination of a guardian.]

5. I have purposefully not nominated my parents or siblings to be the guardians of my child in the event of my disability because they lack an established, close and warm relationship with my child, and I believe it would be detrimental to Jacob to remove him from Andrea and place him with adults who are, for all practical purposes, strangers.

Executed this 4th day of May, 20xx, at Springfield, California.

_____ _____
Sara Wilson

Witnesses:

_____ _____
Name   Signature

_____
Home address and telephone number

_____ _____
Name   Signature

_____
Home address and telephone number

Guardian Nomination form by the National Center for Lesbian Rights, *http://www.nclrights.org.*
Reprinted with permission.

C. Having Your Own Child

We are having babies. With great planning and consideration, lesbians and gay men are bringing much-wanted and well-loved children into the world. Some lesbians and gay men have married just to have children. We won't discuss this here; there's ample literature—both fiction and nonfiction—about the consequences of such arrangements. Aside from marriage, there are other ways to have your own child. Lesbians can get pregnant. Gay men don't have the same biological opportunity, but they can try to make private arrangements with women willing to bear their children.

If you are like most lesbians and gay men who consider having a child, you may be asking any of the following questions:

- Is it possible for my lover and me to raise a child without interference from a sperm or egg donor?
- If a sperm or egg donor now agrees to let me bring up the child myself, how can I be sure he or she will never seek custody?
- If I agree to be a sperm or egg donor, can I later be held liable for support?
- Is it really possible—and legal—for me to pay a woman to give birth to my child?

The answers are complex. A man and a woman can write an agreement concerning their rights and obligations to each other and the child, but neither the child nor the state is bound by the agreement. A child has the right to receive support from both legal parents (unless a parent's rights have been terminated or that parent is not legally considered to be a parent) until she becomes a legal adult. Agreements regarding custody and visitation are recognized by courts, but a court can decide that an agreement isn't in "the best interests of the child" and ignore it.

A lesbian who doesn't want to share parenting with her child's biological father has several choices. The most obvious is not to let him know he's parenting. While this approach can sometimes work, it often presents problems. For one, having casual sex with someone can be dangerous. Second, it often takes more than one or two leaps in the hay to get pregnant. And third, there are moral questions—should a woman feign a relationship with a man just to get pregnant? Should the mother conceal the identity of the father from the child when the mother knows it?

It important that everyone recognize that there are two distinct sets of issues here: 1) Is the donor going to be the legal parent or not; and 2) What role will the donor actually play in the child's life. The decision about being a legal parent will determine whether the donation should be made through a doctor and whether the donor should sign a parentage statement. As to the second issue, all parties involved should work out, through lengthy and careful discussion, the role the donor will play. The parties can then put the decisions about the donor's role into writing, notwithstanding the fact that in many states such agreements are not strictly enforceable under law.

1. When a Lesbian and a Gay Man Parent Together

One arrangement is for a lesbian and gay man to have and raise a child together. They don't have to get married, and often they don't. They won't have an intimate relationship, other than being good friends and the parents of the same child. And if they are both acknowledged as the biological parents of the child, they will both have full legal rights and duties—regardless of their sexual orientation or marital status.

EXAMPLE: Julie wanted a child. She also wanted one of her male friends to be the father so that the child would have the emotional and financial support of a father. She ruled out her straight friends, fearing that they'd be given legal preference if any custody dispute developed. On the other hand, she was concerned about the HIV status of her gay male friends.

Her friend Victor also wanted to be a parent. He agreed to be tested for HIV every month for six months. If the results were negative, he would parent with Julie—she would have custody and he would have visitation. They knew they were each obligating themselves for support until the child reached legal adulthood.

Julie and Victor arranged for counseling, to get support for their arrangement and to test the sincerity of their commitment. They realized that their agreement would probably not be le-gally binding if challenged in court, but they knew it was important to write down their understanding, both for clarity and to refresh their memories in the future.

Here's the agreement they made regarding their daughter, Leslie.

Contract Regarding Child Support and Custody

This agreement is made between Julie Shatz and Victor Lawrence to express our understanding as to our rights and responsibilities to our child. We fully realize that our power to make this contract is limited by state law. With this knowledge, and in a spirit of cooperation and mutual respect, we wish to state the following to be our agreement:

1. Within ten days after the birth, Victor will sign a statement aUlNowledging that he's the father; his name will be on the birth certificate.

2. Our child will be given the last name Shatz.

3. Julie will have physical custody; Victor will –reasonable rights of visitation. Julie will be sensitive to Victor's needs and will cooperate in all practical ways to make visitation as easy as possible.

4. Both of us will do our best to see that our child has a close and loving relationship with each parent.

5. Victor will provide support in the amount of $200 a month for the first year after our child is born. Thereafter, we will arrive at a mutual agreement each year for the amount Victor will pay, taking into account:

    a. The needs of our child

    b. Increases in the cost of living

    c. Changes in Victor's salary and income

    d. Changes in Julie's salary and income.

6. We will make a good-faith effort to jointly make all major decisions affecting our child's health and welfare.

7. If either Julie or Victor dies, our child will be cared for and raised by the other.

8. If any dispute or problem arises between us regarding our child, we agree to seek counseling and professional help to try to resolve those problems.

_____　_____
Date　　　　　　　　　　　　　　Julie Shatz

_____　_____
Date　　　　　　　　　　　　　　Victor Lawrence

⚠️ **Signing a parenthood statement.** *If the biological father will be involved with raising the child and he isn't married to the mother, he should sign a written statement acknowledging paternity as soon as possible after the child's birth. In addition, the mother should sign a statement acknowledging his parenthood. Whether or not he signs a statement, the father is legally responsible for support. Signing a statement is the simplest way to avoid the brambles of the law concerning legitimacy, inheritance, father's rights and the like. Signing just after the baby is born (before any disputes arise) is the best protection for the mother, the baby and especially a father who wants rights of visitation as well as duties of parenthood. Some states, such as California, provide voluntary declaration of paternity forms for this purpose.*

Below is a sample parenthood statement. You will want to prepare three copies—and date, sign and notarize all three. The mother and father should each keep a copy, and the third copy should be kept safe for the child. While legal distinctions between "legitimate" and "illegitimate" children are fast disappearing, they still come up. Having the father sign this statement makes a child legitimate in almost all states, as if the parents had been married.

Acknowledgment of Parenthood

> Julie Shatz and Victor Lawrence hereby acknowledge that they are the biological parents of Leslie Shatz, born April 18, 20XX, in Eugene, Oregon.
>
> Julie Shatz and Victor Lawrence further state that they've welcomed Leslie Shatz into their lives and that it is their intention and belief that they've taken all steps necessary to fully legitimate their child for all purposes, including the right to inherit from and through Victor Lawrence.
>
> Julie Shatz and Victor Lawrence further expressly acknowledge their legal duty to properly raise and adequately support Leslie Shatz.
>
> _____ _____
> Date   Julie Shatz
>
> _____ _____
> Date   Victor Lawrence

2. Lesbians Having Children by Donor Insemination

For lesbians, donor insemination is a highly desirable—and probably the most common—way to become a parent. Sperm is injected into the uterus and, if it fertilizes an egg, a child develops. The woman doesn't have intercourse.

Donor insemination is often used when a married woman is unable to become pregnant through sexual intercourse with her husband. If her husband is able to produce sperm, she will be inseminated with his semen. If he is not, she will be inseminated with the semen of a donor (often chosen because he has characteristics similar to the husband's). In most states, if the donation is handled by a physician, the donor has no legal rights to or obligations toward the child—the husband is legally considered the father.

For lesbians, there are many advantages to conceiving by donor insemination. It can be done without medical personnel or any great expertise—although from a legal point of view, using a physician is normally advisable. Also, unlike adoption, donor insemination avoids entanglement with the state; no social worker comes snooping into your life. Finally, if the woman uses a sperm bank, the identity of the donor can be (and usually is) kept secret, thus eliminating future problems of custody and visitation while the child is a minor. Some sperm banks offer the option of allowing your child to contact the donor once the child turns 18.

But if the mother uses a known donor, is he considered the father? If she had a husband, clearly the answer would be no. For lesbians, there is no easy answer. Donor insemination laws vary from state to state—many states' laws apply only to married women. Several states don't have any laws in this area at all. Interestingly, few states have promulgated any laws governing the legal fate of children born from donated eggs, but most experts believe that the laws regulating donated sperm will be applied to disputes involving donor eggs.

a. The Law on Using a Sperm Donation

As more gay men "come out" about the desire to be parents, you can no longer assume that gay male donors won't be interested in co-parenting. Therefore, you will have to make a conscious decision rather than assume one outcome or the other about this important issue.

If you want to eliminate the potential possibility that your donor will assert himself as the father, go the route of an anonymous donor. You can contact a sperm bank yourself or you can ask your doctor to obtain sperm from a sperm bank for you. Sperm banks are often associated with medical schools and donors are often medical students. You can specify race, religion, complexion and often even height. The donors are asked to provide a thorough medical history (including illnesses of parents and grand-

parents) and are tested for diseases—both acquired (such as syphilis and AIDS) and hereditary (such as sickle-cell anemia). The donor will never have the rights or obligations of a parent. Some sperm banks will allow offspring to contact donors at age 18, but rarely is contact allowed before that age.

Some women object to using a sperm bank—it's impersonal, it usually requires that a doctor get involved and if, heaven forbid, the child should have a rare illness that the sperm bank never tested for, it might be impossible to find the donor. But keep in mind that if you don't use a sperm bank, you are taking a risk that the donor will assert himself as the father.

An increasing number of states offer you some protection. In Oregon, for example, the law states that a man who donates his semen for use in donor insemination with a woman other than his wife loses all parental rights. A court interpreting this law held that it is valid as long as the woman and the donor did not have an agreement giving him rights to parenthood. If they had made such an agreement, the court ruled, then this statute would unconstitutionally take away his right to be a father.

In Colorado, the statute states that the "donor of semen provided to a licensed physician for use in donor insemination in a woman other than the donor's wife" is not considered the legal father. A similar law is in effect in California.

In a case interpreting the Colorado statute, the court focused on the absence of the word "married" before the word "woman" in the law. The court held the law to be ambiguous with respect to known donors and unmarried women, and therefore examined the mother and the donor's conversations, understandings and agreements. This case emphasizes the need to be clear and consistent in your dealings with any known donor.

Using a known donor is complicated, since it is never possible to predict with any certainty how any particular parent—mother, father or donor—will feel once the child becomes a real person. For that reason, we encourage everyone to talk out these issues thoroughly, both the couple privately with one another, and then jointly with the donor.

It's important that you work out who is going to make decisions about the child, and that you feel deep respect and compatibility with each other. Having a child together is a long-term commitment that doesn't have the "divorce" option that you have with a partner. We have watched with great joy some incredibly close and meaningful family connections between donor-dads and moms, but we've also seen some very painful conflicts that erupted when deeper issues had been left unresolved.

If you prefer to use a known donor, you basically have two ways to select him:

- You can use a man you know or are introduced to who has assured you that he doesn't want to be the father. This requires tremendous trust and is very risky.

  In a New York case, for example, a lesbian couple had two children using different donors. The first donor waived all parental rights. So did the second donor (a gay man), but he agreed to be available if the child asked about her biological origin. The child did just that and the donor eventually sued for paternity. New York has no relevant statute and the mother and donor did not write down their agreement. Although the trial court ruled against the donor and upheld the rights of lesbians to create their own families, the Court of Appeal reversed that decision. The case was an emotional drain, lasting two years, and led to much dissension in New York's lesbian and gay community.

- Have a friend select the donor. You and the donor remain anonymous to each other, but your friend knows both identities. Often people take the added precaution of having the intermediary pick up semen from more than one donor and mixing it together so even the intermediary isn't sure whose sperm actually fertilized the egg. This may lessen the chances of conception, however, as antigens in the two semen samples may conflict and inhibit fertilization.

In subsection c, below, we provide agreements you can use if you go the route of a known (either to you or to an intermediary) donor.

b.   Using a Doctor for Insemination

In a few states, using an unknown donor isn't the only way to protect yourself from a man who later claims to be dad. In California, Colorado and Illinois, for example, the statutes state that the "donor of semen provided to a licensed physician for use in donor insemination in a woman other than the donor's wife" is not considered the legal father. If you select the donor but have him deliver his semen to your doctor who performs the insemination, the donor won't be considered the father. But you must use the doctor. In one California case, a court held that where a licensed physician hadn't been used, the donor known to and chosen by the mother was the legal father of the child, entitled to full parental rights and responsibilities.

Several other states have similar laws; however, those states insert the word "married" before the word "woman," leaving open the questions of what happens when a doctor is or isn't used to inseminate an unmarried woman. And in Georgia and Idaho, anyone but a licensed physician is prohibited from inseminating a woman. It's considered practicing medicine without a license.

The bottom line is this: Except in a few states where the law is clear, if you don't want the donor to be considered the father, nothing is guaranteed if you use a known donor. Your safest approach is to use a doctor and have the doctor obtain the semen from a sperm bank. But the honest reality is that physicians in many parts of the country will not inseminate an unmarried woman. So if you want to use a doctor, you may have to shop around. Contact any feminist clinic or a Planned Parenthood office for a possible referral. If you want (or have no choice but) to use a known donor or not use a doctor, be aware of all of the potential risks involved.

Time Out for a Story

Our friends Regina and Susan wanted to have a child. They talked a long time about bringing a baby into their relationship, and were satisfied that the difficulties would be more than balanced by the joy and fulfillment. Regina wanted to bear the child, which was fine with Susan. Neither woman wanted to bring a fourth person (a father) into the relationship.

At one point, Susan suggested that her friend Tom, who was attractive, intelligent, healthy and had nice teeth (she liked the idea of her child having nice teeth), would be wonderful. But Regina pointed out that, no matter how sure they were that Tom didn't want to be involved in raising the child, there would always be the possibility that he would change his mind and seek visitation. And there was no way to guarantee to Tom that neither Regina nor the state would ever ask him for child support. The best they could offer Tom would be a written agreement, saying he wouldn't be financially responsible, but they knew it might not be enforceable.

Finally, Regina and Susan decided that Regina would have a child by donor insemination, with the donor never being involved. They considered saving the doctor and sperm bank fees by having a friend act as a liaison. This made sense, but Regina decided that because she lives in California, she'd use a doctor for the insemination.

Regina and Susan were reassured by the doctor that the donor had no history of inheritable mental or physical illness, or communicable disease. They gave hair, skin and eye color, as well as racial and ethnic background, preferences. After five months of inseminations, Regina became pregnant. She was fortunate to find two other women who had been inseminated about the same time and they started a weekly "support group." They discussed questions common to all mothers and some unique to lesbian mothers who have children by donor insemination. All were concerned about what they would tell their children in later years.

Susan and Regina went to classes on natural childbirth. Finally the great day arrived. Regina gave birth to a beautiful, healthy girl in a San Francisco hospital. They were surprised that their child was a girl, however, because they knew that 75% to 80% of children conceived by donor insemination are boys. The family is doing very well.

c. Donor Insemination Agreements

Here are some agreements for a woman to use when the donor is unknown to her, because she uses a doctor or some other intermediary. You can use the same agreements, with some modifications, if you know the donor. Remember that only a few cases have been decided in this area, so the enforceability of these agreements isn't certain. And let us remind you: Courts do not look favorably upon a woman who argues: "We agreed he wouldn't be the father. Yes, I let him visit the child after the child was born, but I never intended him to be the fa-ther." If you don't want him to be the father, then say no to any contact. You can never predict when his monthly Sunday visits will lead to his mother coming around to see her "grandchild."

While our expertise is in legal and not medical matters, we should point out that most doctors strongly recommend that all sperm be frozen and quarantined before being used by a prospective mother, to ensure that you aren't transmitting HIV virus, hepatitis or any other life-threatening disease. This is what all sperm banks do. If you want more information on this important caution, check with a sperm bank or with the National Center for Lesbian Rights (http://www.nclrights.org).

Donor Insemination Agreement

I, [name of donor], have been given the opportunity to donate my semen for the purpose of donor insemination of a woman whose identity is unknown to me, and wish to protect my interests and those of all concerned. In furtherance of this desire, I freely state that:

1. I understand the purpose of such donor insemination is to produce a child or children.

2. I don't expect to have divulged to me the identity of the woman, or of the child or children who may be produced as a result of such insemination, nor do I expect to learn whether such insemination(s) result in the birth of a child or children.

3. I agree not to seek the identity of the child or children, or of the mother, and I waive all parental rights which I might have regarding the child.

4. I donate my semen with the understanding and agreement that the person who's responsible for its collection will undertake to keep my identity confidential and unknown to anyone except those directly involved in the collection.

5. I agree to submit to a physical examination carried out by a qualified medical doctor, as well as to tests for the detection of any inheritable disease or other defects, after each test and procedure is explained to me; I further agree to supply true and full answers to the doctor in connection with all relevant questions bearing upon my health and family background. It's my understanding that such information will be treated in confidence, and not linked to my identity in any documents outside the confidential files of the doctor (or intermediary) responsible for the semen collection.

6. I understand that any and all financial compensation I receive will be payment for the expenditure of my time in medical examination and semen collection, as well as reimbursement for loss of income and travel expenses because of my donation. This amount is estimated to be $_____. [If the donor wants no compensation, eliminate this clause.]

_____   _____
Date   Donor Signature

_____   _____
Date   Doctor (or Intermediary) Signature

a. Naming the Child

You can name your child anything you want. Many couples give the child the last name of the nonbiological parent, whether or not that parent will be considered a legal parent. In fact, when the nonbiological parent won't be considered a legal parent, giving the child that parent's last name can provide additional evidence that the partners fully intended to be equal parents.

b. Completing the Birth Certificate

If you have a child by donor insemination, you may feel a little odd when you see the "Father's Name" blank on the hospital form used to request the birth certificate. Similarly, gay men who use a surrogate mother to bear their children may feel flummoxed when it comes time to fill in "Mother's Name." Here are your options.

- Don't put the name of the sperm donor (if known) or the surrogate mother, unless you want that person to have rights or responsibilities. Remember to be consistent in your behavior toward and about the donor/surrogate mother.
- Don't put your lover's name (even if it's sex-neutral, like Chris or Lee). This is illegal and could raise many eyebrows—and could even slow down your partner's efforts to adopt your child.
- You can put "unknown."
- Many people simply write in "Name withheld."
- If you want to be bold, you can write by "donor insemination" or "surrogate mother," but consider any later privacy concerns for the child.

You can mark the hospital form "Do Not Report" so that the information isn't given to the newspaper "Births" columnist.

Californians Have Another Option

The California Department of Vital Records and Statistics issues birth certificates for use by same-sex parents doing a second-parent adoption. Instead of blanks for "Mother" and "Father," the Department now designates the blanks "Mother/Parent" and "Father/Parent." Now you can list your lover in the other blank after the adoption. At the time of the adoption, when you fill out the Court Record of Adoption (Form V544), put the biological mother's name in the "Mother" slot and the other mother's name in the "Father" slot. When the Department of Vital Records and Statistics types up the birth certificate, they will replace "Mother" and "Father" with "Parent" and "Parent."

---

c. If the Child Wants to Find the Donor or Surrogate Mother

Several women ask if it's possible to have the best of all worlds—anonymity now, with the possibility that little Justin will be able to find the donor later, perhaps when he's a teenager or older. This is a good question, and should be seriously considered. Many adopted children seek to meet their biological parents and the offspring of sperm donors often want the same option. The solution is to use a sperm bank—or private liaison—that uses what is called an "identity release protocol." Under this system, all parties agree that the offspring can obtain the name, Social Security number and last known address of the donor when he or she turns 18. Your child doesn't have to contact the donor, but having this choice can be very important to most donor-inseminated kids.

D. Adopting a Child

As we discussed in Section A above, doing a second-parent adoption presumes, as the name of this process suggests, that one partner is already a legal parent, either because she or he is the biological parent of the child or has already adopted the child. If neither of you is already the legal parent of the child—even if one or both of you has been acting as a foster parent or legal guardian of the child—your situation is quite different. You will be undertaking an adoption process that is just like that used by straight couples who are adopting a child born to someone other than the two of them. The biological parents' rights will be terminated—unlike what occurs with a second-parent adoption. This means that your adopted child has the right to inherit from you, and not the biological parents, and your child (or your partner) can come after you for payment of child support if you fail to provide it.

It is important to recognize that in some states openly gay people—whether single or coupled—are not allowed to adopt a child. In other states, the law doesn't expressly prohibit such adoptions but in practice they are very difficult to obtain. And sadly, courts throughout this county—as well as many state legislatures—have imposed absolute bans on adoptions by same-sex couples. In some of those states, only one of you will be able to become the legal parent of the child. In other places, even "single" lesbians and gay men can face serious obstacles to adopting a child.

Adoptions always involve a court's approval. Prior to the adoption, the court generally terminates the biological parents' rights (this may be done minutes or weeks, or if an agency is involved, months or years, before the adoption). Then the adoption occurs, and the court issues an order declaring the child adopted and stating that you're the legal parent(s). Before you go to court, an official agency (usually social services or juvenile probation) will investigate you and your home. In most adoptions, the investigating agency recommends whether you'll be allowed to adopt. If the biological parents' rights were terminated prior to the adoption and an agency has already approved you, the adoption won't usually be contested. And unless the judge won't permit an adoption by a lesbian or a gay man, the court proceeding will be routine, with the judge following the agency's recommendation.

Because the process is so legalistic, if you want to adopt you will need to hire an attorney. Adoptions aren't that legally complicated, but a judge will be reassured by the presence of a lawyer, and will probably be disturbed if you have no lawyer present—and this is not the time to make a procedural error. To utter the obvious, a lesbian or gay man adopting a child wants the judge to be as acquiescent as possible. Also, a lawyer with good local connections who has handled gay and lesbian legal issues before will know how to get a favorable social worker or disqualify a hostile judge.

Florida, Utah and Missouri expressly prohibit lesbians and gay men from adopting. Other states are not necessarily supportive of lesbians and gays who want to adopt; bills are regularly introduced into state legislatures to bar such adoptions and courts in numerous states have refused to allow same-sex couples to adopt.

Accordingly, each state requires a customized legal strategy. Although several states no longer officially deem lesbians and gay men "unfit" to raise a child, many lawyers feel it's easier to have just one parent adopt as a single person and then seek a second-parent adoption, rather than have the couple petition jointly. (See Section A, above, for information on second-parent adoptions.)

Although there are no statistics about gay parent adoptions, single people are adopting in increasing numbers. Surely some, perhaps many, of these people are gay.

The increase in single-parent adoptions hasn't solved the major problem with adoption today: The number of children available for adoption is very low. Birth control has reduced the number of "illegitimate" children, traditionally the major source of adopted children. And the stigma against having a child outside of marriage is gone, increasing the number of unwed mothers who keep their children. Agencies are trying to find homes for "hard-to-place" children—usually disabled or older kids. Don't be discouraged, but be realistic. Adoption is a difficult and potentially expensive process. Your chances of adopting a perfectly healthy newborn are slim. But lesbians and gays have done it, and if you long for a child and cannot, or choose not to, give birth, by all means explore adoption.

Start with a local lesbian or gay parents organization. Its members will know what's been done and what's possible in your area. If you proceed, find a friend in the adoption agency—someone sympathetic to your cause. Even in the best situations, be prepared to wait about two years between the initial application and the placement of a child in your home.

1. Methods of Adoption

There are basically four ways to adopt:
- through a public or private agency
- through the mother (or an intermediary)
- through an international agency—that is, a foreign adoption, or
- as a second parent.

a. Agency Adoptions

Many gay men and lesbians adopt through an agency. The agency—either a state agency, such as the county welfare department, or a private adoption agency—locates children available for adoption. (Foster children are often adopted by foster parents this way; in fact, foster parenting is one of the most common avenues for adopting in many states. See Section E, below, on foster parenting.)

Would-be adoptive parents are interviewed by the agency, which has obtained consents to adopt from the biological parent(s). In some instances, the child has already been removed from the home and the parents' rights have previously been terminated by court order. The agency recommends to the court who the adoptive parent(s) will be. Traditionally, most agencies favor married couples over single parents. No agency we know of "favors" les-

bians or gays, though some treat them like any other single people or like a married couple. Unfortunately, however, many agencies will rule out gays and lesbians from adopting. For these reasons, you need to be selective in choosing an agency. There are, however, advantages to using an agency:

- By law, in nearly all states, an agency adoption provides maximum assurance that a child's biological parents won't change their minds.
- The procedures are established, and the agency is likely to be known to the court, which means the judicial procedure should go smoothly.

b. Private Adoptions

In a private adoption, you find the child yourself, or with the aid of a private adoption firm or an individual intermediary (in the states where using a non-agency intermediary is legal). No state agency gets involved, except to investigate the home and report to the court. Private adoptions are legal in most states and are quite common for adopting infants. The adopting parents normally pay the biological mother's medical expenses and sometimes her living expenses, in addition to paying the legal fees. Paying any other "fee," however, is illegal—although legal fees are often so high, it feels as if you are charged an additional fee.

In many states, it's illegal to advertise for an adoption, and using an intermediary to locate or place an adopted child is questionable. In Virginia and Washington, an intermediary may place a child; in Arizona, the intermediary may assist the biological mother in the placement. In California, however, it's a misdemeanor for anyone except a parent or a licensed agency to place a child. Nonetheless, many lawyers "help" with placement.

Once you or your intermediary locate a baby, you'll need the consent of the biological mother, and the biological father, if his identity is known and he hasn't abandoned the child or otherwise forfeited his rights. The biological parent(s) sign a consent-to-adopt form, and then an adoption proceeding is filed in court. The law may require, or the judge may order, an investigation into your home and a report. And although your attorney and friends can help you decide whether the child's biological mother should be told of your sexual orientation, there's usually no reason to tell the agency.

⚠ **Beware of "black market" adoptions.** *Almost everyone has heard the term "black market adoptions," and the idea of people skulking down dark alleys to buy a baby from a mother or an intermediary isn't just unpleasant—it's illegal. One way this "adoption" works is to have the biological mother register at a hospital in the name of the adoptive mother so that the birth certificate contains the "adopting" parent's name. However handled, it leaves the adoptive parent open to blackmail and the risk of losing the child should the biological mother change her mind and try to reclaim the child.*

c. Foreign Adoptions

It may be possible to adopt a child from another country. U.S. immigration laws provide a special visa for a child who's to be adopted by an American citizen. As a practical matter, the child may have to be an orphan, because U.S. immigration laws require that a non-orphan have lived with you for two years before starting their immigration paperwork. There are two methods of adopting an "alien" child.

- The child may be adopted in his or her own country. The child must be personally seen by the adoptive parent(s) before the adoption is completed.
- The child may be admitted to the United States for adoption if the adopting parent(s) have met the pre-adoption requirements of their state of residence.

In either case, it's sometimes possible for a single person to qualify as an adopting parent. Many countries, however, strongly prefer—and even require—that infants be adopted by married couples. Also, the United States isn't alone in its societal bias against lesbian or gay adoptions. So if you are involved in a foreign adoption, you may need to keep your sexual identity private.

Adoptions by lesbians or gay men going abroad are not as rare as they used to be. You must locate the would-be adoptive child or use an agency, and then travel to the child's country and go through its adoption procedures. This can sometimes—perhaps oftentimes—become quite difficult. The adoption "laws" of many countries are murky at best. In Peru, for example, they seem to consist of finding the right person to pay money to. And Tibetan refugees in India can be adopted only if the Dalai Lama says they can.

Despite these difficulties, we know many people who have adopted outside of the U.S. Generally, you must be at least 25 years old (adopting as a single parent) and any investigation of you must be done before the Immigration and Naturalization Service (INS) will issue an immigration visa for the child. Many countries don't quickly issue final adoption decrees. Chile, for instance, issues an interim decree, and requires a two-year wait for a final decree. You must obtain a special visa for the child from the INS to bring the child to the U.S. before the adoption is final.

Foreign adoptions through an agency in your state are slightly more feasible than traveling to a foreign country. Some agencies can, and do, locate foreign orphans to be adopted by U.S. citizens. The prospective adoptive parent is investigated by the adoption agency. If it determines that you are suitable, it certifies to the INS that the state's pre-adoption standards have been met, and INS issues a visa so the child can be brought to the U.S. In general, agencies aren't being asked to find homes for children from Europe, North America or Japan.

Foreign adoptions are costly. You must pay:
- the child's transportation to the United States
- the fees of the adoption agency in the child's country
- the fees of the U.S. adoption agency, and
- attorney's fees and INS charges.

Foreign adoptions, however, have been successful for gay and lesbian people. In a New York case, a gay man was granted certification as an adoptive parent by the Justice Department to adopt a Russian child. This case was an appeal from an INS rejection of his application. As a result of this case, the Justice Department (and now the INS) will not deny an orphan visa petition just because an adoptive parent is gay and lives with a lover who will co-parent. Be prepared to be very patient and persevering.

The United States recently ratified the Hague Convention on Inter-Country Adoptions, an international adoption treaty which permits any country to impose its own restrictions on adoptions which the agency handling the adoption must then abide by. This will enable countries like China to effectively ban openly gay people from adopting children from their country.

d. Second-Parent Adoptions

In the first three of these options, the two of you jointly apply to adopt the child born to someone other than either of you. By contrast, a second-parent adoption, as described in the first section of this chapter, is where one of you is already the legal parent—either through birth or prior adoption from a birth parent—and now you are adding your partner as a second legal parent. Because you don't want to sever the legal ties with the first parent, this process is handled rather like a stepparent adoption, except that the two of you aren't legally married. Few states have actual statutes authorizing this process, and many states don't allow it, so be sure to check with a local attorney who knows local adoption law before deciding how to proceed.

If second-parent adoptions are allowed in your state, then the non-legal parent will apply—with the consent of his or her partner, of course—and the authorities will process the application much like how they process regular joint adoptions. Generally you will need to undergo a home study, which can be expensive (up to $1,500 in some locations) and a judge will need to approve the adoption. While the process is neither simple nor fun, the results are well worth it.

2. Legal Aspects of Adoption

The following information is, by necessity, general. State laws vary considerably; treat what you read here as a starting place for your research.

Age limits. Some states have age restrictions for the adoptive parent. In California, the adoptive parent must be at least ten years older than the adopted child. Other states, such as Delaware, require the parent to be over 21, and some states, such as Rhode Island, simply state "any person older than the child may adopt."

Residence. You, and normally the child, must reside in the state where the adoption case is filed. Many states require that adoptive parents bringing a child into the state for adoption notify the state or a county adoption agency. These laws don't apply if the biological parent brings the child into the state. If a child you want to adopt resides in another state, you may have to establish residence in that state before adopting. Even if you don't establish residence in the child's home state, you will have to comply with the interstate compact on adoption, and thus you may need to have an agency and attorney in both your home state and the other state.

Who may be adopted. Interreligious and interracial adoptions used to be, and sometimes still are, refused by adoption agencies and therefore courts as not considered in the "best interests of the child."

Federal law requires preference be given to the following people in the adoption or foster placement of a Native American child:

- a member of the child's family
- other members of the child's tribe, or
- other Indian families.

The law requires that the tribe be notified of most foster-adoption placements, and warns that some state adoptions can be set aside by tribal courts.

Change of name. All states permit the adoptive parent(s) to change the child's last name at the time of adoption.

Records and birth certificates. Nearly all states seal adoption records, allowing them to be inspected only if the court so orders. Adoptive parents can obtain a new birth certificate which states the child's new name and substitutes the adoptive parents for the biological parents.

Consent of the adopted child. Once the child reaches a certain age, his or her consent is required for an adoption. The age varies from age ten (Michigan) to age 14 (Texas). In a few other states, such as West Virginia and Vermont, the adopted person may have an adoption vacated by filing a dissent within one year after it's final.

E. Foster Parenting a Child

If you have an urge to be a parent, consider whether foster parenting may accomplish your goal. Growing numbers of foster-home placement agencies are placing children with gay and lesbian foster parents. Who winds up in foster homes? Children who, for one reason or another, have been dumped into the cold lap of the Mother State. Many kids have emotional difficulties, and often, either the child is considered delinquent (incorrigible) or the parent has been delinquent (abused or neglected the child, or in jail).

Some of these kids may fall into one of the following categories.

- Gay teenagers who can't get along with their parents—often the underlying problem is the teen's emerging sexual identity. Sometimes these teens are kicked out; often they run away, and occasionally, their parents just seem to have evaporated. These kids, if possible, should be placed in stable gay households.
- Children of gay or lesbian parents removed from the parents' home because of neglect, substance abuse or another problem. These children, too, should be placed in homes resembling the homes they are growing up in— that is, with a gay or lesbian couple.

In some cities, such as New York, San Francisco, Los Angeles and Trenton, agencies have actively recruited gay foster parents for such placements and juvenile judges recognize the appropriateness of making such placements. On the other hand, Nebraska will not place foster children with lesbian or gay parents. Massachusetts and New Hampshire, where nontraditional households are given low priority, have made it very difficult for a lesbian or gay person to be a foster parent. In Massachusetts, the applicant must state his or her sexual orientation, and North Dakota allows only married couples to become foster parents.

Legally speaking, a foster parent is only a temporary guardian of a child. The state has simply granted you a license to be a foster parent, but the ultimate goal is the reunification of the child with his or her parents, not the adoption of the child by you. You may get the opportunity to adopt—and in many states, there is a growing acceptance of adoption by foster parents—but in most instances, the state will try for years to bring the parents and child back together. As a foster parent, you have no long-term legal relationship with the child. The child won't inherit from you unless you provide for him or her in your will. The placement might even be emergency placement for only two days, or it might last for years.

States pay foster parents a monthly amount for support of each foster child. The amount varies among states, but in many urban areas the allowance is several hundred dollars per month. Clearly this isn't generous, and we can't imagine that anyone becomes a foster parent for the pay. Still, if you become a foster parent, the monthly allotment can help pay the bills.

1. Applying for a Foster Child

Single people (except in North Dakota) and, in many states, "roommates" can get foster parents' licenses. And some openly gay households have been licensed. So, if a gay or lesbian couple wants to become foster parents, should one of them apply to the licensing agency as a single person, or should they apply as a couple? We can't tell you how to apply, but we can give you information to help you decide.

If you want to keep your relationship private, have one person apply as a single individual. A single adult, sharing space with another adult, can become a licensed foster parent in most states. But foster care placement is at the agency's or court's discretion, so be prepared to have social workers march into your home to look about. You should plan in advance how "open" to be. And when you make your decision, be consistent; if there's one thing you can count on when dealing with social workers, it's that they'll be back.

In some instances, it may be foolish to tell a foster agency that you're gay or lesbian. Generally, however, maintaining secrecy and applying for a child is risky. The agency may find out the truth; more likely, the child will, and it's not appropriate to ask the child to lie. The question of "to be, or not to be—out" is raised often in this book, but however you answer that question for your own life, kids should be dealt with honestly. If you can locate a sympathetic social worker, you may be able to resolve your coming-out dilemma informally and personally.

2. Placing Gay Kids (and Kids of Gays) in Gay Homes

As we've said, some agencies will approve stable, caring, gay households for placement of gay-identified (the agencies' term) teenagers or children of gay or lesbian parents. These agencies realize that few heterosexual foster parents can adequately deal with gay teenagers and that children of gay and lesbian parents should remain in that environment for their foster placement. With gay teens especially, these agencies know that placing gay kids in large group homes could be problematic.

Be aware that it's often easier for a gay person or couple to become licensed foster parents than it is to actually have children placed in their home. And because foster placement is always considered temporary, the child can be removed at his or her request, your request, or the request of the agency or government probation officers. So there are uncertainties to being a foster parent, especially for a lesbian or gay foster parent.

The changes in gay foster parenting have been brought about largely by the dedicated work of many lesbian and gay people. Several years ago, Sue

Saperstein worked with the director of the San Francisco Department of Social Services to get a gay caseworker in the department to handle the foster placement of gay kids. In response, the San Francisco Foster Licensing Division of the Department of Social Services has licensed lesbian and gay foster homes.

Linda Graham worked with Project Lambda in Boston, helping place gay teenagers in gay households. Amazingly, Project Lambda was funded by an agency of the United States Department of Justice and was very successful for a few years. Ironically, Massachusetts now makes it nearly impossible for gays or lesbians to be foster parents. And in Los Angeles, Gay and Lesbian Adolescent Social Services (GLASS) certifies gay and lesbian people to become licensed foster parents. GLASS also runs four group homes to place gay, lesbian and HIV-positive teens.

Alternative Family Services of San Francisco and Sonoma counties licenses the homes of lesbians and gay men, single people, unmarried heterosexual couples and groups. This private foster-care agency places gay teenagers in gay homes and provides follow-up support.

On the average, a teenager stays in a foster home between six months and a year. Yes, this will shatter your image and dreams of a foster parent-child relationship becoming lifelong with lots of homemade cookies and adorable grandchildren. But the shortness isn't an indication of failure. The reality is that any teenager's life, and especially a foster teenager's life, is chaotic and changing; success of a placement isn't measured by duration, but by the love between the foster parent and the child, and the teenager's growth toward self-sufficiency.

3. Practical Steps to Becoming a Foster Parent

There's a foster-home division in almost every county welfare department. Call it and ask for a list of agencies, both state-operated and private, that license foster homes. Finding an agency willing to place gay-identified teenagers with lesbian and gay couples may take a little work. Ask a local lesbian or gay organization which agencies are sympathetic to placing gay-identified teenagers in gay homes. Agencies or particular social workers willing to make such placements often keep a low profile, believing themselves to be more effective that way.

Because most states have several agencies that place foster children and because you can be licensed by only one agency at a time, investigate carefully. Once you select an agency, the licensing process itself is usually quite simple. You fill out an application, are interviewed by an employee of the agency who is, or should be, concerned only with whether you'd make a good foster parent and are visited at home. In addition:

- you should be able to provide a separate room for the child
- you must have a medical exam
- you must be fingerprinted—ex-felons and ex-sex offenders aren't eligible, and
- if you're asking for a young child, you must demonstrate that you have time to care for the child, or have arranged for child care.

Above all, the most important criteria are stability and responsibility.

You may have a choice of becoming licensed as a foster home for a particular child or getting a general foster-home license and having the agency place a child. When on the general list, you have the option of refusing a child if you and the child don't hit it off. Becoming licensed for a specific child works differently.

Example: Michael and Ron had befriended Scott, a gay boy of 14. Scott was living at an institution and on weekend days caught a bus to Michael and Ron's. They drove him back in the evenings. On Thanksgiving, Scott said to Ron, "Wouldn't it be great to live here all the time?" Ron sighed. "It'd be wonderful—but it's impossible. We all know that." Later, Michael and Ron wondered if it really was impossible. They contacted Scott's social worker, who agreed that placing Scott in Michael and Ron's home would be good for him. The social worker sent Michael and Ron the application forms, and a license was granted. Scott lived happily in Michael and Ron's home.

⚠️ **Getting licensed as a foster parent takes some paperwork.** *Usually the agency will assist you with it, so you shouldn't need an attorney. If, however, you want some help or think you're being discriminated against, you may need to hire a lawyer.*

F. Becoming a Guardian of a Child

A guardian is an adult other than a legal parent who becomes legally responsible for taking care of a minor. Usually, the guardian gets physical custody of the child, and is sometimes given authority to manage the minor's assets. In most states, however, a guardian isn't legally or financially responsible for a child's actions. For example, if a child causes damage by vandalism, a parent (in most states) is liable, but a guardian isn't. There's usually an exception if the guardian agrees, on the child's driver's license application, to be financially responsible for any damage the child causes while driving.

Some guardianships are informal; others are court-appointed. In informal guardianships, the legal parents consent to the arrangement. Informal guardianships are temporary and can be changed at the decision (or whim) of whoever placed the child. They're commonly used when, because of illness, jail sentence or extended travel, a parent asks a relative or friend to temporarily take over parenting. There is no legal process. The parent simply delivers the child to the guardian with a document of authorization.

Formal guardianships involve court proceedings. An adult wanting to be appointed guardian files a petition and the court decides whether the guardianship is "in the best interests of the child." As long as everyone agrees, the judge usually grants the guardianship and issues an order establishing its terms.

If a child is eligible for welfare, the welfare benefits usually follow the child to the guardian's home, but be sure to check your state's laws. Normally, if the guardian is a close relative or meets the welfare department formalities (which are less rigid than with formal guardianships), the benefits will follow.

Example: Ben, a gay man, and Paula were old friends. Paula's son Mark had confided in Ben the summer before coming out to his mother. Paula wasn't shocked to learn that Mark was gay, but was finding him hard to handle. Mark wrote Ben the following letter.

Dear Ben:
Remember how we talked last summer about my parents' divorce? Well, I find there's another reason I want to come to Boston to go to school. I am gay. I just told mother and she said, "No 15-year-old can be gay!" Can you write her and ask if I can come stay with you for the school year? I can't even get any studying done around here! She respects you. Please!
Love,
Mark

Paula wrote to Ben at almost the same time. She had no intention of relinquishing custody or abandoning her duties as Mark's mother. She just knew they needed time apart. Her letter was a little different.

Dear Ben,
I need to talk to you. Mark has just been impossible lately, and nothing I can do or say seems to help. Of course I have known that he's gay for a long time, but he has come out to me very belligerently and accuses me of never understanding him. Frankly, right now, I don't. He has been talking about writing you. I sure hope he does.
Love,
Paula

Paula reflected on the various possibilities and concluded that allowing Mark to live with Ben, a long-time friend and mature gay man, made sense. Fortunately, it made sense to Mark and Ben, too. And Mark's father readily agreed—he'd taken little interest in raising Mark for years and was for any solution that didn't involve work or money on his part. A court proceeding was unnecessary and undesirable. Paula's concern was with Mark's well-being. And going to court could produce a nasty reac-

tion from a judge. So Mark lived happily with Ben during the school year, and returned to his mother during the summer.

1. Informal Guardianship Documents

While written documents aren't essential to establish an informal guardianship, they're desirable. To continue our story, suppose Mark suffered a deep cut on his arm while at Ben's. The wound would have been sewn up by a doctor, under laws authorizing doctors to do what's necessary in an emergency. But what if the doctor also recommended plastic surgery, surgery that had to be done (if at all) within 24 hours? As this is "elective," not "emergency" surgery, the doctor would require Mark's parents' permission before operating. If Ben had no document authorizing him to make medical decisions for Mark, he'd have an obvious problem if he could not find Paula. Or, to switch to a more pleasant example, suppose Mark wanted to go on a school picnic and needed written permission to attend. Ben would need written authorization in order to give permission.

And then there's the question of support. Who pays Mark's living expenses? Paula and Ben discussed it, and then wrote down their agreement. Their agreement also covered school attendance, curfews and the like. And because Mark is a teenager, he was in on the discussion and signed the agreement. After all, if Mark doesn't like what Paula and Ben decide, he can vote with his feet.

Below is a sample agreement. To prepare one of your own, adapt the sample to your specific situation. Make at least four originals: one for the school, one for the hospital and others for the unexpected. These forms aren't court orders, but have them notarized. In most situations, documents like these should suffice when a school official, doctor or someone similar needs proof that the guardian can act for the child. If someone refuses to honor the agreement, point out that you have the legal authority to act for the child. After all, that's what the agreement says. If that doesn't work, call the child's parents fast. And if a school or other public agency insists that you use its form, use it.

For more information about guardianships in California, see The Guardianship Book for California, *by Lisa Goldoftas and David Brown (Nolo).*

Temporary Guardianship Agreement

We, Paula Ruiz of 1811 Main Street, Cleveland, Ohio, and John Ruiz of 493 Oak Street, Cincinnati, Ohio, are the parents of Mark Ruiz, born to us on August 18, 1990. We hereby grant Ben Jacobs, of 44 Tea Road, Boston, Massachusetts, temporary guardianship of Mark Ruiz. We grant to Ben Jacobs the power to act in our place as parents of Mark Ruiz, to authorize any medical examination, tests, operations or treatment that in Ben Jacobs's opinion are needed or useful to Mark Ruiz.

We also hereby grant to Ben Jacobs the power to act in our place as parents of Mark Ruiz in connection with any school, including, but not limited to, enrollment and permission for activities.

During the period while Ben Jacobs acts as guardian of Mark Ruiz, the costs of his upkeep and living expenses shall be paid as follows. [Insert what has been agreed on.]

_____   _____
Date   Paula Ruiz

_____   _____
Date   John Ruiz

_____   _____
Date   Mark Ruiz

_____   _____
Date   Ben Jacobs

Notarization

Authorization to Consent to Medical, Surgical or Dental Examination or Treatment of a Minor

---

I, Paula Ruiz, being the parent with legal custody of Mark Ruiz, born August 18, 1990, hereby authorize Ben Jacobs, into whose care Mark Ruiz has been entrusted, to consent to any X-ray, examination, anesthetic, medical or surgical diagnosis, or treatment and hospital care to be rendered to Mark Ruiz under the general or special supervision and upon the advice of a physician or surgeon licensed to practice medicine in any state of the United States, or to consent to an X-ray, examination, anesthetic, dental or surgical diagnosis, or treatment and hospital care to be rendered to Mark Ruiz by a dentist licensed to practice dentistry in any state of the United States.

This authorization is valid from September 1, 20___, to June 30, 20___.

_____ _____
Date   Paula Ruiz

_____ _____
Date   Ben Jacobs

Notarization

---

2. Court-Appointed Guardianships

A court-ordered guardianship makes sense if the parent is mentally ill or incarcerated, or if a third party—usually a relative—may try to intervene and get custody. It also may be necessary to obtain benefits, deal with school authorities or manage the child's money, because an adult must be legally au-thorized to care for the child's financial assets. The guardianship process differs from state to state, and you will probably need to consult with an attorney to learn your local procedures.

If you are facing a contested guardianship, where relatives or other persons object to the guardianship, you'll definitely need an attorney's help. If you anticipate problems with the guardianship process, you should see an attorney before you begin.

Because the court proceeding and the social service investigation for an uncontested guardianship vary from state to state, and because attitudes toward gays and lesbians can vary widely, be sure to discuss your situation with a knowledgeable lawyer sympathetic to, and aware of, lesbian and gay concerns. Unless you're convinced you won't face a bi-ased, hostile judge, don't file a formal guardianship. And while heterosexual couples can safely handle their own guardianships, you'll probably want to hire a lawyer.

G. Arrangements Between a Teenager and the Adults Who'll Care for the Teen

When a teen comes to live with gay or lesbian adults—through foster parenting or a guardianship—the teen and the adults should consider making an agreement. The purpose isn't to sue each other if the garbage isn't dumped, but to formulate and memorialize understandings and expectations. Our sample agreement concerns Eric, a 16-year-old who has come to live with John and David.

Contract Between a Teenager and the Adults He Will Live With

1. **First Things**

   General: Eric is coming into John and David's home; we are making this agreement to help make our family life together as harmonious and enjoyable as possible. We realize that circumstances change and we agree to review this agreement every six months.

   Disputes: All disputes will be carried out verbally. This means no punching. It also means that we will do our best to communicate openly and not assume that the others should automatically know our concerns.

   Eric's Parents: Eric's parents will be encouraged to visit if they wish to do so and will be made as welcome as possible.

2. **Finances**

   John and David will receive $300 from the welfare department as stipend for Eric's support. The money will be used as follows:

   > $100 for rent
   >
   > $100 for food
   >
   > $50 for clothing
   >
   > $50 for Eric for spending money.

   John and David will contribute more to Eric's support than they are compensated by welfare. Further, Eric's $50 per month spending money isn't conditioned upon his doing chores. John will be the banker.

3. **Hours**

   Eric agrees to be home by 7:00 pm on school nights and by 1:00 am on weekends. He agrees to let John and David know what he's doing. He also agrees to call home by 6:30 pm on school nights and by 9:00 pm on weekends to request any later hours.

   John and/or David agree to be home by 6:30 pm on weeknights and by 1:00 am on weekends, and agree to leave a note on the refrigerator and/or call if there's any change.

4. **Meals**

   Dinner is considered a special time, and will be served around 7:30 pm. Everyone is expected to be present if at all possible.

5. **Drugs**

   Eric will obey all laws regulating drug use.

6. **School**

   Eric will be enrolled in public school and agrees to attend regularly.

7. **Chores**

   Eric will keep his room neat—but it's his room and as long as he confines his mess to this area, there will be peace. Eric won't spread his belongings around the rest of the house. If he does, they will be placed in his room.

   John and David will shop, do the general cleaning, cook, keep the household accounts, do the wash and do the maintenance around the house.

   Eric is responsible for his own room; he will clean up after dinner and wash dishes twice a week. He will also take out the garbage—without being asked—and pitch in on small chores and large cleaning jobs. We will divide the yard work.

8. Time Together

John agrees to be home at least two nights a week and David agrees to be home two nights a week. Tuesday night and Saturday afternoons are times together and no one can make plans unless they include everyone—except if we all agree otherwise.

9. Stereo Equipment

The stereo equipment is David's. He admits he's fanatic about it, but it was expensive. So everyone agrees only David will use it. He will attempt to either play music everyone enjoys or use earphones. He's willing to put albums, tapes and CDs on for others. The radio and TV can be used by all, and the volume is to be kept at a moderate level.

10. Smoking

Smoking is permitted only in the back room.

11. Space

Eric has his room and is free to lock it if he chooses. John and David have their room, and they may lock it if they choose. Everyone's privacy is respected.

12. Guests

John and David aren't used to sharing their home with a lot of people so Eric is permitted only one guest at a time and only when someone else is home unless other arrangements have been made; Eric is responsible for his guest's behavior.

13. Social Worker

We agree to meet with Jeff Lakely, the social worker, every other week and candidly discuss our joys and problems.

14. Length of this Agreement

Eric, David and John understand that their living together must be enjoyable for everyone, and that they must all give a lot for it to work. If one person can't make it work, he will terminate the agreement and it will expire.

_____   _____
Date   Eric Farmer

_____   _____
Date   David Roberts

_____   _____
Date   John Torres

Medical and Financial Matters: Delegating Authority

All lesbians and gay men, whether coupled or not, should consider what will happen if they become seriously ill or suffer a medical emergency. Ask yourself several questions: Who do you want to have authority to act for you if you are incapacitated and cannot make your own healthcare decisions? Who do you want to be allowed to visit you in intensive care? Who do you want to have legal authority to handle your finances if you can't?

You can control these matters by preparing some simple legal documents which will ensure that your desires are carried out if you become incapacitated. Using different documents, discussed below, you can provide for your healthcare and treatment, and management of your finances.

Unfortunately, if there has been no advance preparation, there is no assurance that your wishes will be respected or followed. In a well-known case from some years ago, Karen Thompson was denied contact with, and authority to act for, her incapacitated lover, Sharon Kowalski. Sharon had been seriously injured in a car accident. Her mother and father ran to court to remove her from Karen's care after learning that the women were lovers. Karen and her lawyer persisted, however, and after a seven-year battle, the Minnesota Court of Appeals finally named Karen as Sharon's legal guardian. By then, however, Sharon had lost years of Karen's aid in her recovery, which could never be made up.

Other common situations involve people with serious illnesses. Often, the lover and other people the patient regards as "family" are excluded from visiting him in the hospital by his biological family. Sometimes, biological family members have religious or medical ideas that the ill person rejects. Because hospitals and doctors conventionally look to the immediate family for authority to act (absent a document giving the lover that power), the lover is sometimes forced to look on in horror while the doctor is instructed in ways which the lover knows are contrary to his mate's wishes.

There are more than just medical care decisions to make when a person is ill or incapacitated. Someone must pay bills, deposit checks and take care of other financial matters. The authority to make financial decisions traditionally belongs to a spouse, not a lover or friend. But you can use a simple legal document called a durable power of attorney for finances to name and authorize another person to manage your money matters.

This chapter explains how you can handle medical and financial matters during a medical crisis. The materials are both for people who suffer from long-term illnesses, and for people foresighted enough (which we hope all our readers are) to prepare documents that will cover your concerns if an emergency develops.

California's Domestic Partners Law

Under California's new domestic partnership law, which became effective January 2001, a member of a registered gay or lesbian couple has legal authority to represent his or her partner in custodianship proceedings and other healthcare matters. To gain this and the many other rights extended under this law, couples must register with the California Secretary of State, http://www.ss.ca.gov.

Registering as domestic partners is an important act for many couples, but this should not replace the health and medical care documents we describe here. The documents we talk about in this chapter grant authority to your partner over issues that the California's domestic partner law does not reach.

AIDS Referral Organizations. *As we are all sadly aware, the AIDS epidemic has been responsible for the incapacity and deaths of thousands of people. AIDS has made people aware of their mortality and their need to be responsible to themselves and their loved ones. We provide information on organizations that provide legal assistance or legal referrals for people with HIV or AIDS in Chapter 10, Section C.*

All medical crises are frightening and stressful. Our close friend Jan was diagnosed with AIDS. Within about a week and a half after diagnosis, he had recovered sufficiently to leave the hospital. We were all so elated that he was out of the hospital and doing better that we didn't want to consider death. We became jubilant as he improved. His mother baked a dozen pies and after a week his parents flew back home. Within a month, however, Jan had to go back into the hospital. Because his fever was so high, he was unable to make any personal, let alone business, decisions. His parents flew out again.

We knew we had to prepare for future times when Jan would be unable to make medical or business decisions. We also had to prepare for his death. We were fortunate because Jan's parents talked with and listened to Jan's lover, business partner and friends. We had to figure out who would have the power to decide business and financial matters, medical care, hospital visitation and burial plans if Jan didn't recover sufficiently to make his own decisions. When Jan became coherent, we urged him to consider this and to prepare the necessary documents.

Jan died in the summer. No legal papers can lessen that tragedy. The documents we provide here, though, can help to prevent needless additional pain and confusion, as well as the denial of ill gay and lesbian people's wishes.

Terminal Illnesses and Hospices

In recent years, hospice programs have been set up throughout the country to help terminally ill people maintain control over how they live and ultimately die. There are over 2,000 hospices in the U.S. Cancer patients make up the highest proportion of users of hospices. In addition, thousands of AIDS patients use hospices each year.

Typically, the terminally ill person stays at home, where care is provided by family, close friends and medical professionals. Special counseling is given to the terminally ill person and those close to him. Hospice programs help ensure that a terminally ill person gets the type of medical care he wants. For example, if a patient is opposed to being connected to respirators or other life support systems, a hospice can provide alternatives.

Information about hospices throughout the country can be obtained from the National Hospice Help Line, 800-658-8898.

A. Healthcare Decisions

The increasing use of life-sustaining medical technology over the last decades has raised fears in many that our lives may be artificially prolonged against our wishes. The right to die with dignity, and without the tremendous agony and expense for both patient and family caused by prolonging lives artificially, has been addressed and confirmed by the U.S. Supreme Court, the federal government and the legislatures in every state.

This individual right also protects against the situation where doctors might wish to provide a patient with less extensive care than he would like. For example, a doctor may be unwilling to try experimental treatments or maintain long-term treatments on a patient who she feels has slim chances of recovering.

In 1990, the United States Supreme Court held that every individual has the constitutional right to control his own medical treatment. The Court also expounded that "clear and convincing evidence" of a person's wishes must be followed by medical personnel—even if those wishes are directly opposed by the patient's family.

1. Documents Protecting Choices of Medical Care

In response to the legal right to control one's own medical treatment, every state now has laws authorizing individuals to create a simple document that provides the "clear and convincing evidence" of that person's wishes concerning life-prolonging medical care. Depending upon the state, the document may be called by one of several different names: living will, medical directive, directive to physicians, declaration regarding healthcare or durable power of attorney for healthcare.

The directions expressed in the document are to be followed if an individual is no longer capable of communicating to medical personnel his choices regarding life-prolonging and other medical care.

Most medical care documents are drafted to specifically provide that the person creating those documents must be incapacitated and unable to make his own medical care decisions before the documents become effective. In legalese, this is called a "springing" document or power, because it only springs into effect if and when it's needed. You can also impose further limits on when your healthcare documents become effective, restricting them, say, to when you have a coma or terminal condition.

We feel there's no reason for this kind of restriction. If you cannot make your own medical decisions, even if you're not in a coma or in a terminal condition, you will want the person you've named to be able to make decisions for you.

2. Differences Among Types of Medical Care Documents

The two basic types of documents to direct medical care are a declaration and a durable power of attorney for healthcare. Both are grouped under the broader labels of "medical care documents" or "healthcare directives."

The basic difference between the two types of documents is simple. The declaration is a statement you make directly to medical personnel which spells out the medical care you do or do not wish to receive if you become incapacitated. It functions as a contract with the treating doctor, who must either honor the wishes for medical care that you have expressed or transfer you to another doctor or facility that will honor them. The earliest declarations were called living wills—confusing terminology because they are not true wills, but documents stating a person's decision to receive or not to receive certain medical treatment.

In a durable power of attorney, you appoint someone else (your "attorney-in-fact") to see that your doctors and healthcare providers provide you with the kind of medical care you wish to receive. In some states, you can also give the person you appoint the broader authority to make decisions about your medical care on your behalf, such as when to hire and fire doctors.

This type of document may, in your state, go by another name, such as "Declaration Regarding Healthcare," "Designation of Healthcare Surrogate" or "Patient Advocate Designation." A few states combine both documents (the declaration and the power of attorney) into a single form.

⚠️ **You must use your state's forms.** *Each state has its own specific rules and requirements for making healthcare directives and powers of attorney. In almost all states, you must use your state's particular forms to ensure your documents are valid.*

How to Make Your State-Specific Healthcare Documents

You can use Nolo's *Quicken Lawyer Personal* software to create healthcare documents tailored to the laws of your state. You can also contact your state's medical association for these forms, or you can download fill-in-the-blank forms for each state at http://www.partnershipforcaring.org. In addition, any large hospital—by law, any hospital that receives federal funds—must provide patients with appropriate healthcare directive forms. Check with the patient representative at the hospital. Finally, local hospices or organizations that provide support for AIDS or cancer patients will probably have your state's forms, and they may be able to provide guidance in filling them out.

In an Emergency: DNR Orders

In addition to your declaration and durable power of attorney for healthcare, you may want to secure a "do not resuscitate" order, or DNR order. A DNR order documents the wish that you not be administered cardiopulmonary resuscitation (CPR) and will alert emergency medical personnel to this wish. DNR orders were first used in hospital settings to alert hospital staff that CPR should be withheld from a patient, but now they are frequently used in situations where a person might require emergency care while outside of the hospital, such as when paramedics must be summoned.

You may want to consider a DNR order if:
- you have a terminal illness
- you are at an increased risk for cardiac or respiratory arrest, or
- you have strong feelings against the use of CPR under any circumstances.

In most states, any adult may secure a DNR order. But some states allow you to create an order only if you have been diagnosed as having a terminal illness.

If you want a DNR order, or you want more information about DNR orders, talk with a doctor. A doctor's signature is required to make the DNR valid—and in most states, he or she will obtain and complete the necessary paperwork. If the doctor does not have the form or other information you need, call the Health Department for your state and ask to speak with someone in the Division of Emergency Medical Services.

If you obtain a DNR order, discuss your decision with your lover or other caretakers. They should know where your form is located—and who to call if you require emergency treatment. Even if you are wearing identification, such as a bracelet or necklace, keep your form in an obvious place. Consider keeping it by your bedside, on the front of your refrigerator, in your wallet or in your suitcase if you are traveling. If your DNR order is not apparent and immediately available, or if it has been altered in any way, medical personnel who attend you will most likely perform CPR.

When Your State Form Is Not Enough

When it comes to medical directives, there are many state differences in the forms and formats used. Some state laws mention that a specific form must be followed for a directive to be valid. Because the Supreme Court ruled in the *Cruzan* case that every individual has a constitutional right to direct his or her own medical care, however, the most important thing for you to keep in mind is that your directions should be clear and in writing to doctors and other medical personnel. If you feel strongly about a particular kind of care—even if your state law or the form you get does not address it—it is a good idea to include your specific thoughts in your written document. If you are using a state form that does not adequately address your concerns, write them in on the form with the additional request that your wishes be respected and followed.

---

3. What to Include in a Medical Directive

Most laws controlling healthcare directives allow individuals to direct their own medical care if they are diagnosed to be in a permanent coma or if they have a terminal condition. A few states set out other medical conditions that may activate a directive. A trend is to allow individuals the right to direct what "comfort care"—care which doctors feel may alleviate pain and which may or may not prolong life—should be provided or withheld.

The problem many people have in filling out their state forms on directing healthcare is that they are not sure how to fill in the blanks—and are not sure what much of the terminology means. Although medical technology and treatments are evolving over time, filling out the forms is not as difficult as it may seem at first. In most healthcare documents, you can direct:

- that all life-prolonging procedures be provided
- that all life-prolonging procedures be withheld, or
- that some be provided, while others are withheld.

The following medical procedures and treatments are usually considered to be in the category of "life-prolonging."

Blood and blood products. Partial or full blood transfusions may be recommended to combat diseases that impair the blood system, to foster healing after a blood loss or to replenish blood lost through surgery, disease or injury.

Cardiopulmonary resuscitation. CPR is used when a person's heart or breathing has stopped. CPR includes applying physical pressure, using mouth-to-mouth resuscitation, using electrical shocks, administering intravenous drugs to normalize body systems and attaching you to a respirator.

Diagnostic tests. Diagnostic tests are commonly used to evaluate urine, blood and other body fluids and to check on all bodily functions. Diagnostic tests can include x-rays and more sophisticated tests of brainwaves or other internal body systems.

Dialysis. A dialysis machine is used to clean and add essential substances to the blood—through tubes placed in blood vessels or into the abdomen—when kidneys do not function properly.

Drugs. The most common and most controversial drugs given to seriously ill or comatose patients are antibiotics—administered by mouth, through a feeding tube or by injection. Antibiotics are used to arrest and squelch infectious diseases. Drugs may also be used to eliminate or alleviate pain. Because high doses of pain control drugs can impair respiration, such drugs sometimes hasten death in a seriously ill patient.

Respirator. A mechanical respirator or a ventilator assists or takes over breathing for a patient by pumping air in and out of the lungs. These machines dispense a regulated amount of air into the lungs at a set rate—and periodically purge the lungs. Patients are connected to respirators by a tube that goes through the mouth and throat into the lung or that is surgically attached to the lung.

Surgery. Surgical procedures such as amputation or a brain shunt are often used to stem the spread of life-threatening infections or to keep vital organs functioning. Major surgery such as a hysterectomy or a heart bypass are also typically performed on patients who are terminally ill or comatose.

In addition to the life-prolonging procedures discussed above, you may want to craft your directive to include your wishes about comfort care and artificially administered food and water.

Comfort care. The laws of many states assume that people want relief from pain and discomfort and specifically exclude pain-relieving procedures from definitions of life-prolonging treatments that may be withheld. If that was all there was to it, most people would agree with this and welcome the relief. But the medical community disagrees over whether providing food and water or drugs to make a person comfortable or alleviate pain will also have the effect of prolonging the person's life.

Some people are so adamant about not having their lives prolonged when they are comatose or likely to die that they choose to direct that all comfort care and pain relief be withheld in those circumstances even if a doctor thinks those procedures are necessary. Other people are willing to have their lives prolonged rather than face the possibility that discomfort or pain would go untreated.

Artificially administered food and water. If you are close to death from a terminal condition or in a permanent coma and cannot communicate your preferences, it is likely that you will also not be able to voluntarily take in water or food through your mouth. The medical solution is to provide you with food and water—as a mix of nutrients and fluids—through tubes inserted in a vein, into your stomach through your nose or into your stomach through a surgical incision.

Intravenous feeding, where fluids are introduced through a vein in an arm or a leg, is a short-term procedure. Tube feeding through the nose

(nasogastric tube), through the stomach (gastrostomy tube), intestines (jejunostomy tube) or largest vein, the vena cava (total parenteral nutrition), can be carried on indefinitely.

Similar to the controversy that rages over comfort care, medical experts are split over whether artificial food and water prolongs life or is medically necessary. Many patients face the decision with a strong predilection.

To make an informed decision about which procedures you do and do not want, as well as about others which might pertain to your particular medical condition, it may be a good idea to discuss your medical directive with your physician. She can explain the medical procedures more fully and can discuss the options with you. You will also find out whether your doctor has any medical or moral objections to following your wishes. If she does object and will not agree to follow your wishes regardless of those objections, you will probably want to change doctors.

4. Using a Durable Power of Attorney for Healthcare

Even when you have specified your wishes in a declaration regarding life-prolonging and comfort care medical treatment, certain decisions may still be difficult to resolve. They may include:

- when, exactly, to administer or withhold certain medical treatments
- whether or not to provide, withhold or continue antibiotic or pain medication, and
- whether to pursue complex, painful and expensive surgeries which may serve to prolong life but cannot reverse the medical condition.

To deal with these situations, you can use a durable power of attorney for healthcare (sometimes called a healthcare proxy or patient advocate designation) to appoint someone you trust to make these decisions in accordance with your wishes and in your best interest. To help the appointed person make and carry out these decisions, the power of attorney or proxy form may include specific authorizations:

- to give, withhold or withdraw consent to medical or surgical procedures
- to consent to appropriate care for the end of life, including pain relief
- to hire and fire medical personnel
- to visit you in the hospital or other facility even when other visiting is restricted
- to have access to medical records and other personal information, and
- to get any court authorization required to obtain or withhold medical treatment if, for any reason, a hospital or doctor does not honor the document.

The most important factor in choosing your attorney-in-fact is to select a person you totally trust. Most readers will choose their lover. If your lover can't serve because of health reasons or because he or she is not likely to be a strong advocate, be sure you pick a person who truly understands you and your life, and who, of course, you can rely on totally.

It is also a good idea to appoint a second person as attorney-in-fact if your first choice is unable or unwilling to serve. Make it clear, however, that the second person is only a backup. It is not a wise choice to appoint two people to do the job together; that is likely to complicate the process.

⚠ **Do not appoint your doctor as attorney-in-fact.** *Although your doctor is an important person for your attorney-in-fact to consult concerning all healthcare decisions, you should not appoint your doctor to act as attorney-in-fact. The laws in most states specifically forbid treating physicians from acting in this role—to avoid the appearance that they may have their own interests at heart and may not be able to act purely according to your wishes.*

5. Preparing Your Healthcare Documents

You do not need to consult a lawyer to prepare a declaration, power of attorney for healthcare or other medical directive form. While you may have to make difficult decisions about what types of care you want or do not want, these are not legal issues. It is wise to discuss what you want in depth with your attorney-in-fact. In grim reality, making a medical decision for a loved one can be confusing and wrenching. You want your attorney-in-fact to understand as much as possible what you want. And it can be a huge comfort if he or she knows that you've expressed how difficult carrying out your instructions or making a decision for you can actually be.

6. What to Do With Your Completed Documents

Once you have completed the documents directing your medical care, there are several steps you should take.

Signing, witnessing, notarizing. Every state law requires that you sign your documents—or direct another person to sign them for you—as a way of verifying that you understand them and that they contain your true wishes.

Most state laws also require that you sign your documents in the presence of witnesses. The purpose of this additional formality is so that there is at least one other person who can attest that you were of sound mind and of legal age when you made the documents.

Some states also require that you and the witnesses appear before a notary public and swear that the circumstances of your signing, as described in the documents, are true. In some states, you have the option of having a notary sign your document instead of having it witnessed.

Making and distributing copies. Ideally, you should make an effort to make your wishes for your future healthcare widely known. Keep a copy of your healthcare directives, and give other copies to:

- any physician with whom you now consult regularly
- any attorney-in-fact or healthcare proxy you have named, including any back-up
- the office of the hospital or other care facility in which you are likely to receive treatment, and
- any other people or institutions you think it's wise to inform of your medical intentions, such as a hospice program.

Qualifications for Witnesses

Many states require that two witnesses see you sign your healthcare documents and that they verify in writing that you appeared to be of sound mind and signed the documents without anyone else influencing your decision.

Each state's qualifications for these witnesses are slightly different. In many states, for example, a spouse, other close relative or any person who would get property from you at your death (this includes anyone you name in your will) is not allowed to act as a witness for the document directing healthcare. And many states prohibit your attending physician from being a witness.

The purpose of the laws restricting who can witness your documents is to avoid any appearance or possibility that another person was acting against your wishes in encouraging specific medical care. States that prevent close relatives or potential inheritors from being witnesses, for example, justify their restrictions by noting that these people may have a conflict of interest.

B. Physician-Assisted Suicide

Behind closed doors, many doctors acknowledge that they have helped seriously ill patients end their own lives—many of them by writing large prescriptions for drugs, ostensibly to help patients with sleeping or pain problems.

Doctor-assisted suicide is currently a crime in the vast majority of states. But legislation arises each year in states to allow voters to consider the desirability of allowing doctor-assisted lethal injections for incurably ill patients. Some states have established commissions to study and make recommendations on the issue.

The Internet provides a lot of current information about the legalities and practicalities of physician-assisted suicide. One of the most complete websites is the Euthanasia World Directory, at http://www.finalexit.org.

C. Burial and Body Disposition

Burial and body disposition are potential problems for survivors. We know of a biological family that claimed the body of a person who died from AIDS and refused to give the service and disposition the deceased had wanted. Instead, the family members gave their own, which conflicted drastically with the deceased's spiritual values. We even know a surviving partner who was excluded entirely from a burial service. In the past few years, a number of states have passed laws making it illegal for family members to violate a deceased person's wishes as to burial services and body disposition. Whether or not you live in one of these states, however, many painful situations can be avoided by proper planning and advance discussions, so lovers, friends and biological families know what's wanted.

1. Written Instructions

After death, a body must be disposed of quickly. If you haven't left written instructions, nearly every state gives control to your blood relatives—your lover can be excluded. If your lover has the resources to sue to gain control over your body, he may succeed, but these cases are messy and expensive. One man who sued and won was Michael Stewart. When his lover died leaving no instructions, the family took the body and prepared for a religious funeral. Michael sued, arguing that he knew what his lover wanted—and a religious funeral wasn't it. The court gave Michael the right to stop the funeral, due to their spouse-like relationship.

In most states, written body disposition instructions are legally binding. Written instructions let you state your wishes and name someone to carry them out. Contrary to what many believe, your will is not the best place to leave these instructions. A will is not likely to be found and acted upon until quite some time after your death. If you anticipate objections from your family, make sure to write your instructions in a separate document, then sign and date it. Here are two examples:

Examples

> I have made arrangements with the Tri-City Funeral Society regarding my funeral and burial. I appoint Alfred Gwynne to be responsible for implementing these arrangements regarding my death.

> I have made the following arrangements regarding my death:
>
> 1. I have made an agreement with Hillman Hospital, San Francisco, California, to donate any of my organs or body parts needed by the hospital.
>
> 2. After any such donation, I direct that my remains be cremated, and my ashes scattered at sea. I have made written arrangements with the Nicean Society regarding my cremation.
>
> 3. I direct that Anna Rodriguez, my good friend and executor, be solely responsible for ensuring that these instructions are carried out.

2. Choices Regarding Disposition of the Body

In preparing for your death, you have a number of choices regarding disposition of your body, including esoteric ones like cryonics—body-freezing with the hope of being brought back to life sometime later. Among the most common are:

- A traditional funeral at a commercial mortuary or funeral home, which can include embalming. It may also include burial and religious or social ceremonies for the survivors.
- A funeral you arrange with the help of a funeral society—these exist in many states and provide information about low-cost funerals and burials, and simple, dignified memorial services. You can find the nearest organization by contacting the Continental Association of Funeral and Memorial Societies, 800-458-5563.
- Cremation, either through a for-profit cremation company, mortuary or funeral home.

- Donation of your body to a medical school.
- Donation of body parts and organs to hospitals or organ banks.

For decades, funerals and burials were controlled by commercial funeral parlors, which were both secretive and expensive. The business of funerals first came under attack in the 1960s, especially through Jessica Mitford's fine book *The American Way of Death*. Since then, reforms have been instituted in most states. Today it's usually possible to find good funeral services at a reasonable price if you ask knowledgeable friends for recommendations, and monitor costs closely—and most importantly, plan in advance to target the services that fit in with your budget.

We don't have space to give you an exhaustive rundown on each alternative, but here are a few significant points.

- Embalming is generally not necessary. It is usually required by law only when a body must be transported out of the state or country.
- Commercial funerals can cost many thousands of dollars. So shop around—compare services offered and check the prices charged by non-profit funeral societies. Mortuaries are required by law to give you a list of their goods and services if you ask for one.
- Burial is expensive—especially given the high costs of "perpetual care" that many cemeteries charge for maintaining the gravesites.
- Donation of your body to a medical school requires specific arrangements in advance. You can find out more about body donation options from the National Anatomical Service, which operates a 24-hour phone service out of New York, at 718-948-2401, and St. Louis, at 314-726-9079.
- Kidneys, corneas, pituitary glands, heart tissues, even knee parts have been transplanted. Some states have adopted the Uniform Anatomical Gift Act, which lets you authorize the donation of body parts simply by carrying a short, signed donor card with you. It's useful, though, to arrange with a hospital or organ bank to receive, and use, your donation. Bodies from which organs have been transplanted

may be returned for burial—or may be cremated in a designated plot.

- Cremations have increased over the past few years. Cremation is the burning of the body, followed by the inurnment or scattering of the ashes. Some state laws allow ashes to be scattered over private land; other states forbid it. Cremations are offered by most commercial funeral homes and by for-profit organizations such as the Neptune Society. Be careful how you specify the service you want. Some funeral homes provide—and charge for—the presence of a coffin at the memorial service, even if you have been cremated.
- Many funeral-burial businesses have couple rates, allowing a couple to pay for services in advance. We know of a business that refused to give its couple rate to a gay couple. This discrimination is legal. However, it is illegal in most states for a mortuary to refuse to handle or to charge more for handling a body that has died from AIDS.

D. Estate Planning Note

When you prepare for a death or possible medical emergency, consider what will happen to your property after you die. This is what lawyers call "estate planning," and it's particularly important for seriously ill people. After you die, your property will be transferred either by your estate planning documents, such as a will, living trust or joint tenancy document, or by laws imposed by your state. No other method is possible. Oral statements made before your death about who should get your property have no legal effect. A durable power of attorney for finances (discussed just below) ceases to be effective when you die, so you can't use that document to transfer your property. Even while you are alive, an attorney-in-fact doesn't have the power to make a will or estate plan for you.

Without estate planning documents, your lover has no rights over any aspect of what happens to you and your property after your death. Unless you've made written instructions, your lover can't receive any of your property, decide how to distribute or dispose of it of or arrange for your burial and body disposition.

These dire consequences can be avoided by proper estate planning, which we discuss in Chapter 5. If you do nothing else, at least prepare a will, so you, not your state's laws, determine who gets your property.

E. Durable Power of Attorney for Finances

During a medical crisis, you may be unable to manage your own financial affairs. Exhaustion, recurring dementia, long periods of treatment or other hardships may leave you unable to tend to practical matters. If this happens, you'll need someone to take care of basic tasks such as paying bills, making bank deposits, watching over investments or collecting insurance and government benefits. If you don't plan ahead and you become incapacitated, a court will decide who should handle your finances—and it might not appoint the person you would have chosen. Fortunately, there's a simple way to name a trusted person to handle your money matters: prepare a durable power of attorney for finances.

With a durable power of attorney for finances, you can:

- name the person who will handle your financial tasks (this person is called your attorney-in-fact)
- appoint someone to replace your attorney-in-fact if he or she cannot serve
- state exactly how much authority you want your attorney-in-fact to have over your finances, and
- specify when the document should become effective (when the attorney-in-face has authority to act for you).

Most durable powers of attorney for financial matters become effective if and only if the principal (that's you) has become mentally incapacitated to

the degree the principal can't manage his or her own affairs. This is called a "springing" durable power of attorney.

In addition, you can use your document to place limits on the power of your attorney-in-fact. For example, you might want to forbid your attorney-in-fact from selling your home, or require her to use money from specified bank accounts to pay certain bills. You can include such restrictions in the "special instructions" section of the document.

Important Terms

Principal: The person who creates and signs the power of attorney document, authorizing someone else to act for him or her. If you make a durable power of attorney for finances, you are the principal.

Attorney-in-Fact: The person who is authorized to act for the principal. In many states, the attorney-in-fact is also referred to as an agent of the principal.

Alternate Attorney-in-Fact: The person who takes over as attorney-in-fact if your first choice cannot or will not serve. Also called successor attorney-in-fact.

Durable Power of Attorney: A power of attorney that will remain in effect even if the principal becomes incapacitated, or will take effect only if the principal becomes incapacitated. This is the kind of power of attorney you make with *Quicken Lawyer Personal* software by Nolo.

Incapacitated: Unable to handle one's own financial matters or healthcare decisions. Also called disabled or incompetent in some states. Usually, a physician makes the determination.

Springing Durable Power of Attorney: A durable power of attorney that takes effect only if a physician determines that the principal cannot handle his or her own financial affairs. In some states, this document may be called a conditional power of attorney. The form included in this book gives you the option of making your power of attorney springing.

The most important decision you'll make when you create a durable power of attorney for finances is choosing your attorney-in-fact. It's crucial to name someone you trust completely. In most situations, the attorney-in-fact does not need extensive experience in financial management: common sense, dependability and complete honesty are enough. Your attorney-in-fact can get any reasonably necessary professional help—from an accountant, lawyer or tax preparer, perhaps—and pay for it out of your assets.

You will probably want to name your partner as your attorney-in-fact, though some people may feel a close friend or family member is the best person for the job. Keep in mind that it's best to appoint just one person to serve as your attorney-in-fact. Appointing more than one person opens the door to conflicts between them and may disrupt the handling of your finances. That said, however, it *is* important to name at least one trusted person as an alternate attorney-in-fact—someone to take over if your first choice can't serve.

All states permit some form of durable power of attorney for finances. At the end of this chapter we provide a sample durable power of attorney for finances, so you can get a general idea of what one looks like. This sample form has been filled out by the principal. However, do not try to use or adapt this personal form for your own personal use. Get the form best suited for your state.

Getting your state's durable power of attorney form. *You can make a durable power of attorney for finances that's tailored to your state's laws by using* Quicken Lawyer Personal *software by Nolo. Californians can also use the Nolo book* Medical Directives and Powers of Attorney for California, *by Shae Irving.*

Your financial institutions may use different forms. *Many banks and other financial institutions have their own durable power of attorney for finances forms. It's a good idea to use the financial institution's form in addition to your own form. Using the form that your financial institution is most familiar with will make it easier for your attorney-in-fact to get things done.*

After you've prepared your durable power of attorney for finances, you must take just a few simple steps to make sure the document is legally valid.

Notarization. You must sign your power of attorney in the presence of a notary public for your state. In some states, notarization is required by law to make the power of attorney valid. But even where law doesn't require it, custom does. A power of attorney that isn't notarized may not be accepted by people or institutions with whom your attorney-in-fact must deal.

Witnesses. Most states don't require a power of attorney to be signed in front of witnesses. The few states that do and the number of witnesses required are listed below. Witness requirements normally consist of the following:

- Witnesses must be present when you sign the document in front of the notary.
- Witnesses must be mentally competent adults.
- Your attorney-in-fact can't be a witness.

In case they're ever needed, it's a good idea to choose witnesses who live nearby and will be easy to contact.

Recording. You may need to put a copy of your durable power of attorney on file in the land records office of any counties where you own real estate. This office is called the County Recorder's or Land Registry Office in most states.

Just two states, North Carolina and South Carolina, require you to record a power of attorney for it to be durable—that is, for it to remain in effect if you become incapacitated. In other states, you must record the power of attorney only if it gives your attorney in fact authority over your real estate. If the document isn't in the public records, your attorney-in-fact won't be able to sell, mortgage or transfer your property.

States That Require Witnesses

State	# of Witnesses	Other Requirements
Arizona	1	Witness may not be your attorney-in-fact, the spouse or child of your attorney-in-fact, or the notary public who acknowledges your documents.
Arkansas	2	The attorney-in-fact may not be a witness.
Connecticut	2	The attorney-in-fact may not be a witness.
California	2	Witnesses are required only if your document is not notarized. The attorney-in-fact may not be a witness.
District of Columbia	2	Witnesses are necessary only if your power of attorney is to be recorded. The attorney-in-fact may not be a witness.
Florida	2	The attorney-in-fact may not be a witness.
Georgia	2	The attorney-in-fact may not be a witness. In addition, one of your witnesses may not be your spouse or blood relative.
Illinois	1	The attorney-in-fact may not be a witness.
Michigan	2	Witnesses are necessary only if your power of attorney is to be recorded. The attorney-in-fact may not be a witness.
Oklahoma	2	Witnesses may not be your attorney-in-fact, or anyone who is related by blood or marriage to your or your attorney-in-fact.
Pennsylvania	2	The attorney-in-fact may not be a witness.
South Carolina	2	The attorney-in-fact may not be a witness.
Vermont	2	Witnesses are necessary only if your power of attorney is to be recorded. The attorney-in-fact may not be a witness.
Wisconsin	2	Witnesses may not be your attorney-in-fact, anyone related to you by blood or marriage, or anyone entitled to a portion of your estate under your will.

Durable Power of Attorney for Finances

WARNING TO PERSON EXECUTING THIS DOCUMENT

THIS IS AN IMPORTANT LEGAL DOCUMENT. IT CREATES A POWER OF ATTORNEY FOR FINANCES. BEFORE EXECUTING THIS DOCUMENT, YOU SHOULD KNOW THESE IMPORTANT FACTS:

THIS DOCUMENT MAY PROVIDE THE PERSON YOU DESIGNATE AS YOUR ATTORNEY-IN-FACT WITH BROAD LEGAL POWERS, INCLUDING THE POWERS TO MANAGE, DISPOSE, SELL AND CONVEY YOUR REAL AND PERSONAL PROPERTY AND TO BORROW MONEY USING YOUR PROPERTY AS SECURITY FOR THE LOAN.

THESE POWERS WILL EXIST UNTIL YOU REVOKE OR TERMINATE THIS POWER OF ATTORNEY. IF YOU SO STATE, THESE POWERS WILL CONTINUE TO EXIST EVEN IF YOU BECOME DISABLED OR INCAPACITATED. YOU HAVE THE RIGHT TO REVOKE OR TERMINATE THIS POWER OF ATTORNEY AT ANY TIME.

THIS DOCUMENT DOES NOT AUTHORIZE ANYONE TO MAKE MEDICAL OR OTHER HEALTHCARE DECISIONS FOR YOU.

IF THERE IS ANYTHING ABOUT THIS FORM THAT YOU DO NOT UNDERSTAND, YOU SHOULD ASK A LAWYER TO EXPLAIN IT TO YOU.

1. Principal and Attorney-in-Fact

I, _Jonathan Chen_

of _147 Iris Street, Detroit, Michigan 48231_,

appoint _Lucas Wilkes, 229 Apple Street,_
Detroit, Michigan 48231

as my attorney-in-fact to act for me in any lawful way with respect to the powers delegated in Part 6 below. If that person (or all of those persons, if I name more than one) is unable or unwilling to serve as attorney-in-fact, I appoint the following alternates, to serve alone in the order named:

First Alternate

Edward Chen
Name
2461 Derby Street
Address
Lincoln, Nebraska 68501

Second Alternate

_____
Name

_____
Address

_____

2. Authorization of Attorneys-in-Fact

If I have named more than one attorney-in-fact, they are authorized to act:

☐ jointly.

☐ independently.

3. Delegation of Authority

☒ My attorney-in-fact may delegate, in writing, any authority granted under this power of attorney to a person he or she selects. Any such delegation shall state the period during which it is valid and specify the extent of the delegation.

☐ My attorney-in-fact may not delegate any authority granted under this power of attorney.

4. Effective Date

☒ This power of attorney is durable. It is effective immediately, and shall continue in effect if I become incapacitated or disabled.

☐ This power of attorney is durable. It shall take effect only if I become incapacitated or disabled and unable to manage my financial affairs.

5. Determination of Incapacity

If I am creating a springing durable power of attorney under Part 4 of this document, my incapacity or disability shall be determined by written declaration of ☐ one ☐ two licensed physician(s). Each declaration shall be made under penalty of perjury and shall state that in the physician's opinion I am substantially unable to manage my financial affairs. If possible, the declaration(s) shall be made by

_____

_____

_____ .

No licensed physician shall be liable to me for any actions taken under this part which are done in good faith.

6. Powers of the Attorney-in-Fact

I grant my attorney-in-fact power to act on my behalf in the following matters, as indicated by my initials next to each granted power or on line (14), granting all the listed powers. Powers that are struck through are not granted.

INITIALS

____JC____ (1) Real estate transactions.

____JC____ (2) Tangible personal property transactions.

_J.C._   (3) Stock and bond, commodity and option transactions.

_J.C._   (4) Banking and other financial institution transactions.

_J.C._   (5) Business operating transactions.

_J.C._   (6) Insurance and annuity transactions.

_J.C._   (7) Estate, trust and other beneficiary transactions.

_J.C._   (8) Living trust transactions.

_J.C._   (9) Legal actions.

_J.C._   (10) Personal and family maintenance.

_J.C._   (11) Government benefits.

_J.C._   (12) Retirement plan transactions.

_J.C._   (13) Tax matters.

_J.C._   (14) ALL POWERS (1 THROUGH 13) LISTED ABOVE.

These powers are defined in Part 14, below.

7. Special Instructions to the Attorney-in-Fact

_____

_____

_____

_____

_____

_____

_____

_____

_____

_____

_____

_____

_____

_____

_____

8. Compensation and Reimbursement of the Attorney-in-Fact

☒ My attorney-in-fact shall not be compensated for services, but shall be entitled to reimbursement, from my assets, for reasonable expenses. Reasonable expenses include but are not limited to reasonable fees for information or advice from accountants, lawyers or investment experts relating to my attorney-in-fact's responsibilities under this power of attorney.

☐ My attorney-in-fact shall be entitled to reimbursement for reasonable expenses and reasonable compensation for services. What constitutes reasonable compensation shall be determined exclusively by my attorney-in-fact. If more than one attorney-in-fact is named in this document, each shall have the exclusive right to determine what constitutes reasonable compensation for his or her own duties.

☐ My attorney-in-fact shall be entitled to reimbursement for reasonable expenses and compensation for services in the amount of $_____. If more than one attorney-in-fact is named in this document, each shall be entitled to receive this amount.

9. Personal Benefit to the Attorney-in-Fact

☒ My attorney-in-fact may buy any assets of mine or engage in any transaction he or she deems in good faith to be in my interest, no matter what the interest or benefit to my attorney-in-fact.

☐ My attorney-in-fact may not benefit personally from any transaction engaged in on my behalf.

☐ Although my attorney-in-fact may receive gifts of my property as described in Part 7 of this document, my attorney-in-fact may not benefit personally from any other transaction he or she engages in on my behalf.

10. Commingling by the Attorney-in-Fact

☐ My attorney-in-fact may commingle any of my funds with any funds of his or hers.

☒ My attorney-in-fact may not commingle any of my funds with any funds of his or hers.

11. Liability of the Attorney-in-Fact

My attorney-in-fact shall not incur any liability to me, my estate, my heirs, successors or assigns for acting or refraining from acting under this document, except for willful misconduct or gross negligence. My attorney-in-fact is not required to make my assets produce income, increase the value of my estate, diversify my investments or enter into transactions authorized by this document, as long as my attorney-in-fact believes his or her actions are in my best interests or in the interests of my estate and of those interested in my estate. A successor attorney-in-fact shall not be liable for acts of a prior attorney-in-fact.

12. Reliance on This Power of Attorney

Any third party who receives a copy of this document may rely on and act under it. Revocation of the power of attorney is not effective as to a third party until the third party has actual knowledge of the revocation. I agree to indemnify the third party for any claims that arise against the third party because of reliance on this power of attorney.

13. Severability

If any provision of this document is ruled unenforceable, the remaining provisions shall stay in effect.

14. Definition of Powers Granted to the Attorney-in-Fact

The powers granted in Part 6 of this document authorize my attorney-in-fact to do the following.

(1) Real estate transactions

Act for me in any manner to deal with all or any part of any interest in real property that I own at the time of execution of this document or later acquire, under such terms, conditions and covenants as my attorney-in-fact deems proper. My attorney-in-fact's powers include but are not limited to the power to:

(a) Accept as a gift, or as security for a loan, reject, demand, buy, lease, receive or otherwise acquire ownership or possession of any estate or interest in real property.

(b) Sell, exchange, convey with or without covenants, quitclaim, release, surrender, mortgage, encumber, partition or consent to the partitioning of, grant options concerning, lease, sublet or otherwise dispose of any interest in real property.

(c) Maintain, repair, improve, insure, rent, lease and pay or contest taxes or assessments on any estate or interest in real property I own or claim to own.

(d) Prosecute, defend, intervene in, submit to arbitration, settle and propose or accept a compromise with respect to any claim in favor of or against me based on or involving any real estate transaction.

(2) Tangible personal property transactions

Act for me in any manner to deal with all or any part of any interest in personal property that I own at the time of execution of this document or later acquire, under such terms as my attorney-in-fact deems proper. My attorney-in-fact's powers include but are not limited to the power to lease, buy, exchange, accept as a gift or as security for a loan, acquire, possess, maintain, repair, improve, insure, rent, convey, mortgage, pledge and pay or contest taxes and assessments on any tangible personal property.

(3) Stock and bond, commodity, option and other securities transactions

Do any act which I can do through an agent, with respect to any interest in a bond, share, other instrument of similar character or commodity. My attorney-in-fact's powers include but are not limited to the power to:

(a) Accept as a gift or as security for a loan, reject, demand, buy, receive or otherwise acquire ownership or possession of any bond, share, instrument of similar character, commodity interest or any investment with respect thereto, together with the interest, dividends, proceeds or other distributions connected with it.

(b) Sell (including short sales), exchange, transfer, release, surrender, pledge, trade in or otherwise dispose of any bond, share, instrument of similar character or commodity interest.

(c) Demand, receive and obtain any money or other thing of value to which I am or may become or may claim to be entitled as the proceeds of any interest in a bond, share, other instrument of similar character or commodity interest.

(d) Agree and contract, in any manner, and with any broker or other person and on any terms, for the accomplishment of any purpose listed in this section.

(e) Execute, acknowledge, seal and deliver any instrument my attorney-in-fact thinks useful to accomplish a purpose listed in this section, or any report or certificate required by law or regulation.

(4) Banking and other financial institution transactions

Do any act that I can do through an agent in connection with any banking transaction that might affect my financial or other interests. My attorney-in-fact's powers include but are not limited to the power to:

(a) Continue, modify and terminate any deposit account or other banking arrangement, or open either in the name of the agent alone or my name alone or in both our names jointly, a deposit account of any type in any financial institution, rent a safe deposit box or vault space, have access to a safe deposit box or vault to which I would have access and make other contracts with the institution.

(b) Make, sign and deliver checks or drafts, and withdraw my funds or property from any financial institution by check, order or otherwise.

(c) Prepare financial statements concerning my assets and liabilities or income and expenses and deliver them to any financial institution, and receive statements, notices or other documents from any financial institution.

(d) Borrow money from a financial institution on terms my attorney-in-fact deems acceptable, give security out of my assets, and pay, renew or extend the time of payment of any note given by or on my behalf.

(5) Business operating transactions

Do any act that I can do through an agent in connection with any business operated by me that my attorney-in-fact deems desirable. My attorney-in-fact's powers include but are not limited to the power to:

(a) Perform any duty and exercise any right, privilege or option which I have or claim to have under any contract of partnership, enforce the terms of any partnership agreement, and defend, submit to arbitration or settle any legal proceeding to which I am a party because of membership in a partnership.

(b) Exercise in person or by proxy and enforce any right, privilege or option which I have as the holder of any bond, share or instrument of similar character and defend, submit to arbitration or settle a legal proceeding to which I am a party because of any such bond, share or instrument of similar character.

(c) With respect to a business owned solely by me, continue, modify, extend or terminate any contract on my behalf, demand and receive all money that is due or claimed by me and use such funds in the operation of the business, engage in banking transactions my attorney-in-fact deems desirable, determine the location of the operation, the nature of the business it undertakes, its name, methods of manufacturing, selling, marketing, financing, accounting, form of organization and insurance and hiring and paying employees and independent contractors.

(d) Execute, acknowledge, seal and deliver any instrument of any kind that my attorney-in-fact thinks useful to accomplish any purpose listed in this section.

(e) Pay, compromise or contest business taxes or assessments.

(f) Demand and receive money or other things of value to which I am or claim to be entitled as the proceeds of any business operation, and conserve, invest, disburse or use anything so received for purposes listed in this section.

(6) Insurance and annuity transactions

Do any act that I can do through an agent, in connection with any insurance or annuity policy, that my attorney-in-fact deems desirable. My attorney-in-fact's powers include but are not limited to the power to:

(a) Continue, pay the premium on, modify, rescind or terminate any annuity or policy of life, accident, health, disability or liability insurance procured by me or on my behalf before the execution of this power of attorney. My attorney-in-fact cannot name himself or herself as beneficiary of a renewal, extension or substitute for such a policy unless he or she was already the beneficiary before I signed the power of attorney.

(b) Procure new, different or additional contracts of health, disability, accident or liability insurance on my life, modify, rescind or terminate any such contract and designate the beneficiary of any such contract.

(c) Sell, assign, borrow on, pledge, or surrender and receive the cash surrender value of any policy.

(7) Estate, trust and other beneficiary transactions

Act for me in all matters that affect a trust, probate estate, guardianship, conservatorship, escrow, custodianship or other fund from which I am, may become or claim to be entitled, as a beneficiary, to a share or payment. My attorney-in-fact's authority includes the power to disclaim any assets from which I am, may become or claim to be entitled, as a beneficiary, to a share or payment.

(8) Living trust transactions

Transfer ownership of any property over which he or she has authority under this document to the trustee of a revocable trust I have created as settlor. Such property may include real estate, stocks, bonds, accounts with financial institutions, insurance policies or other property.

(9) Legal actions

Act for me in all matters that affect claims in favor of or against me and proceedings in any court or administrative body. My attorney-in-fact's powers include but are not limited to the power to:

(a) Hire an attorney to assert any claim or defense before any court, administrative board or other tribunal.

(b) Submit to arbitration or mediation or settle any claim in favor of or against me or any litigation to which I am a party, pay any judgment or settlement and receive any money or other things of value paid in settlement.

(10) Personal and family maintenance

Do all acts necessary to maintain my customary standard of living, and that of my spouse and children and other persons customarily supported by or legally entitled to be supported by me. My attorney-in-fact's powers include but are not limited to the power to:

(a) Pay for medical, dental and surgical care, living quarters, usual vacations and travel expenses, shelter, clothing, food, appropriate education and other living costs.

(b) Continue arrangements with respect to automobiles or other means of transportation, charge accounts, discharge of any services or duties assumed by me to any parent, relative or friend, contributions or payments incidental to membership or affiliation in any church, club, society or other organization.

(11) Government benefits

Act for me in all matters that affect my right to government benefits, including Social Security, Medicare, Medicaid or other governmental programs, or civil or military service. My attorney-in-fact's powers include but are not limited to the power to:

(a) Prepare, execute, file, prosecute, defend, submit to arbitration or settle a claim on my behalf to benefits or assistance, financial or otherwise.

(b) Receive the proceeds of such a claim and conserve, invest, disburse or use them on my behalf.

(12) Retirement plan transactions

Act for me in all matters that affect my retirement plans. My attorney-in-fact's powers include but are not limited to the power to select payment options under any retirement plan in which I participate, make contributions to those plans, exercise investment options, receive payment from a plan, roll over plan benefits into other retirement plans, designate beneficiaries under those plans and change existing beneficiary designations.

(13) Tax matters

Act for me in all matters that affect my local, state and federal taxes. My attorney-in-fact's powers include but are not limited to the power to:

(a) Prepare, sign and file federal, state, local and foreign income, gift, payroll, Federal Insurance Contributions Act returns and other tax returns, claims for refunds, requests for extension of time, petitions, any power of attorney required by the Internal Revenue Service or other taxing authority, and other documents.

(b) Pay taxes due, collect refunds, post bonds, receive confidential information, exercise any election available to me and contest deficiencies determined by a taxing authority.

I understand the importance of the powers I delegate to my attorney-in-fact in this document. I recognize that the document gives my attorney-in-fact broad powers over my assets.

Signed this _____ 6th _____ day of _____ October _____, _____ 20xx _____.

State of _____ Michigan _____, County of _____ Wayne _____.

_____ Jonathan Chen _____   _____ 123-45-6788 _____

Signature   Social Security Number

WITNESSES

On the date written above, the principal declared to me that this instrument is his or her financial power of attorney, and that he or she willingly executed it as a free and voluntary act. The principal signed this instrument in my presence.

_____   _____
Name   Name

_____   _____
Address   Address

_____   _____

_____   _____
County   County

CERTIFICATE OF ACKNOWLEDGMENT OF NOTARY PUBLIC

State of _____ }
                                   } ss
County of _____ }

On _____, before me, _____,

a notary public in and for said state, personally appeared _____,

personally known to me (or proved on the basis of satisfactory evidence) to be the person whose name is subscribed to the within instrument, and acknowledged to me that he or she executed the same in his or her authorized capacity and that by his or her signature on the instrument the person, or the entity upon behalf of which the person acted, executed the instrument.

WITNESS my hand and official seal.

_____

Notary Public for the State of _____

[NOTARIAL SEAL]   My commission expires: _____

PREPARATION STATEMENT

This document was prepared by:

Jonathan Chen
_____
Name

147 Iris Street
_____
Address

Detroit, Michigan 48231
_____

Looking Ahead: Estate Planning

Few people look forward to the day when they will die; making plans for that inevitable time can seem dull, even macabre. But it's vitally important that lesbians and gay men—especially those who are coupled—plan what they want to happen to their property after they die. This is called estate planning. Generally, if you die without a will (or a living trust or other legal means for transferring property), your property will be distributed under your state's "intestacy" laws. These laws require that all your property pass to certain specified relatives, namely a spouse, children, parents and siblings. State death laws don't recognize lesbian and gay relationships (except for Vermont couples who register their civil unions and Hawaii couples who register as reciprocal beneficiaries). (For more on the laws governing couples in Vermont and Hawaii, see Chapter 3.)

If you have a living together contract, you may think you've done enough. But that's definitely not the case. A living together contract defines how a couple owns property while both partners are alive. It's not a substitute for a will or living trust, documents that legally specify what happens to a person's property after he or she dies. It's not hard to do basic estate planning. It's foolish not to do at least the minimum, which is preparing a basic will.

If you don't take steps to "plan your estate"—that is, you don't draft a will, create a living trust or follow any of the other suggestions in this chapter—your surviving lover can try to obtain your property by arguing that your living together agreement gives her rights to that property. But it's far from certain that her claim would succeed. She might have to sue, which will be time-consuming, expensive and nasty. Don't risk it. Rather, be sure to specify, in an appropriate legal document, what will happen to your property at your death. If you and your partner have mixed property and it's unclear who owns what, you can resolve that in a clearly defined living together contract.

We know quite a few horror stories involving people's families suddenly swooping down on a surviving lover to claim all the deceased person's property. Some years ago, an article in a national gay and lesbian news magazine described the plight of one man whose lover died and left no will. The deceased's family quickly appeared and started removing property from the couple's apartment. "His mother took the pillows and pillowcases off the bed," the lover said. "I ended up having to fight for my own clothes. We wore the same size."

Deciding what you want done with your property after you die isn't the only benefit of estate planning. If you and your lover are raising a child together but only you are the recognized legal parent, you can nominate your lover as a personal guardian for your child. Further, you can appoint the person you want to be responsible for supervising the distribution of your property—called your executor. You can also summarize your wishes for memorial services and body disposition or specify that the arrangements are to be made by your lover, though we recommend that you do this in a document separate from your will. (See Chapter 4, Section C, for a more detailed discussion of burial and body disposition.)

Section C in this chapter covers wills, the most basic of all estate planning documents, and contains a sample completed will form. There is also a basic will form at the end of this chapter.

Section D covers more extensive estate planning. Transferring all your property by a will can have drawbacks. The principal one is probate, a legal proceeding where your will is filed with a court, your assets identified, your debts paid and your property distributed to your heirs. Probate is usually expensive and time-consuming. By planning ahead, you can eliminate or lessen the need for probate, and sometimes save your heirs on death taxes. Section D can help you to decide whether your estate planning needs will be taken care of through a will or if something more is warranted.

Before we plunge into particulars of wills and estate planning, let us acknowledge that giving attention to the practical consequences of death, while important, is quite minor when compared to the misery, grief and tragedy of the death of a loved one. We share the thoughts of a friend who lost his lover of nearly three decades.

A. Reflections on the Death of a Mate

Recognizing that one individual's reactions to death are no basis for generalization, I offer the following only as a personal response to a question about the feelings a survivor experiences when an abiding homosexual relationship is ended by the death of one of the partners. My only qualification for doing so lies in being such a survivor after a mutual love of nearly thirty years.

From what I perceive through observation, through literature, or by intuition, I strongly suspect that, except for easier distribution of property in a legally binding relationship, there may not be great differences of impact for the survivor whether the love has been homosexual or heterosexual. The death of a mate obviously leaves one emotionally and, in the case of a long illness, physically spent. What are the significant feelings that survive after the initial shock of finality has exhausted itself in the busy-work that ensues around the affairs of the decedent? Despair isn't quite one of them, for if a close relationship has endured two or three decades, each partner has already recognized and yielded to the necessity for mutual independence and steadfast self-reliance. Nonetheless, there's a transient sense of cosmic inquiry: "What am I doing here?" which may easily deteriorate to, "What am I doing anywhere?" But the daily business of living—and it may seem a business without profit—does supersede such disorientation.

The feelings that continue, and which most poignantly harbor the pain, can be identified, I believe, as essentially two. The first of these is the piercing loneliness of having no focus for one's affection after so long a time. The emptiness of not loving is an infinite void, and it summons the most painful recognition of loss. Such feelings, however, though perpetual, aren't near the surface and reveal themselves most forcefully in what seems to be the dullness of leisure or in the sadness of reflection.

Lying nearer the surface are the daily—sometimes hourly, for a little while perhaps constant—reminders that feed the second and more persistent pain, one that will never be totally consumed. Couples inevitably develop their own language, visual as well as verbal, based on shared experiences, shared jokes, mutual acceptance of difficulty, shared joys and sorrows, reciprocal devotion. Layers are thereby added to the relationship much as alluvial deposits are washed down to enrich life's texture in a less psychologically ornamented environment. The survivor continues to use that language, for it's a part of him, although he now lacks an auditor who grasps its overtones, undertones and essential meanings. When those symbols, and the figure in the carpet which they represent, appear—whether verbally, cerebrally or viscerally—and no one's there to recognize an allusion, to be counted on for sympathetic amusement at one's own folly, to recognize an earlier situation now cryptically cited to give sharpened meaning to the present, the vacancy is felt as the ebbing away of an adult lifetime.

For those of us who aren't artists, the structure which houses those symbols may be the closest we shall ever come to the creation of poetry. Like poetry, the form of communication and its underlying history make up an economical construct of imagery that distills experience. To borrow a verb from Gerard Manley Hopkins, the distillation "explodes" as mutual recognition, as ineffable joy, as reciprocal contemplativeness—in short, as the impact of art. The irreversible decay of the only context in which the construct obtained, and in which a man's life has been elevated out of the limitations of self-concern into felicitous union, is what I perceive to be the basis of grief. Although the "grief returns with the revolving year," it is, in the fullness of time, merged into a sense of one's own good fortune, into the joyful remembrances of things past, and into an appreciation for what the relationship still contributes to one's future.

B. Death and Living Together Contracts

In Chapter 6, we explain that most states enforce written living together contracts that cover property. If you have a contract stating that you're the half-owner of specific property, your partner has no power to dispose of your share, either during life or at death. While a living together contract will serve the purpose of establishing who owns what, do not rely on a living together contract (even one that provides that the survivor inherits the deceased partner's property) as a valid means for transferring property at death.

If you and your lover have no written contract, you could face big trouble proving, after his or her death, what the two of you informally agreed to as to property ownership. Generally, property is legally owned by the person whose name is on the title document (assuming there is one), such as a real estate deed or car registration. Suppose your lover had his name on most of the property but your intent was to share ownership equally. If your lover dies without a will, you would face an uphill battle trying to convince any court you had an ownership interest in property held in his name. And even if you could prove it in the end, this would be difficult, costly process. You'd have to persuade a judge or jury that you had an oral contract about property, or that you had contributed to the purchase or creation of the property. The best way to avoid this is to prepare a will and a living together contract, and leave a lawsuit to others.

C. Wills

A will is a document in which you specify who gets your property when you die. These people and institutions are called your "beneficiaries." The advantages of a will are the following:

- A will is relatively easy to make.
- You can leave your property to anyone you wish. No laws prohibit you from leaving your property to your lover (or anyone else, for that matter).
- A will is easy to change or revoke; you're not stuck with it once you make it.
- Your will is your own business. Discussing it with your lover is probably a good idea, but you're not required to reveal its contents to anyone.

As we've mentioned, the drawback to using a will is probate. After reading Section D, you may decide to take steps to avoid probate. Even if you do, you should definitely also make a will. First, you may have property at your death that you hadn't thought of, or known of, when planning your estate, such as a suddenly inherited house, a gift of an expensive stereo or computer, big winnings at the races or a personal injury lawsuit recovery. If you have a will, you can simply pass the "residue of your estate" (any property you own not specifically left to beneficiaries in your will or by other methods) to your lover. Second, in a will you can name who will supervise distribution of your property. Third, you can nominate a guardian for your minor child—something you can't do in other estate planning devices, such as a living trust.

Once you decide what property you want to transfer by will, don't delay in preparing the document. There is no benefit to postponing the drafting of your will; delay only increases the risks of the consequences of an untimely death—that is, your parents or siblings inheriting all of your property, rather than your property going to whom you've chosen.

1. Who Can Make a Will?

Anyone who's legally an adult and "of sound mind" can make a valid will. An adult is anyone 18 years or older (19 or older if you live in Wyoming). You have to be very far gone before your will can be invalidated on the grounds that you weren't "of sound mind." If you understand this book, you're competent to draft a will.

2. Will I Need a Lawyer to Prepare My Will?

Most people can safely prepare their will without hiring a lawyer. If you have a moderate estate (in tax terms, under $1 million) and envision a straightforward distribution of property, you should be able to prepare your will yourself. After all, your intent is simply to define who gets your property when you die. You can probably state that in two or three sentences. Why should making your wishes about property distribution legal become complicated?

If you have a large estate and desire extensive estate planning (complicated trusts, "pour-over" wills—that sort of thing), you'll need to have your will prepared by a lawyer. But ordinary folks don't need such costly planning. Lawyers often try to scare people into buying their expensive services by claiming that each will requires "expert, professional attention," then routinely have their secretaries use the same form-book wills, over and over and over again.

Preparing Your Own Will. *If you want to explore preparing your will on your own, check out Nolo's books and software in the list of Estate Planning Resources at the end of this chapter.*

3. Providing for Your Children

Many lesbian and gay couples have children, whether from donor insemination, an earlier marriage or adoption. (See Chapter 3 for more information.) Either member of such a couple can leave property to their own or their lover's children without problems. You simply name the children in your will and leave them whatever you want. Or, you and your lover can leave all property to each other, and then name the children as alternate beneficiaries.

Providing for your minor children, however, does inevitably raise concerns. If you die before they're grown, who will care for them and how can you leave property to them? Let's look at each of these concerns separately.

a. Custody and Care

The legal parents of a minor child are the people entitled to custody of that child. If there is only one legal parent, that parent can direct, but not mandate, who will have custody of the child if the legal parent dies. When there are two legal parents (whether members of a same-sex couple or the divorced parents of a child), each is entitled to custody. If one dies, the other automatically gets custody, unless a compelling reason—such as the incompetence of the surviving parent—dictates otherwise.

Some lesbian and gay couples share legal custody of a child. But many lesbian and gay parents do not. In most cases, only one member of the couple—the biological parent or sole adoptive parent—is the sole custodial parent. In such a situation, if the legal parent dies, another adult must have legal responsibility for caring for a minor child. This adult is called the child's personal guardian. Only a legal parent can name a personal guardian in his or her will for a minor child.

The nomination of a minor child's personal guardian in a will is not legally binding. Children are not property and cannot be transferred by will. The final decision is made by a judge, usually using the standard of the "best interest of the child." But a personal guardian nominated by a parent is usually the one confirmed by a court. Normally, only when someone contests the custody proceeding, or the guardian is obviously unfit to serve, will a court reject the guardian nominated by the parent.

If you and your partner are raising a child together but only one of you is the legal parent, the legal parent should nominate the other as the child's personal guardian. Otherwise, the surviving lover may have an uphill battle to gain custody. You can also name an alternate guardian, in case the first choice can't serve.

b. Gifts of Property

Either parent can leave property to the couple's minor child, regardless of who is the recognized legal parent. Of course, before you can consider leaving money or property to your child, you must have something to leave. If you have little beyond a big mortgage and car payments, consider buying a moderate amount of term life insurance to help provide for your child if you die, until he is on his own. Because term life insurance pays benefits only if you die during the covered period (often five or ten years), it's far cheaper than other types of life insurance.

Assuming you have property to leave to your child, your first concern is who will manage it if you die before your child is mature enough to have it. Except for property of little value, the law requires that an adult manage property inherited by minors until they turn 18 (and you can delay this age for property you leave in a will). If you don't designate a manager in your estate plan, a court will appoint one for you. These court procedures are time-consuming, costly and may produce a result you wouldn't approve of. Here are several ways to do it yourself:

- **Leave property directly to your children's other parent.** This makes the most sense if you and your partner are co-raising a child and only you are the recognized legal parent. You can use the basic will at the end of this chapter for this purpose.
- **Use the provisions of the Uniform Transfers to Minors Act (UTMA).** In all states but South Carolina and Vermont, you can use the UTMA to name a custodian to manage property you leave to your minor children for their benefit until the children are 18 or 21 (up to 25 in California, Alaska and Nevada). The UTMA works particularly well if you leave your children $100,000 or less, because money or property in this range will likely be spent for the child's education and living expenses by age 21. To use the UTMA, you can use one of Nolo's specialized estate planning or will-drafting products. (See the Estate Planning Resources information at the end of this chapter.)
- **Create a child's trust.** For large estates ($100,000 or more) and for states where the UTMA is not available, consider establishing a simple child's trust, in either your will or living trust. The trustee of a child's trust manages the money for your child and doles it out for education, healthcare and other needs

under the terms of the trust. The child's trust ends, and any remaining money is turned over to your child outright, at whatever age you designate. Again, see the Estate Planning Resources list at the end of the chapter.

 Name the same person to care for your child and any property you leave that child. *It's wise to nominate the same person you nominated as personal guardian to serve as custodian of your children's money and other property (in your will, or under the UTMA or in a child's trust), unless that person doesn't have good financial sense. If you face this problem, you are better off naming two different people; one to care for your child and another to manage her finances. Make sure the two people you name get along, because they will have to work together if you die before your child is an adult.*

4. Typical Will Provisions

You can use a will to do the following:

- Leave anything you own to anyone or any institution you choose. You never have to state your relationship to the beneficiary—it's no one's business. Once you draft your will, you don't have to hold onto property just because it's left to someone in your will. If you left your Renoir painting to your friend Bob in your will, but sell the painting before you die, Bob's out of luck.
- Forgive debts owed to you.
- Nominate a personal guardian for your minor children.
- Name a property guardian to manage your minor children's property.
- Set up simple trusts for your children or leave UTMA gifts.
- Name the person who will supervise the distribution of your property left by your will. This person is called your executor or personal representative. You can name your lover, or anyone you trust, to be your executor. Some states require out-of-state executors to post a bond, so it is a good idea to name

an executor who lives in the same state you do.

- Disinherit people. You can't completely disinherit a spouse—but this is a problem few of our readers will face.

Disinheriting

You can disinherit almost anyone by simply not mentioning him or her in your will. To disinherit your child (or the child of your deceased child), however, requires more explicit action. The traditional method is to state the disinheritance expressly in your will—"I disinherit my son William Jones and direct that he receive nothing from my estate."

The basic will at the end of this chapter provides a general clause that will result in a child's or children's disinheritance if you don't leave property to them. Specifically, the will states: "If I do not leave property in this will to one or more of my children or my grandchildren named above, my failure to do so is intentional." If you want to use an express disinheritance clause, you'll find a sample in *Nolo's Simple Will Book*, by Denis Clifford.

Some states have laws, called "pretermitted heir" statutes, which are designed to prevent accidental disinheritance of children. These laws provide that if you fail to mention a child born after your will was made, that child receives a set percentage of your estate. So, if you have a child after writing your will, you should revise the will to leave something to that child.

---

5. Technical Requirements in Preparing a Will

For your will to be valid:

- It must be typed or computer printed.
- It must state that it's your will—"This is the will of (your name)" suffices.

- It must be signed and dated by you after declaring to witnesses that it's your will. Some authorities recommend you say, "This is my will," and the witnesses answer, "He says it's his will." It sounds like Gilbert and Sullivan, but it can't hurt. More importantly, the witnesses must know the document is your will, but they aren't expected (or required) to read it.
- It must be signed and dated by three witnesses who are not beneficiaries under the will. They sign after you do. In most all states, only two witnesses are legally required. Using a third, however, can't hurt and means the will is valid in all states.

6. Are Handwritten Wills Valid?

Handwritten wills, or "holographic" wills, are valid in some states, but not others. Handwritten wills usually do not have to be witnessed. Regardless of your state's rule, however, your will should be typed and witnessed, not handwritten and unwitnessed. Holographic wills often receive suspicious treatment by courts. They must be letter-perfect and can't have any cross-outs, machine-printed dates or technical errors. If you're trapped in the woods and the wolves are coming to get you, write out a will and say your prayers. When you return to civilization, prepare a typed or printed will and sign it before witnesses.

7. Are Joint Wills Valid?

A joint will is one document through which two people leave their property. After the first person dies, the joint will specifies what happens to the property of the second person when she dies. We don't recommend joint wills; the survivor, we believe, should have the freedom to dispose of her property as she wants. If you're thinking of using a joint will despite our recommendation, see a lawyer.

8. Is My Will Valid If I Move to a New State?

If your will is valid in the state where you prepare it, that will remains valid if you move to another state. However, if you move to Louisiana, you should prepare a new will because Louisiana's laws are based on a different system than those of all other states. Also, you might want to draft a new will after you move, if your personal or financial situation has changed. To make simple changes, you can revoke your will and write a new one, or add a "codicil" changing your executor.

9. A Sample Will

We show you a sample will below, so you can gain an idea what a basic one looks like. In this will form, Samuel Traplan has handwritten the information that he wants in his final will. He must then type up the will, then sign and witness it.

This sample will is a bare-bones will. It's far better to have basic will than none at all, but most people will want a more thorough will, which they can prepare using one of Nolo's will-writing resources. If you want to prepare just a bare-bones will, we provide a form from which you can draft one at the end of this chapter.

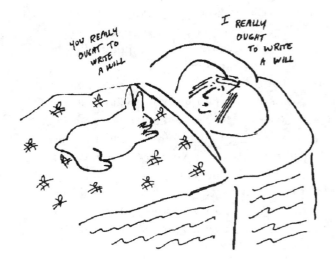

Sample Will

Will of _Samuel Troplon_

I, _Samuel Troplon_ ,

a resident of _Queens_ County, _New York_ , declare that this is my will.

1. Revocation

I revoke all wills and codicils that I have previously made.

2. ~~Prior Marriages~~

~~I was married to _____ and am now divorced.~~

3. Children

A. I have __1__ children now living, whose names and dates of birth ~~is~~:

Name _Nina Yanes_

Date of Birth _July 5, 1994_

[Repeat as often as needed.]

The terms "my children" as used in this will shall include any other children hereafter born to or adopted

by me.

B. I have the following children of my deceased child _____.

Name _____

Date of Birth _____

[Repeat as often as needed.]

C. If I do not leave property in this will to one or more of my children or my grandchildren named above,

my failure to do so is intentional.

D. If at my death any of my children are minors, and a personal guardian is needed, I recommend that

_____ _Michael Haight_ _____ be appointed guardian of the persons of my minor

children. If _____ _Michael Haight_ _____ cannot or refuses to serve, I nominate

_____ _Elizabeth Troplon_ _____ as guardian of the persons of my minor children.

E. If at my death any of my children are minors and a property guardian is needed, I name

_____ _Michael Haight_ _____ to be appointed guardian of the property of my minor

children. If _____ _Michael Haight_ _____ cannot or refuses to serve, I name

_____ _Elizabeth Troplon_ _____ to be appointed guardian of the property of my

minor children.

4. Gifts

A. I make the following gifts of money or personal property:

1. I give every child or grandchild listed in Clause 3 $1.00 (one dollar) in addition to any other property I may give them elsewhere in this will, or otherwise.

2. I give the sum of $ ___20,000___ to _____Nina Yanes_____ if ~~he~~/she/~~it~~ survives me by 60 days; if ~~he~~/she/~~it~~ doesn't, this gift shall be made to ___Michael Haight___.

[Repeat as often as needed.]

3. I give ___my car___ to ___Nina Yanes___ if ~~he~~/she/~~it~~ survives me by 60 days; if ~~he~~/she/~~it~~ doesn't, the gift shall be made to ___Michael Haight___.

[Repeat as often as needed.]

4. I forgive and cancel the debt of $ _____ owed to me by _____.

[Repeat as often as needed]

B. I make the following gifts of real estate:

1. I give my interest in the real estate in ___163 Astoria Heights___, commonly known as _____, to ___Michael Haight___ if he/~~she~~/~~it~~ survives me for 60 days. If he/~~she~~/~~it~~ doesn't survive me for 60 days, that property shall be given to ___Nina Yanes___.

[Repeat as often as needed.]

5. Residue

I give the residue of my property subject to this will as follows:

A. To ___Nina Yanes___ if ~~he~~/she/~~it~~ survives me by 60 days.

B. If not, to ___Michael Haight___ if he/~~she~~/~~it~~ survives me by 60 days.

C. If neither ___Nina Yanes___ nor ___Michael Haight___ survives me by 60 days, then to ___Elizabeth Troplon___.

6. Executor

A. I nominate ___Michael Haight___ as executor of this will, to serve without bond. If ___Michael Haight___ shall for any reason fail to qualify or cease to act as executor, I nominate ___Elizabeth Troplon___ to serve without bond.

B. I grant to my executor the right to place my obituary of ~~her~~/his choosing in the papers ~~she~~/he thinks appropriate.

7. No Contest

If any person or persons named to receive any of my property under my will in any manner contests or attacks this will or any of its provisions, that person or persons shall be disinherited and shall receive none of my property, and my property shall be disposed of as if that contesting beneficiary had died before me leaving no children.

8. Simultaneous Death

If ____*Nina Yanes*_____ and I should die simultaneously, or under such circumstances as to render it difficult or impossible to determine who predeceased the other, I shall be conclusively presumed to have survived _____*Nina Yanes*_____ for purposes of this will.

9. Signature and Witnessing

I subscribe my name to this will this _____ of _____, _____, at _____,

_____, _____.

On this ____*7th*___ of___*March*_____, ___*1996*___, ___*Samuel Traplon*_____ declared to us, the undersigned, that this instrument was [his/~~her~~] will, and requested us to act as witnesses to it. [He/~~she~~] thereupon signed this will in our presence, all of us being present at the time. We now, at [his/~~her~~] request, in [his/~~her~~] presence, and in the presence of each other, subscribe our names as witnesses and declare we understand this to be [his/~~her~~] will, and that to the best of our knowledge the testator is competent to make a will, and under no constraint or undue influence.

We declare under penalty of perjury that the foregoing is true and correct.

_____
Witness's Signature

_____
Address

_____
Witness's Signature

_____
Address

_____
Witness's Signature

_____
Address

10. Preparing a Basic Will Using Our Form

You can use the will form at the end of this chapter to prepare a basic will. While we urge you to go deeper into preparing a will, we include this form so you can at least prepare some kind of will promptly. Here are some guidelines for preparing a basic will using this form.

- **Do it in two steps.** After reading this chapter, prepare a rough draft of your will, using or adapting the form at the end of this chapter. Once you're satisfied you've covered everything, type the will on 8-1/2" x 11" white typing paper. (You can use a computer.)
- **Complete only the clauses that pertain to you.** If you were never married, delete Clause 2, "Prior Marriages." Then renumber the remaining clauses when you type it up. Thus, clause "3: Children" would become "2: Children."
- **Use plain language and common sense.** If you write "I leave my car to my sister Sue," she will receive whatever car you own when you die. If you write, "I leave my Toyota to my sister Sue," and sell it before you die and buy a Porsche, Sue gets no car. Courts try to give effect to the "intent" of the will writer, but they can't contradict clear words.
- **Don't make changes before you sign your will.** If you want to change your will before it's signed and witnessed, don't just cross something out and initial the change. Instead, you'll need to retype it. And after the will has been completed—signed, dated and witnessed—you can make changes only by using a "codicil," or by revoking your will and preparing an entirely new one. (See Section C12, below.)

Completing the Will Form

Here we cover some basics of how to complete the clauses of the will at the end of this chapter.

Your Name and Address

Use your full name and use it the same way throughout the will.

Your address is important because if, at the time of your death, you had connections with more than one state, each state may try to impose death taxes. Giving your residence will help minimize this, and will help establish in which county your will is to be probated. (It's probated in the county where you made your home.) If you have real ties to more than one state, see a lawyer to figure out how to keep more than one from trying to impose death taxes.

Clause 1. Revocation

This clause covers all prior wills, including any handwritten document that could be construed as a will.

Clause 2. Prior Marriages

Fill in this clause only if you've ever been married. If you have, mention the marriage and that it ended (we're assuming it has). If you are still legally married, you will want to see a lawyer before completing your will. Remember, a marriage entered into for immigration purposes is still a legal marriage.

Clause 3. Children

If you have any children, list them all, and all children of any child of yours who has died. Your children are those for whom you are a legally recognized parent—that is, children you have given birth to, biologically fathered or legally adopted. If you are co-parenting, but are not legally recognized as a parent, you would not include the children here. Instead, you can provide for them in Clause 4.

As previously mentioned, if you wish to disinherit a child using this will, you can do so by leaving nothing to that child. The child will be disinherited under the terms of Clause 3.C.

If you have custody of minor children, you can nominate a personal guardian for those children in Clause 3.D. See the discussion in Section C3, above.

You can also use Clause 3.E to name a property guardian for your minor children; this person will manage any property you leave your children and can manage any other property they acquire before they become 18. Again, see the discussion in Section C3, above.

Clause 4.A. Gifts of Money or Personal Property

In Clause A, you name beneficiaries for your money and personal property. Your personal property is everything but your real estate, which you give away in Clause B. Clause A lets you make direct, unconditional gifts to a single beneficiary, either a person or organization. If you want to leave a certain item of property to be shared by two or more people, see Nolo's other will resources or a lawyer. And, if you want to place conditions on a gift—for example, "I leave my boat to Ronald but only if he graduates from culinary school"—you'll need to see a lawyer.

If you leave someone money, you might want to add to the bequest "but in no event more than [number] percent of my (net or probate) estate" just in case there's not as much there as you'd planned.

You can also name an alternate beneficiary if the beneficiary doesn't survive you. If you don't name such a person, and the beneficiary dies before you, your property becomes part of your "residue" in Clause 5, and goes to your residuary beneficiary.

Many people don't want to leave something to someone who will never benefit from it, and so they require the beneficiary to survive them by some specified period of time. We require the beneficiary to survive you by 60 days in order to receive the property. You can specify any other reasonable period you want, such as 30 or 100 days (two years isn't reasonable).

If you plan to give specific items of property to a beneficiary, describe them with sufficient detail so there is no question as to what property you mean. If you want to leave many small items to someone, however, and you don't want to list them all, you can state that you give "all my furniture [or "my tools" or "my records"] to [name]." If you don't care who gets your minor pieces of personal property, you can add a clause stating that these items "are to be distributed as my executor deems proper."

In Clause 4.A.4, you can also forgive (forget) debts owed you. Forgiving a debt is in reality making a gift to the debtor, who would otherwise owe the money to your estate.

Clause 4.B. Gifts of Real Estate

In Clause B, you name beneficiaries for your real estate. As with personal property, it's wise to include a survivorship period, and to name an alternate beneficiary if the primary beneficiary doesn't survive the survivorship period. If the beneficiary (and alternate beneficiary, if you name one) doesn't survive you, the real estate becomes a part of your residue.

When you make a gift of real estate, all mortgages and other debts (such as tax liens) on the property go with it. If you want to give real estate free of a mortgage, see one of Nolo's other will resources.

Clause 5. Residue

The "residue" in your will is exactly what it sounds like—all property subject to your will left over after the specific gifts in Clause 4 have been distributed. You can select any person or organization you want to receive the "residue" of your estate. It's prudent to name an alternate beneficiary for your residue. If you want to be really careful, you can name a second alternate beneficiary to receive your will residue if the first two don't survive within the 60 (or however many you choose) days. Many people simply leave the bulk of their estate to their residuary beneficiary, rather than list all their property in Clause 4.

Clause 6. Executor

Your executor should be someone you trust and can rely on, and who will be available and competent when you die. You should name at least one successor executor in case your first choice dies before you, declines to serve or is incompetent when you die. If your will names no executor or no alternate when an alternate is needed, the probate court appoints one.

If you don't state that the executor is "to serve without bond," the probate court may require the executor to post a sum of money. This means either that a large amount of cash from the estate is tied up or that the estate must pay a bondsman's fee—usually 10% of the amount of the bond.

If you name an out-of-state executor, the court may require a bond, even if you stated "to serve without bond."

Clause 7. No Contest

This clause is designed to discourage will contests. We have not included any general disinheritance clause, or a clause giving $1 to all nieces and nephews. As discussed, your children are a special case and can be disinherited specifically if you want or you can do so under the terms of the will by not leaving them property. There's no need to specifically exclude other people; most will drafters and contemporary will-form books omit a general disinheritance clause.

 A lawyer can help you if you think anyone in your family will challenge your will. *If your relatives object to your sexual orientation, it's possible that they will challenge your will on grounds that you were incompetent, or under "undue influence," when you made your will, especially if you have considerable money. This may be even more likely if you leave your property to your lover, other gay or lesbian friends or a gay and/or lesbian organization. Although will contests are rare, they do happen, especially in cases of people with AIDS. Anyone diagnosed with AIDS should prepare a will as early after diagnosis as possible, to minimize the chance that the will will be successfully challenged on the grounds that you weren't mentally competent when you signed it.*

If there's any real possibility that a relative will challenge your will, take action to establish that you are competent and not under undue influence when you sign it. If worse comes to worst, this evidence can be used in court after your death.

One possibility is to have your will prepared by and signed in front of a lawyer, who can testify that you were obviously competent. Another possibility is to write your will yourself and pay a lawyer only for review and the signing. If you're truly concerned about a challenge, explore various possibilities. Consult a lesbian/gay attorney service which can provide lawyers experienced with will contests. Consider using a lawyer who's familiar with video-taping, so when you sign your will, you can look into the camera and tell the world how sane you are. Or follow the approach of one lawyer who advises her lesbian and gay clients to insert a clause like the following, which shows you considered leaving your property to your relatives:

> *I don't make my gifts to Ben Tymons out of any lack of love for my parents, sister, brother, Aunt Susan, Uncle Jonathan, cousin Cynthia, cousin Harold or other relatives, but rather because my relatives are adequately cared for and I specifically wish to benefit my friend Ben who has been a source of great love and comfort to me over many years.*

Many lawyers encourage their clients to sit down with their family members and speak directly about their intentions. This isn't an easy task, but it can have a very powerful emotional impact and can help avoid later conflicts.

Clause 8. Simultaneous Death

This clause covers the unusual situation in which you die at the same time as a beneficiary. Most states have adopted the Uniform Simultaneous Death Act. This law presumes that when two people die together, and it's impossible to know who died first, the beneficiary is presumed to have died first. This way, the will writer's property passes to his or her alternate beneficiaries, and not to the briefly surviving beneficiary and then to that beneficiary's beneficiaries. If you name alternate beneficiaries with survivorship periods, this shouldn't be a problem. Even so, it doesn't hurt to include this provision in your will.

If you own property in joint tenancy, and you and the other joint tenant died simultaneously, you're presumed to have died last. Thus your share passes through your will and the other joint tenant's share passes in her or his will. (See Section D2d, below, for more information on joint tenancy.)

If you own insurance, and you and the beneficiary die simultaneously, the proceeds of the policy are distributed as if the beneficiary had died before you—that is, to any alternate beneficiary named in the policy or under the residuary clause of your will.

Clause 9. Signature and Witnessing

Sign and date your will in front of your three witnesses, who then sign the witness clause in front of each other. In many states, a will can be witnessed by what's called a "self-proving affidavit," which can simplify or even eliminate witnesses' need to go to court after the will writer dies. Explanations of self-proving affidavits and sample forms are in Nolo's will-writing books and software.

11. Storing and Copying Your Will

Store your will in a safe place, one that your executor has ready access to. A safe deposit box is generally not a good idea because your executor probably won't have access to the box after you die.

You can make copies of your will for any person you want to have one. But do not sign any copies directly (photocopies of your signature on the original are okay). The reason for this is to prevent any possibility of duplicate wills, which can cause trouble later if you revoke or amend your will.

12. Changing or Revoking Your Will

Suppose you want to make a minor change in your will. For example, Mary died, and the library of lesbian fiction you were going to leave her you now want to leave to Martha. Or suppose you want to revoke your will entirely—let's say you and your lover just split up. What do you do?

a. Changing Your Will

When you should change your will is a matter of common sense. Don't make impromptu changes. At the same time, you can't just ink out a provision in your will or handwrite a change in the margin. Changes must be made formally.

The form used to make legal changes to a will is called a "codicil." You can use a codicil to make an addition, modification or deletion after your will is drafted, signed and witnessed. A codicil is a sort of legal "P.S." to a will, and must be executed with the same formalities. If possible, it should be typed on the last page of the will itself, or on an additional page or pages. It must be dated and signed by the will writer and three witnesses. They don't have to be the ones who witnessed the will, but try to use them if they're available.

Codicils are usually used for relatively minor matters, like the change of the beneficiary for the lesbian fiction library in the example above. If you want to make a major revision, don't use a codicil. A will that has been substantially rewritten by a codicil is confusing, awkward to read, and may not clearly show the relationship of the codicil to the original will. For major revisions, draft a new will; the first provision in our will—"I revoke all wills and codicils that I have previously made"—will revoke your earlier will and any codicils to it. (See subsection b, below, for information on revoking a will.)

Below is a sample codicil shown in completed draft stage, like the sample will above. This is the codicil form we provide at the end of this chapter. Follow our same instructions for completing your will. When you're done, make several copies and attach the original codicil to your original will. Attach a copy of the codicil to each copy of your will.

(Sample) Codicil

First **Codicil to the Will of** _Samuel Troplon_ **dated** _May 14, 20xx_.

I, _Samuel Troplon_ , a resident of _Queens_ County, _New York_ ,
declare this to be the first codicil to my will dated _May 14, 20xx_

First. I revoke Item _A2_ of Clause _VI_ , and substitute the following:

I give the sum of $5,000 to my friend Tim Grayson, if he survives me by 60 days; if he doesn't, this gift shall be made to Becky Alwith.

Second. I add the following new Item _____ to Clause _____:

I give the sum of $5,000 to the Gay Men's Health Crisis Center.

Third. In all other respects I confirm and republish my will dated _March 7, 1996_, this _14th_ day of _May, 20xx_ , at _Queens, New York_ .

Samuel Troplon

On the date written below, _Samuel Troplon_ declared to us, the undersigned, that this instrument, consisting of _____ pages, including this page signed by us as witnesses, was the first codicil to [his/~~her~~] will and requested us to act as witnesses to it. [He/~~she~~] thereupon signed this codicil in our presence, all of us being present at the same time. We now, at [his/~~her~~] request, in [his/~~her~~] presence, and in the presence of each other, subscribe our names as witnesses, and declare we understand this to be [his/~~her~~] will, and that to the best of our knowledge the testator is competent to make a will, and under no constraint or undue influence.

Executed on _____, at _____, _____.

We declare under penalty of perjury that the foregoing is true and correct.

_____
Witness's Signature

_____
Address

_____
Witness's Signature

_____
Address

_____
Witness's Signature

_____
Address

b. Revoking Your Will

Wills are easy to revoke. A will writer who wants to revoke her will or codicil should do so by:

- writing a new will, expressly stating that she's revoking all previous wills, or
- destroying the old will—burn, tear, conceal, deface, obliterate or otherwise destroy it with the intent to revoke it. If you destroy your will, do it in front of witnesses. Otherwise, after you die, it may be difficult to determine if you really intended to destroy it, or in fact, if you did. Someone may have a copy and claim the original will was unintentionally lost, and your would-be inheritors would have a real mess, and probably a lawsuit, on their hands.

D. Estate Planning Beyond a Will

Lesbians and gay men with substantial amounts of money or property can obtain significant benefits for their surviving beneficiaries by more extensive estate planning than simply writing a will. If you have little property, planning beyond a will is probably not necessary. Likewise, if you are young (under age 40) and healthy, you can probably wait until later in life to bother with further estate planning. Our rough rule is that anyone over 40 or ill at any age, with more than $50,000 to $100,000 in assets, can probably benefit from some estate planning beyond a will, which means determining and setting up the least expensive and most efficient methods of transferring your property after death.

As we've discussed, property that passes through your will must go through probate. Probate can be expensive. These fees are taken out of your property and reduce the amount your beneficiaries receive. If you leave your property to be transferred by an estate planning device which avoids probate, you can eliminate probate fees.

In this section, we provide you with an overview of the primary estate planning methods. If you want to look farther, be assured that estate planning need not be as forbidding as many "professionals" would have you believe it is. They have a financial interest in making what they do seem as complicated (expensive) as possible. People with moderate estates can normally do most of the planning themselves, if they have good information. Start with *Plan Your Estate*, by Denis Clifford and Cora Jordan (Nolo).

1. Estimate the Value of Your Property

The first step for many people is to take stock of their net worth. You can do this in any way that makes sense to you. If you have just a few major assets, make a rough estimate of the value each. Or, prepare a thorough list of your property. If you have a substantial estate, this can help you determine if your estate will be likely to owe federal estate taxes, which are assessed for a net estate worth more than $1 million in 2002 or 2003. (Basic federal estate tax rules are set out in Section 3, below.)

A property list may help your survivors identify and locate all of your property. Nolo's *Personal RecordKeeper* software can help you make your list.

Here is an example of a net value list.

Net Estate of Leslie Grayson

Personal Property	Value	Location or Description
Cash	$500	Safe Deposit Box
Savings accounts	$8,500	Tyson Bank
Checking accounts	$1,500	Tyson Bank
Listed (private corporation) stocks and bonds		
	$11,000	Matco Corporation
	$14,000	Break-Monopoly Company
Money owed me including promissory notes, mortgages, leases and accounts receivable	$5,000	Jason Michaels (sold him my car)
Vested interest in profit-sharing plan, pension rights, stock options, etc.	$17,000	401(k) from Invento Corporation
Automobile and other vehicles (include boats and recreation vehicles; deduct any amounts owed)		
	$6,000	Honda motorcycle
	$12,000	BMW
Household goods, net total	$10,000	In my house
Artwork	$33,000	Various pieces around my home
Miscellaneous	$3,000	Silver set in my house
Real estate		
Current market value	$275,000	1807 Saturn Drive, Newark, Delaware
Mortgages and other liens	($125,000)	
Equity (current market value less money owed)	$150,000	
My share of equity (co-owned)	$75,000	
Business interest—33% interest in Invento Corporation, maker of small telephone-related inventions	$250,00	Acquired in 1999; estimate of present market value of interest
AETCO life insurance policy, No. 12345B	$50,000	Name of insured: Leslie Grayson Owner of policy: Leslie Grayson Beneficiary: Robin Anderson
Total value of assets	$496,400	
Debts (not already calculated such as real estate mortgage)	($3,000)	
Taxes (excluding estate taxes)	($12,000)	
Total (other) liabilities	($15,000)	
Total net worth	$481,4000	

2. Probate Avoidance

As we discussed earlier, probate is a court proceeding where your will is filed—or your property transferred under intestate laws if you didn't write a will or arrange for a transfer of your property by other methods—your assets are identified, your debts and taxes are paid and any remaining property is distributed to your beneficiaries. Probate is expensive. Lawyers and executors receive fees, often substantial fees, for what's usually routine, albeit tedious, paperwork. Probate also takes considerable time, normally a minimum of several months and often more than a year. By contrast, property transferred outside of probate can usually be received by the beneficiaries within a few days of the deceased's death.

Probate has acquired a rather notorious aura. Most people may not know exactly what it involves, but they sense it's a lawyer's rip-off. There's a lot of truth in that. Probate is largely an institutionalized racket. No European country has the expensive, form-filled probate process America has. Even in England, where our probate system got its start in feudal times, probate was simplified in 1926. Now, only in case of conflict do a court and lawyers get involved.

Probate fees are usually set by state law. Computation methods vary from state to state. In some states, fees are often based on the size of the estate. But however calculated, rest assured that the lawyer's fee will be generous.

The well-established methods of transferring property to avoid probate include:

- revocable living trusts
- pay-on-death bank or stock accounts
- joint tenancy, and
- life insurance.

Each has advantages and drawbacks, which we briefly discuss below.

a. Revocable Living Trusts

A revocable living or "inter vivos" (Latin for "among the living") trust is usually the best way for a person to avoid probate. A revocable living trust is created by establishing a trust document and giving the trust a name (such as "The R. P. Payne Living Trust"). Because the trust states that it is revocable, you have the right to revoke or change any portion (or all) of it at any time before you die, as long as you are still mentally competent.

In the trust document, you name yourself as both the grantor (the person setting up the trust) and the initial trustee (the person managing the trust property). You list the property owned by the trust. You name your beneficiary or beneficiaries— the people you want to receive the trust property after you die. You also name a successor trustee to manage the trust after you die or become incapacitated. The successor trustee can be a beneficiary. You must sign the trust document and have it notarized. It doesn't have to be witnessed or recorded. Finally, you must transfer all trust property with documents of title into the trustee's name. For example, if you place your house in the trust, you must execute and record a new deed transferring the house from you to yourself as trustee of the trust.

When you die, your successor trustee transfers your trust property to your beneficiaries without any court proceeding. While you are still alive, the trust is essentially a paper transaction, with no real-world effects. You maintain full control over the property in the trust—you can spend, sell or give it away—and can end the trust whenever you want. Trust transactions are reported as part of your regular income tax return; no separate tax forms are required. The only real downside is that property with a legal document title, such as real estate and stocks, must actually be transferred into the trustee's name.

EXAMPLE: Wayne creates a living trust with himself as the initial trustee and his lover, Mark, as successor trustee. In the trust, Wayne makes several small gifts to friends, and names Mark as the beneficiary of Wayne's principal assets— a house and an apartment building. Wayne then executes and records deeds transferring title to the house and apartment house into the name of the trustee. When Wayne dies, Mark, acting as successor trustee, distributes the small gifts to Wayne's friends, and executes new deeds transferring the house and apartment house to the beneficiary—that is, himself.

For more information on living trusts, see the list of Nolo's Estate Planning Resources at the end of this chapter.

b. Pay-on-Death Bank Accounts

A "pay-on-death" bank account, sometimes called a bank trust or Totten trust, allows you to name one or more beneficiaries to receive all money or property in the account when you die. The property goes directly to the beneficiary, avoiding probate. You manage the account as you would any other bank deposit account. The only difference is that you name someone on the account form—such as your lover—as beneficiary of the account, to receive the balance after you die. During your life, you retain full and exclusive control over the account— you can remove any funds in the account for any reason, make deposits, close the account or whatever else you want.

There are no drawbacks to a pay-on-death bank account. Most banks have standard forms allowing you to create this type of trust—either by opening a new account or transferring an existing account. Pay-on-death account fees are normally no higher than the fees for other types of bank accounts.

c. Pay-on-Death Securities Accounts

In almost all states, you can add a transfer-on-death designation to brokerage accounts, or to individual securities (stocks and bonds) under the Uniform Transfers-on-Death Securities Registration Act. In these states, if you register your stocks, bonds, securities accounts or mutual funds in a transfer-on-death form, the beneficiary or beneficiaries you designate will receive these securities promptly after your death. No probate will be necessary. If you live in one of these states, your broker can provide the forms you'll need to name a beneficiary for your securities or security account.

States That Allow Transfer-on-Death Registration of Securities

Transfer-on-death securities registration is available in every state but Louisiana, New York, North Carolina and Texas. The District of Columbia allows transfer-on-death registration.

---

d. Joint Tenancy

Joint tenancy is a form of shared property ownership. What makes it unique is the "right of survivorship." Right of survivorship means that when one joint tenant dies, his share in the joint property automatically passes to the surviving joint tenants. (See Chapter 7, Section D.) If there's more than one survivor, each acquires an equal share of the deceased tenant's original interest. It's not possible to leave your share of joint tenancy property to someone other than the joint tenants when you die. If you attempt to leave joint tenancy property in a will, the will provision will be ignored. In order to avoid confusion, however, it's a good idea to mention in your will that certain property is held in joint tenancy and therefore not covered by the will.

Any property can be bought and owned in joint tenancy, although it's most commonly used with real estate. (We discuss that in Chapter 7, Section D.) Joint tenancy is a good probate avoidance device for property you acquire, 50-50, with your lover—assuming each of you wants your share to pass to the other after death. You can also create joint tenancy ownership in property you own alone by transferring title of the property from yourself to yourself and someone else as joint tenants. You may owe gift taxes, however, if you give property worth more than $10,000 to the new joint tenant. Also, transferring the property into joint tenancy means you are irrevocably giving up ownership of half the property while you are still alive. Usually, a living trust is a better probate avoidance device than a transfer into joint tenancy for solely owned property.

Joint tenancy has drawbacks. Any joint tenant can sell his interest in the joint tenancy at any time, thereby destroying the joint tenancy. If a joint tenant sells or gives away his share, the new owner and the remaining owners are called "tenants in common." Tenants in common don't have rights of survivorship. If a tenant in common dies, her share passes by her will, or by state law if she died without a will. Another drawback of joint tenancy is that joint tenants must own equal shares of the property. If you own unequal shares, joint tenancy won't work. In some cases, having joint tenancy property can also increase the estate taxes of the first co-owner who dies.

e. Life Insurance

Normally, life insurance proceeds are paid directly to the policy's beneficiary you've chosen, without going through probate. The proceeds of a life insurance policy are subject to probate, and included in the value of the probate estate, only if the beneficiary is the "estate" itself, not a specific person or organization. Only in the rare case of a large estate with no other assets to pay the death taxes and probate costs is there any reason to name the estate as the beneficiary.

3. Death Taxes

All property owned at the time of death is subject to federal estate, or death, taxes. Also, a number of states impose state death taxes as well. Death taxes are imposed whether the property is transferred by will (through probate) or by another device (outside of probate). Death taxes are harder to reduce or avoid than are probate fees, but there are some ways to achieve savings.

a. Federal Estate Taxes

Federal estate taxes are assessed against the net worth of the estate (called the "taxable estate") of a person who died. A set amount of property is exempt from tax, depending on the year of death. The table below lists the estate tax thresholds.

The Federal Estate and Gift Tax Law

Year	Estate tax exemption	Gift tax exemption	Highest estate and gift tax rate
2002	$1 million		50%
2003	$1 million		49%
2004	$1.5 million	$1 million	48%
2005	$1.5 million	$1 million	47%
2006	$2 million	$1 million	46%
2007	$2 million	$1 million	45%
2008	$2 million	$1 million	45%
2009	$3.5 million	$1 million	45%
2010	Estate tax repealed	$1 million	top individual income tax rate (gift tax only)
2011	$1 million unless Congress extends repeal		55% unless Congress extends repeal

Federal law authorizes several additional exemptions to estate tax:

- The marital deduction, exempting all property left to a surviving spouse. This is one reason lesbian and gay couples want to be allowed to marry.
- The charitable deduction, which exempts all property left to qualified tax-exempt charities.
- The family small business exemption, which under certain circumstances can exempt up to $1.3 million of your estate if the major asset in your estate is a family business.

Federal law also allows deductions for some lesser debts, including:

- costs of last illness, burial and probate fees and expenses, and
- certain debts, including a portion of any state death taxes assessed.

To estimate if your estate will be likely to owe estate tax, keep in mind these rules:

- All property you legally own will be included in your federal taxable estate.
- The worth of a house, or any other property, is your equity in it, not the market value—unless you own it free and clear.
- Property which you have transferred but still control, such as property you placed in a living trust, will be included in your estate.
- The total value of *all* property held in joint tenancy will be included in your taxable estate, minus the portion the surviving joint tenant can prove he contributed. The government presumes that a deceased person contributed 100% of any joint tenancy property, and the survivor contributed nothing. If the survivor can prove he contributed all or some of the money for joint tenancy property, the taxable portion will be reduced accordingly.

EXAMPLE 1: Eighteen years ago, Joe and Ben bought a lemon-yellow Jaguar XKE together, and have preserved it in mint condition. It's always been owned in joint tenancy, but the records proving that each person contributed half the purchase price have long since been lost. Joe dies. The government will include the current market value of the entire car in Joe's taxable estate unless Ben can somehow prove that he contributed half the cost.

EXAMPLE 2: The same facts, except Ben contributed all the money used to buy the car and maintain it, and kept the records. Joe dies. Even though the car was owned in joint tenancy, none of its value is included in Joe's taxable estate because Ben can prove that Joe didn't contribute any money to buy or maintain it.

The tax rates on property that is not exempt from estate tax are stiff. The technical workings of estate tax calculations are complex; they require the services of an estate lawyer or other tax expert. But the basic rules are easy to grasp. If an estate is over the exempt amount, the tax rate on the nonexempt portion is the rate for full value of the estate. Then the tax on the exempt portion is deducted. What this means is that the effective tax rate starts at 39% or more depending on the year of death.

EXAMPLE: Pete dies in 2001 with a net estate worth $1,075,000. The exempt amount for this year is $1 million. So $75,000 of the estate is subject to tax. But the tax rate applied is not the tax rate for an estate of $75,000 but that for estates of $1 million, which is 39%. Then the tax due on the exempt portion of the estate is forgiven. So, the tax on the $75,000 is $29,250.

The estate tax rate is graduated, so the larger the estate, the higher the tax rate. During 2002, the rate tops out at 50% for estates worth over $3 million.

b. State Death Taxes

Only the states listed below impose death taxes. All other states have no effective death tax. We say "effective" because many states have a "pick up" tax that attempts to capture a portion of any federal tax paid. But this is only a matter only between the state and federal government, not anything you need to plan for.

States That Impose Death Taxes

Connecticut (phasing out by 2005)

Indiana

Iowa

Kentucky

Louisiana (phasing out by 2004)

Maryland

Nebraska (county inheritance tax only)

New Hampshire

New Jersey

If you live in a state subject to state death taxes, you might be penalized for leaving property to anyone other than legal family. Many states provide different classes of death tax exemptions. The amount of exemption varies, depending on the legal relationship of the deceased person to the beneficiary. Usually, the largest exemption is for property left to a spouse, the next largest for property left to minor children, then for property given to other blood relatives and finally, maybe, an exemption for property left to "strangers" (including a lover). A few states don't provide any exemption for property left to "strangers." Some states vary the tax rate itself, depending on whom the property is left to. Generally, the rate is lowest for property left to a spouse, highest for property left to "strangers."

What this means is that if you live in a state with death taxes and want to know their impact on your estate, you'll have to check your state's laws to determine the precise rules. (There's a state-by-state breakdown of death tax rules in Nolo's *Plan Your Estate*, by Denis Clifford and Cora Jordan.) The state death tax rate is much less than the federal estate tax rate, but, because "strangers" are taxed the most, the taxes will be much higher on property you leave your lover than they'd be if you were married.

The state of your "domicile" (generally where you live) when you die is the state that imposes death taxes. If, however, you own real estate in another state that has death taxes, that state will impose its death taxes on the property in that state.

Domicile is a legal term of art, which refers to your principal residence—that is, where you intend to have your home. Usually, this is easy to figure out from voting records, your driver's license and many other forms that identify you. If you move around a lot, however, you risk having your estate subjected to more than one state's death tax. Pick one place and declare that your legal home. If you're very wealthy, get some legal advice on this point—as George Bush did about being a legal resident of Texas, despite the fact that he's a New Englander through and through.

c. Changes to Federal Estate Tax Law

You've undoubtedly heard that Congress has "repealed" the estate tax. Actually, the new tax law Congress passed in 2001 is much more confusing than a simple repeal.

The new estate tax law:

- Increases the personal exemption from $1 million in 2002-2003, rising to $3.5 million in 2009, as shown in the chart above
- Repeals the estate tax entirely for one—and only one—year (2010)
- Revives the estate tax, with an exemption of $1 million, for 2011 and thereafter, and
- Greatly restricts the "stepped-up" basis rules for inherited property in 2010. It is unclear if the stepped-up basis rules will be revived when the estate tax returns in 2011.

For technical, as well as political, reasons, Congress could not simply flat-out repeal the estate tax law. The law they passed is a mess, in the opinion of professional estate planners. How can anyone with substantial assets sensibly engage in long-range estate tax planning? It would be extremely difficult to create three different, sensible, valid, plans—one if you die before 2010, another if you die in 2010, and yet another if you die in 2011. Worse, even if you could, with the help of experts, prepare a tri-part plan, it couldn't cover what you should do if (actually, most experts say *when*) Congress again revises the estate tax law.

How Congress might revise the estate tax law the next time around is uncertain. It will depend upon political and economic realities that cannot be predicted now.

For now, what can you sensibly do to devise a plan that makes sense through 2009? You need to understand that you will likely have to revise your plan:

- If you have the good fortune to live to 2009; or
- When Congress revises the estate tax law.

To learn the latest information on the estate tax law, you can check Nolo's website at: http://www.nolo.com.

d. Avoiding or Reducing Federal and State Death Taxes

Estate tax planning is often thought to be a form of lawyer's magic, or chicanery, to escape death taxes. Certainly there's some gimmickry in many schemes used by the rich to escape or reduce death taxes, although not as much as there used to be. The truth, however, is that for folks rich enough to be subject to them, death taxes aren't easy to escape.

Make tax-free gifts. (See Section 4, below.)

Establish trusts. Tax saving trusts are desirable only for net estates over the federal estate tax threshold. Because of the complex nature of tax savings trusts, a serious discussion is beyond the scope of this book. If you have a substantial estate, you may save considerably on estate taxes by using trusts, particularly if:

- The bulk of your estate will be left to a person who's old or ill and likely to die soon. When that person dies, the property you left her will be taxed again. If you set up a trust in your will leaving the old or ill person only the income from the trust and the right to use the principal only for an IRS-approved reasons (including medical costs) during her life, with the principal going to someone else, this "second tax" can be avoided. This is called an "AB" trust.

- You leave all your property to your children. It will be taxed when you die and then taxed again when the children die. For years, one of the death tax dodges of the very rich was to leave their wealth in trust for their grandchildren, escaping taxation on the middle generation. Tax law changes curtailed this by introducing a "generation-skipping transfer tax." Currently you can leave up to $1 million in a trust for your grandchildren and escape estate taxes on the middle generation. This exemption increases to match increases in the federal estate tax exemption (see chart above). Any amount over this exemption is subject to federal estate taxes in each generation. So if you have children, grandchildren and a hunk of money, consider establishing a generation-skipping trust. If so, you'll definitely need to see a good estate planning lawyer.

Using a Charitable Trust

An irrevocable charitable trust allows you to make a gift to charity, such as a lesbian and gay group or an AIDS organization, and also name someone to receive income from the donated property. You donate property while you are alive to a charity you select. Then the charity makes set payments, as defined by you in the trust document, to a beneficiary you've named—called the "income beneficiary." This beneficiary can be you, another person, or both, such as you and your lover. The payment can be either a fixed sum or a set percentage of the value of the trust assets. The payments can be made for a set year period, or for the life of the income beneficiary. After this period expires, all remaining trust income is turned over to the charity.

You have to want to make a gift to a charity to bother with a charitable trust. But if you do want to make a charitable gift, this type of trust offers other benefits. First, the person who creates the trust receives an income tax deduction for the worth of the donated property. Second, a charitable trust can be particularly desirable if property has appreciated. The charity can sell it for its current market value, without having to pay capital gains tax. The money the charity receives from the sale becomes part of the trust property. Third, for someone whose estate will be liable for federal estate taxes all the donated property is removed from the estate, thereby lowering or eliminating those taxes.

This type of trust is called, in legalese, a "charitable remainder trust." For more information, see *Plan Your Estate*, by Clifford and Jordan (Nolo).

Transfer ownership of certain property, particularly life insurance, before death. Life insurance proceeds are not part of the deceased's federal taxable estate if he did not own the policy for at least three years before his death. If he did, the proceeds are included in his taxable estate. The IRS presumes you're trying to avoid taxes if you give the gift within three years of your death, and assesses taxes anyway. The IRS is strict in determining ownership. If you retained any significant power over an insurance policy (called, in insurance lingo, "maintaining incidents of ownership") within three years of death, you will be held to be the owner. Significant powers include the rights to:

- change or name the beneficiaries of the policy
- borrow against the policy, pledge any cash reserve it has or cash it in
- surrender, convert or cancel the policy
- select a payment option, such as lump sum or in installments, and
- make payments on the policy.

There are two basic ways an insurance policy can be owned by someone other than the insured. First, a person having what's called an "insurable interest" can take out, and pay for, a policy on the insured's life. Insurance companies don't allow lesbians and gays to have an "insurable interest" in their lovers; they require marriage, or a business (economic) relationship. Second, you can buy a policy and transfer ownership to another, even if that person doesn't have an "insurable interest" in the insured. Of course, anyone has an "insurable interest" in his or her own life. So, you can buy a policy and assign it to your lover. Life insurance policies are usually transferred by making a gift to the new owner. Transfer forms should be available from your insurance company. It's the new owner who is now responsible for paying the premiums.

Once you give a gift of a life insurance policy, that's it. Gifts are final. If you break up, your ex-lover has the right to continue to own the policy. You couldn't compel him to cancel it. Thus, you can retain control over your life insurance policy, or reduce your taxable estate. But you can't do both.

4. Gifts and Gift Taxes

At first hearing, the concept of gift taxes may not sound fair. (You mean the feds even tax generosity?) Well, sort of. But think of it this way. If a rich person could "give" away all his property tax-free just before death, there wouldn't be any point to death taxes. So Congress has defined the point at which giving gifts becomes a matter for the tax collector. The current rule, stated simply, is that gifts of up to $10,000 per person per year are tax-free. If Adrian gives $13,000 to Justin, gift taxes are assessed on $3,000; if Adrian gives $10,000 to Justin and $10,000 to Jack, no gift taxes are assessed. Also, if Adrian gives $10,000 to Justin each year for three years, no gift taxes are assessed.

Because federal estate and gift taxes are connected, taxable gifts made during life have an effect on estate tax owed at death.

> **EXAMPLE:** Kelly gives Irene $60,000. The first $10,000 is exempt from gift tax but the remaining $50,000 is subject to it. This means $50,000 of Kelly's personal estate tax credit has been used up. If Kelly dies in 2003, when the exemption is $1 million, her (remaining) exemption will be $950,000.

Document Any Large Gifts to Your Partner

Any non-commercial transfer of property between unmarried couples is a legal gift. If the value of the gift is over $10,000, the person making the gift is legally required to file a gift tax return. No gift taxes must actually be paid, however, until the giver uses up her $1 million dollar lifetime exemption from gift taxes.

Why bother with the hassle of filing a gift tax return if you won't even have to pay a tax? Because without documenting the gift, you could encounter income tax problems down the line. If you two to decide to sell a property after you've made a gift of a portion of it to your partner, how do you establish to the IRS that each of you is a co-owner? You might have to file a retroactive gift tax return and be hit with fines and penalties.

> **EXAMPLE:** Annie moves in with Candace, who owns her house. After five years together, they have a formal commitment ceremony. As one part of that ceremony, Candace announces that she's giving Annie one half interest in the house. But they do not record a new deed, nor does Candace file a gift return. Three years later, the couple sells the house. When Annie claims half the profits on her income tax, the IRS disallows it, asserting that legally Candace remains the sole owner.

The $10,000 annual gift tax exemption can be used to lower the eventual value of your estate.

EXAMPLE: Sarah, who is in her late 60s, has an estate of over $1,000,000. She wants to help a couple she's close to, Marcy and Louise. She gives each $10,000 a year. In five years she has removed $100,000 from her estate tax free.

If you're wealthy, other options are available that involve gifts, including major charitable gifts. These devices aren't useful for people with average incomes or estates, so we don't cover them. Anyone making, or contemplating making, a really substantial charitable gift should check it out with a tax attorney or tax accountant.

5. Individual Retirement Accounts As Estate Planning Devices

You can name one or more beneficiaries to receive any funds remaining at your death in an individual retirement account, such as an IRA, 401(k) or profit-sharing plan. However, you should note that except for a Roth IRA, an individual retirement account is a "wasting asset." Once you reach age 70 and 1/2, you must withdraw a certain percentage of your account each year. The withdrawal percentage is calculated on the basis of the combination of your life expectancy and that of your (oldest) beneficiary. So, if you live a long life, much of the funds in your account will have been withdrawn.

Still, it's obviously wise to name a beneficiary for any individual retirement account you own. If you die prematurely, or if, for whatever reason, significant funds remain in the account at your death, your beneficiary will receive that money directly, without probate. Therefore, there's rarely a reason to leave any retirement funds to a living trust, which would only complicated the distribution process.

 Nolo's Estate Planning Resources. *Nolo publishes the following estate planning books and software:*

- Quicken Lawyer Personal *software, by Nolo, is a complete estate planning tool. You can use the software to prepare a customized will, living trust, healthcare directive and durable power of attorney for finances.*

- Nolo's Simple Will Book, *by Denis Clifford, gives all the instructions necessary for drafting and updating a will.*

- Plan Your Estate, *by Denis Clifford and Cora Jordan, covers every significant aspect of estate planning. It is especially valuable for people with larger estates (over $1 million).*

- Make Your Own Living Trust, *by Denis Clifford, provides a thorough explanation of this most popular probate avoidance device, including forms and explanation for an AB trust.*

- 8 Ways to Avoid Probate, *by Mary Randolph, a thorough discussion of all the major ways to transfer property at death outside of a will.*

- The Quick and Legal Will Book, *by Denis Clifford, contains thorough forms and instructions for preparing a basic will.*

- Nolo's Law Form Kit: Wills, *by Denis Clifford and Lisa Goldoftas, provides you with a quick and easy, legally valid will.*

- 9 Ways to Avoid Estate Tax, *by Mary Randolph and Denis Clifford, provides suggestions on how to lower the value of your estate before your death.*

Will

Will of _____

I, _____, a

resident of _____ County, _____, declare that this is my will.

1. Revocation

I revoke all wills and codicils that I have previously made.

2. Prior Marriages

I was married to _____ and am now divorced.

3. Children

A. I have _____ children now living, whose names and dates of birth are:

Name _____

Date of Birth _____

[Repeat as often as needed.]

The terms "my children" as used in this will shall include any other children hereafter born to

or adopted by me.

B. I have the following children of my deceased child _____.

Name _____

Date of Birth _____

[Repeat as often as needed.]

C. If I do not leave property in this will to one or more of my children or my grandchildren named

above, my failure to do so is intentional.

D. If at my death any of my children are minors, and a personal guardian is needed, I recommend that

_____ be appointed guardian of the persons of my minor

children. If_____ cannot or refuses to serve, I nominate

_____ as guardian of the persons of my minor children.

E. If at my death any of my children are minors and a property guardian is needed, I name

_____ to be appointed guardian of the

property of my minor children. If _____

cannot or refuses to serve, I name _____

to be appointed guardian of the property of my minor children.

4. Gifts

A. I make the following gifts of money or personal property:

    1. I give every child or grandchild listed in Clause 3 $1.00 (one dollar) in addition to any other property I may give them elsewhere in this will, or otherwise.

    2. I give the sum of $ _____ to _____ if he/she/it survives me by 60 days; if he/she/it doesn't, this gift shall be made to

    _____.

    [Repeat as often as needed.]

    3. I give _____

    to _____ if he/she/it survives me by 60 days; if he/she/it doesn't, the gift shall be made to _____.

    [Repeat as often as needed.]

    4. I forgive and cancel the debt of $ _____ owed to me by _____.

    [Repeat as often as needed]

B. I make the following gifts of real estate:

    1. I give my interest in the real estate in _____,

    commonly known as _____, to

    _____ if he/she/it survives me for 60 days. If he/she/it doesn't survive me for 60 days, that property shall be given to

    _____.

    [Repeat as often as needed.]

5. Residue

I give the residue of my property subject to this will as follows:

A. To _____ if he/she/it survives me by 60 days.

B. If not, to _____ if he/she/it survives me by 60 days.

C. If neither _____ nor _____ survives me by 60 days, then to _____.

6. Executor

A. I nominate _____ as executor of this will, to serve without bond. If _____ shall for any reason fail to qualify or cease to act as executor, I nominate _____ to serve without bond.

B. I grant to my executor the right to place my obituary of her/his choosing in the papers she/he thinks appropriate.

7. No Contest

If any person or persons named to receive any of my property under my will in any manner contests or attacks this will or any of its provisions, that person or persons shall be disinherited and shall receive none of my property, and my property shall be disposed of as if that contesting beneficiary had died before me leaving no children.

8. Simultaneous Death

If _____ and I should die simultaneously, or under such circumstances as to render it difficult or impossible to determine who predeceased the other, I shall be conclusively presumed to have survived _____ for purposes of this will.

9. Signature and Witnessing

I subscribe my name to this will this _____ of _____, _____, at _____, _____, _____.

On this _____ of_____, _____, _____ declared to us, the undersigned, that this instrument was [his/her] will, and requested us to act as witnesses to it. [He/she] thereupon signed this will in our presence, all of us being present at the time. We now, at [his/her] request, in [his/her] presence, and in the presence of each other, subscribe our names as witnesses and declare we understand this to be [his/her] will, and that to the best of our knowledge the testator is competent to make a will, and under no constraint or undue influence.

We declare under penalty of perjury that the foregoing is true and correct.

_____
Witness's Signature

_____
Address

_____
Witness's Signature

_____
Address

_____
Witness's Signature

_____
Address

Codicil

_____ Codicil to the Will of _____ dated _____.

I, _____, a resident of _____ County, _____,

declare this to be the first codicil to my will dated _____.

First. I revoke Item _____ of Clause _____, and substitute the following:

_____

_____

_____

Second. I add the following new Item _____ to Clause _____:

_____

Third. In all other respects I confirm and republish my will dated _____, this _____ day of

_____, at _____.

_____

On the date written below, _____ declared to us, the under-

signed, that this instrument, consisting of _____ pages, including this page signed by us as witnesses,

was the first codicil to [his/her] will and requested us to act as witnesses to it. [He/she] thereupon signed

this codicil in our presence, all of us being present at the same time. We now, at [his/her] request, in [his/

her] presence, and in the presence of each other, subscribe our names as witnesses, and declare we

understand this to be [his/her] will, and that to the best of our knowledge the testator is competent to make a

will, and under no constraint or undue influence.

Executed on _____, at _____,

_____.

We declare under penalty of perjury that the foregoing is true and correct.

_____
Witness's Signature

_____
Address

_____
Witness's Signature

_____
Address

_____
Witness's Signature

_____
Address

Living Together Contracts for Lesbian and Gay Couples

A contract is no more than an agreement to do (or not to do) something. It contains promises made by one person in exchange for another's actions or promises. Marriage is a contractual relationship, even though the terms of the contract are rarely stated explicitly, or even known, by the marrying couple. Saying "I do" commits a couple to a well-established set of state laws and rules governing, among other things, the couple's property rights. While it might be upsetting to some people that they weren't informed of all of the rules before they reached the altar, they are binding should disagreements arise during the relationship—or if one spouse dies or the couple splits up.

Unlike married couples, gay and lesbian couples do not automatically agree to any contractual agreement when they start a relationship. Gay and lesbian partners may have an obligation to a landlord or mortgage company if they rent or buy a place together, but that obligation would be no different if they were roommates. Getting together, in and of itself, or forming a personal opinion about what is fair or what should happen, does not create a contractual relationship. If the couple chooses to make an agreement, however, or in some states if they act as though an agreement exists, that agreement will often be considered an enforceable contract—a "nonmarital agreement," in legal terms.

Many unmarried couples buy property, mix assets and invest together, often without writing down or talking about their intentions. Then, if problems around money and property come up, they try to work out an understanding or reach a compromise. Sometimes they visit a therapist or ask their friends to help. If they split up, they quietly divide their accumulations and go their separate ways, and are not required to go through a court process or follow the legal rules of marriage and divorce.

Unfortunately, some couples don't quietly divide the property and move apart. They battle in a courtroom, forcing the courts to deal with their claims. The first unmarried couples to bring their disputes to court were heterosexual couples, and most courts responded to these claims by trying to figure out what the couple had agreed to and dividing their property accordingly. By doing so, the courts ruled that unmarried couples generally have the right to create whatever kind of living together contracts they want when it comes to financial and property concerns, and noted that courts should enforce these contracts whenever there's a dispute.

A chapter that tells you how to create contracts designed so you can break up amicably would be pretty depressing—few people starting a relationship or working to protect the relationship they've built plan on splitting up. Instead, we present material on living together contracts so the two of you can figure out what you intend, which, we hope, should lessen disagreements and misunderstandings even when things are going well. Talking out your intentions will bring you closer, and help you overcome your fears about money, property and your future.

And if you do in fact split up, having an agreement helps you avoid taking your troubles to court. The risks, trauma and expense of litigation are far less likely to be visited on those who have taken the time to define their understanding in an agreement.

Love and Law

"The heart signs no documents," E.M. Forster pithily stated. Living together contracts are not what keeps a couple together. If we were sure we knew how to maintain love, we'd certainly reveal that here. But since we're distinctly not sure, all we can say is that love has to do with feelings of the heart.

A. Living Together Contracts Are Legal

As we mentioned, the legal rules governing living together contracts have been made by courts and judges, and not by legislatures, for the most part. The leading court case is called *Marvin v. Marvin*, and involved the actor Lee Marvin and the woman he lived with, Michele Triola Marvin. (She used his last name even though they were not married.) In the case, the California Supreme Court announced new legal principles involving the right of unmarried couples to make contracts. First, the court ruled that marital property laws do not apply to couples not legally married. Then, the court recognized that unmarried couples are here to stay, saying:

> *The fact that a man and a woman live together without marriage, and engage in a sexual relationship, doesn't in itself invalidate agreements between them relating to their earnings, property, or expenses. Neither is such an agreement invalid merely because the parties may have contemplated the creation and continuation of a nonmarital relationship when they entered into it.*

The court concluded this passage by stating that agreements between non-married partners are invalid only when they are based on an exchange of sex for money. The court in *Marvin* declared four contract principles:

- Unmarried couples may make written contracts.
- Unmarried couples may make oral contracts.
- If a couple hasn't made a written or oral contract, the court may examine the couple's actions under the judicial microscope to decide whether an "implied" contract exists.
- If a judge can't find an implied contract, she may still presume that the parties intend to deal fairly with each other and find one lover indebted to the other by invoking well-established legal doctrines of equity and fairness.

Several cases in many different states since the *Marvin* decision have upheld the application of these principles to contracts made by gay and lesbian partners. Depending on the state, however, a court will follow different legal rules. Most states enforce contracts between gay and lesbian partners, although in some states only written contracts will be enforced. A small number of states prohibit contracts between unmarried couples on the basis that they foster immorality, and a few haven't considered the question. In a state where sodomy is illegal, for example, a judge might refuse to enforce a contract on the ground that the underlying relationship is criminal. In fact, this is exactly what happened initally in a Georgia case, decided while sodomy was still a crime there. After a lesbian couple split up, one woman sued the other to enforce their written agreement. The trial judge refused because of their "illegal and immoral" relationship. The Supreme Court of Georgia reversed, saying that nothing in the agreement required them to engage in illegal activity.

Furthermore, even in states where sodomy is legal, any contract that even hints of sex as the basis for the deal will be thrown out of court. A California appellate court refused to uphold a gay living together contract, declaring that it explicitly referred to rendering services as a lover in exchange for assets, and was therefore, in effect, an agreement for prostitution. So don't make any reference to sex in your contract. Identify yourselves as "partners," not "lovers." The less cute you are the better.

We're not suggesting that you not discuss your sexual relationship when preparing your contract. A force as powerful as passion can destroy, as well as enhance, any relationship. But discussing what's sexually expected, permitted, condoned or forbidden isn't the same as mentioning sexuality in a property contract. It is especially important that you not make monogamy a condition for any financial provision, however important fidelity may be for you.

⚠ **Enforcing your agreement.** *Most courts faced with enforcing a living together contract uphold written ones, reject implied ones unless there is very clear evidence supporting the claims and fall somewhere in the middle with oral ones. When one partner says there was an oral contract while the other emphatically denies it, a judge is unlikely to find that the contract existed, unless other evidence (such as a witness to a discussion about the contract or subsequent action) substantiates it. General vows, such as those uttered in a commitment ceremony, usually aren't considered to be legally binding. Paradoxically, when one partner dies and the other claims there was an oral contract entitling him to property, a judge is more likely to sympathize with the survivor and find a contract, especially if no one refutes it.*

As we emphasized above, however, the purpose of this chapter is to help you write down your understanding about your life as a couple. This chapter doesn't contain strategies on legally enforcing your living together contract in a courtroom. If it ever comes to that, you will need to read Chapter 9 and seek help beyond this book.

And keep in mind that although you have the right to rely on the tenets of contract law—meaning that written, oral and even implied contracts should be enforceable and a court can invoke the doctrine of fair dealings in your favor—this doesn't mean that you should put all your faith in legal protections. The law is still hostile to lesbians and gay men, and going to court to prove your contract will be time-consuming, expensive and emotionally draining. In other words, it's better that you truly trust your partner before you take a precipitous financial step together than to rely on the notion that your contract will bail you out.

> **EXAMPLE:** Patti and Katherine move in together. After graduating from college, Patti enters dental school. Katherine, too, intended to finish school, but postponed her plans and supported them both until Patti finished. They had many conversations about their long-term plans, but wrote nothing down about sharing the benefits of Patti's new career. After four years, Patti passed her dental boards. Katherine was ready to resume her education, but Patti fell in love with a classmate and moved out. Katherine was left with the flea market furniture, the flea-ridden dog and the feeling she was ripped off—and Patti went on to enjoy a flourishing new career and luxurious life with her new partner.
>
> Remember—they had no contract. Assuming that Patti and Katherine intended to treat each other fairly, we can reasonably assume that because Katherine put Patti through dental school, Patti would reciprocate and pay Katherine's school expenses. Would a court find an implied agreement? Could Katherine prove an oral one? Maybe, but maybe not, even though Katherine has a sympathetic case.

B. When You Need a Living Together Contract

Obviously, you don't need a contract if you have no assets or are in a brief relationship. But in a long-term and serious relationship, whether you're basking in the glow of just having joined forces or you've been together 20 years, you should consider the legal consequences of how you live. If you mix assets or share expenses, please do everyone a big favor and put your agreement in writing, especially if significant money or property is involved. If you're both stone-broke NINKs (no income, no kids) with no property and little prospect of getting any soon, put away the pen and paper and take a nap in the sun.

Why should you put your contract in writing? The sooner you agree on if and how to share your property, the less confusion and misery you are likely to face later.

C. What to Include in a Living Together Contract

A living together contract can be comprehensive, covering every aspect of your relationship, or it can be specific, covering only your new house purchase. (We provide sample contracts specifically for purchasing a house together in Chapter 7.) These contracts need not be like the fine-print monsters foisted on you when you buy insurance or a car. You can, and should, design your contract to say exactly what you both want, in words you both understand. A simple, comprehensible and functional document using common English is much better than one loaded with "heretofores" and "pursuants."

Let us make one suggestion, however: If you want your living together contract to include the day-to-day details of your relationship, make two agreements. The first one should pertain only to property and finances. Then, if one of you ever sues the other in court, the property and finance terms should be the only ones a judge ever sees. Write up a second agreement if you wish about who will do the dishes, who will walk the dog, how many overnight guests you'll allow and whose art goes in the living room. A court probably won't—and shouldn't be asked to—enforce this kind of agreement. As a result, if you do just one agreement that includes the personal as well as financial clauses, a court might get distracted by the personal clauses, declare the contract illegal or frivolous, and refuse to enforce the more important financial clauses.

1. Property and Finances Clauses

Your living together agreement should cover all of your property—including the property you had before you began the relationship as well as the property either or both of you accumulate during it.

Property owned before living together. You each probably had some property before you met. Just because you move in together doesn't mean you can't continue to solely own your TV, oriental tapestry and floppy-eared cocker spaniel, while your lover holds onto her car and collected works of Virginia Woolf. Making an agreement about the property you bring into the relationship may seem unnecessary, but it's not. Think about trying to separate it all ten years from now, when you've both been referring to everything around the house as "ours."

You can deal with use of valuable items as well as ownership. Who gets to use the property? Who pays for upkeep? For instance, Alan owns a boat which he'll want to keep it if he and Fred ever split up. Fred agrees to help with upkeep in exchange for using it without acquiring any ownership interest. It's up to you how detailed to get.

Property inherited or received by gift during the relationship. Many people will want to keep separate the property they inherit or receive by gift. Others will want to "donate" the property to the relationship. Again, it's up to you. If you plan to keep inherited or gift property separate, don't forget to cover questions of use and control. Remember though, any property given to *both* of you is legally owned by both—this includes gifts you receive at

your union ceremony or anniversary party, even if given by a relative or friend of just one of you.

Property bought during the relationship. Many people make purchases item by item, understanding that whoever makes the purchase owns the property. George buys the kitchen table and chairs, and Ham buys the lamp and stereo. If they split up, each keeps the property he bought.

Purchases also can be pooled. Ham and George can jointly own everything bought during the relationship, and divide it all 50-50 if they separate. A consistent approach to property ownership may simplify things, but is required by neither law nor logic. Ham and George could choose a combination of the two methods. Some items may be separately owned, some pooled 50-50 and some shared in proportion to how much money each contributed toward the purchase price or how much labor each put into upkeep.

Expenses during the relationship. How will you divide the day-to-day costs for food, utilities, laundry, housing and the like, especially if expenses go up or incomes go down? Even if you substitute margarine for butter, or vin ordinaire for Chateau Mouton-Rothschild, you must adopt a plan. We can't help you choose what you buy, but we have some suggestions of how to share expenses.

- **Share and share alike.** A few of our friends live like this. One couple has only one checking account. They both deposit their paychecks into it and pay all household bills out of it. Over the course of their relationship, they've each been in school or unemployed. Their incomes shift and who earns more varies year to year. They figure it all evens out in the end, and whatever savings or debts accumulate are viewed as equally shared, regardless of who had the higher income.

- **Split 50-50.** We know several couples who do this. Any time one of them buys something for the house or pays a bill, he writes his name on the receipt and throws it into a jar. Every few months, they empty out the receipt jar and total up how much each has spent. One then writes the other a check to even things up.

- **Each contributes in proportion to her income.** This works especially well for people with great income discrepancies. We know a couple who live this way. One earns nearly $100,000 a year and the other gets Social Security. The woman on Social Security was going crazy trying to keep up with her lover. Finally, they saw that they had a serious problem and adopted a plan under which all expenses were divided 80-20. It saved their relationship.

2. Cooling Off Clause

Consider including a clause to remind yourselves of your commitment should the stress of a moment threaten to drive you apart. We call this a "cooling off" clause. Although it's not always enforceable in court, it's an excellent expression of intention. It can simply state that if one person wants to leave the relationship, he will take some time to cool off before grabbing the cat and the good wine glasses and heading for the hills. Imperfect souls that we are, we make a lot of hasty, irrational decisions when we're hurt or angry that we later come to regret. A cooling off provision can break the routine and give you time to try to work things out.

Noel Coward understood the value—and the limits—of this kind of agreement in *Private Lives*. If either spouse called "Solomon Isaacs" during a fight, a truce would immediately begin. It worked well until one day, when the husband cried "Solomon Isaacs" and his wife broke a record over his head, shouting "Solomon Isaacs, yourself." Yes, cooling off clauses don't always cool people off.

Here are a few sample cooling off clauses:

Option 1. In the event either person is seriously considering ending the relationship, that person will take a vacation, finding another place to stay, whether with a friend or at a hotel, for at least one week before making a final decision. At least two more weeks will pass before we divide the property. In addition, we agree to attend at least one counseling session if either one of us wants it.

Option 2. Either of us can request a cooling off period for any reason, including that we are fighting. We will spend one week separately. At the end of the week, we will meet for a meal and try to discuss our difficulties rationally, and with affection for each other.

Option 3. At the request of either one of us, we agree to attend a minimum of four counseling sessions with a friend or professional before making any irrevocable decisions concerning our relationship.

Although our clauses don't do so, you can specify who will do the mediation. Your choices are a professional mediator, an attorney-mediator, your therapist, a trusted friend, a group of three colleagues, the minister of the local gay church or anyone else you know. Be creative to get the best person for the two of you. Several years ago, a New York couple split up. They needed help resolving a few issues and wanted someone who shared their experiences as African-American lesbians. They called the late poet/writer Audrey Lorde, who met with and assisted them. You might also look to see if a local gay and lesbian group has any organized mediation or arbitration services.

3. Arbitration and Mediation Clause

If you split up and disagree over a provision in your contract, you have several ways to resolve the conflict. Traditionally, people went to court and let a judge decide. But happily there are alternatives to court. Our top suggestion is mediation and, if necessary, binding arbitration. Both are cheaper, faster and usually less painful than litigation. You can include a mediation-arbitration clause in your contract and spell out exactly how you want to proceed.

Mediation is an informal process where you, your lover and the person or persons who will help you work together to reach a mutually satisfactory compromise. You then write out your agreement, agree to be bound by it and sign it. No decision is imposed on you. Many therapists serve as mediators for couples splitting up, as do some attorneys.

Arbitration is quite a bit different. It, too, can be informal, but you and your lover each present your version of the dispute to a person or persons you've designated and empowered to make a decision. Unlike mediation, an arbitrated decision is made by the arbitrator, not by the two of you. The parties usually agree in advance to be bound by the arbitrator's decision—otherwise, there's little point to the process. This means that if one of you sues in court, the court will merely enforce the arbitrator's decision. Business and labor disputes have been resolved through arbitration for years, partly because a dispute settled quickly is as important as who wins and who loses.

Below is a sample mediation-arbitration provision you can add to any agreement. If you don't like ours, take a look at other mediation and arbitration provisions in contract forms books available at local law libraries.

Meditation-Arbitration Clause

Any dispute arising out of this agreement shall be mediated by a third person mutually acceptable to both of us. If we can't agree on a mediator, we will each appoint a representative and the two of them will choose the mediator. The mediator's role shall be to help us arrive at our solution, not to impose one on us. If good-faith efforts to arrive at our own solution with the help of a mediator prove to be fruitless after a minimum of four sessions, either may make a written request to the other that our dispute be arbitrated. This shall be done as follows.

1. Either of us may initiate arbitration by making a written demand for arbitration, defining the dispute and nominating one arbitrator.

2. Within five days from receipt of the demand, the other shall either accept the proposed arbitrator or name a second arbitrator.

3. The two nominated arbitrators shall within ten days nominate a third person, who shall serve as the arbitrator.

4. Within seven days, an arbitration meeting will be held. Neither of us may have a lawyer present, but we may consult with an attorney beforehand and we may present evidence and bring relevant witnesses.

5. The arbitrator shall make his or her decision within 15 days after the hearing. Their decision shall be in writing, will be binding upon us and will be enforceable by a local court.

6. If the person to whom the demand for arbitration is directed fails to respond within five days, the other must give an additional five days' written notice of his or her intent to proceed. If there is no response, the person initiating the arbitration may proceed with the arbitration before the arbitrator he or she has designated, and his or her award shall have the same force as if it had been settled by the mutually selected arbitrator.

⚠ **Name your arbitrator in advance.** *Sometimes, arbitration organizations, such as the American Arbitration Association, will not accept a case unless they were named in the arbitration agreement. In such a situation, if you can't find someone to do the arbitration, you may be forced to go to court to ask the judge to appoint the arbitrator, which is exactly what you were trying to avoid.*

D. Sample Living Together Contracts

Throughout this section there are a number of sample living together contracts. We suggest that you read this section carefully, including looking over the sample contracts. When you are ready to make your own contract, type up your own contract using the language from the sample agreements that most closely match your situation and your goals. The contracts in this section are designed to cover the major areas of concern to most lesbian and gay couples.

By the time you finish modifying one of our agreements, your changes may pretty much replace the original. You've created your own contract. If you're at all nervous about the legality of the new document, especially if it refers to significant amounts of money or if property is involved, have a lawyer look at it. (See Chapter 10.) But be careful when dealing with attorneys. Many charge very high prices and have little experience with lesbian and gay couples. To find a lawyer who works with gay men and lesbians, look in a local gay or feminist paper or directory. Then call to ask about the fee. Remember—you've already done most of the work; you're just asking the lawyer to check it over. You shouldn't be charged much more than $500 for such a review.

⚠ **Signing the contract.** *Whether you use one of our living together contracts or design your own, photocopy the final draft so you each have a copy. You and your lover each initial every page and then sign and date both copies. It makes no difference who keeps which—both are "originals." Hav-*

ing it notarized isn't necessary unless, in some states, it covers real estate. If that is required in your state, you must notarize your signatures and then, if you wish, you can record the agreement at your county records office. Notarization doesn't make the contract legal or enforceable. It simply proves that your signatures aren't forged, which can never hurt.

Creating a contract that touches upon the very core of your relationship is bound to be an emotional experience. If either of you begins to feel overwhelmed, stop and regroup. Some couples will design a good agreement in an hour; other couples will take a month.

It's probable that one or both of you will engage in the dangerous practice of "strategic ambiguity" as to one or another of the issues that should be included in your living together contract. What is "strategic ambiguity"? It is when you deliberately work to keep things vague in your relationship so you can avoid facing a difficult issue. For example, if you are paying most of the rent each month because you make more money, you may not want to confront the question of whether this is a gift or a loan to your partner—and your partner may be equally uncomfortable talking about it. You may hope that your relationship will last forever and thus obviate the need for ever discussing the question. But in our opinion, based upon watching many couples deal with these sensitive issues, we think it's better to face things openly—even if you have to hear or say something that makes you uncomfortable—than to pretend that these financial realities do not matter. This is not easy work, but unless you deal directly with these questions, you won't be able to create the agreements you need to have if your relationship is going to flourish in the long term.

1. Short and Simple Living Together Contracts

The living together agreements we provide later in this chapter are quite thorough. For those of you who don't want such detailed agreements, we provide first two simple, one-page living together agreements.

Keeping Income and Accumulations Separate

Roosevelt Jackson and Alan Stein make the following agreement:

1. They are living together now and plan to continue doing so.

2. All property owned by either Roosevelt or Alan as of the date of this agreement remains his separate property and cannot be transferred to the other unless the transfer is done in writing.

3. The income of each person, as well as any accumulations of property from that income, belongs absolutely to the person who earns the money. Joint purchases are covered under Clause 7.

4. If Roosevelt and Alan separate, neither has a claim against the other for any money or property, for any reason, with the exception of property covered under Clause 7, or unless a subsequent written agreement specifically changes this contract.

5. Roosevelt and Alan will keep separate bank and credit accounts, and neither will be responsible for the debts of the other.

6. Living expenses, which include groceries, utilities, rent and day-to-day household upkeep, will be shared equally. Roosevelt and Alan agree to open a joint bank account into which each agrees to contribute $750 per month to pay for living expenses.

7. If Roosevelt and Alan make joint purchases, ownership of each specific item will be reflected on any title slip to the property. If the property has no title slip, or if the slip is insufficient to record all details of their agreement, Alan and Roosevelt will prepare a separate, written, joint ownership agreement. Any such agreement will apply to the specific jointly owned property only, and won't create an implication that any other property is jointly owned.

8. This agreement sets forth Roosevelt and Alan's complete understanding concerning real and personal property ownership and takes the place of any and all prior contracts or understanding whether written or oral.

9. This agreement can be added to or changed only by a subsequent written agreement.

10. Any provision in this agreement found to be invalid shall have no effect on the validity of the remaining provisions.

_____   _____
Date   Roosevelt Jackson

_____   _____
Date   Alan Stein

Combining Income and Accumulations

Aline Jones and Mary Wiebel agree that:

1. We live together now and plan to continue doing so.

2. All property earned or accumulated prior to our living together belongs absolutely to the person earning or accumulating it, and cannot be transferred to the other unless it's done in writing.

3. All income earned by either of us while we live together and all property accumulated from that income belongs equally to both of us, and should we separate, all accumulated property will be divided equally.

4. Should either of us receive real or personal property by gift or inheritance, the property belongs absolutely to the person receiving the inheritance or gift and it cannot be transferred to the other unless it's done in writing.

5. In the event that either of us wishes to separate, we will divide equally all jointly owned property under Clause 3 and honor the separate property provisions of Clauses 2 and 4.

6. Once we divide the jointly owned property, neither of us will have any claim to any money or property from the other for any reason.

7. This agreement represents our complete understanding regarding our living together, replaces any and all prior agreements, whether written or oral, and can be added to or changed only by a subsequent written agreement.

8. Any provision in this agreement found to be invalid shall have no effect on the validity of the remaining provisions.

_____ _____
Date   Aline Jones

_____ _____
Date   Mary Wiebel

2. Contracts for Jointly Acquired Items

Many couples adopt the basic keep-things-separate approach. Often, however, they want to own some major items together. The basic keep-things-separate contract in the previous section provides a structure for joint ownership of some property. You prepare a separate written contract covering each jointly owned item. The following contracts accomplish this task. Modify one or the other to meet your needs, sign it and staple or clip it to your basic keep-things-separate contract.

If you completed a combine-income-and-accumulations contract, you don't need this joint-ownership agreement. You already provide for equal ownership.

Joint Outright Purchase

Carol Takahashi and Louise Orlean agree as follows:

1. We will jointly purchase and own a carved oak table costing $1,000.

2. If we separate and both want to keep the table, we will agree on its fair market price and flip a coin. [For a very expensive item, you may want to add a mediation-arbitration clause.] The winner keeps the table after paying the loser one-half of the agreed-upon price. If we can't agree on a price, we will abide by the decision of a neutral appraiser.

3. If we decide to separate and neither wants the table, or if we both want it but can't arrive at a price we agree is fair, we will sell the table at the best available price and divide the proceeds equally.

4. Any provision in this agreement found to be invalid shall have no effect on the validity of the remaining provisions.

_____ _____
Date   Carol Takahashi

_____ _____
Date   Louise Orlean

Sometimes, only one partner can make a purchase. This commonly occurs when the purchase is made with a credit card in only one person's name. Here's a contract to make sure that the item bought on credit is jointly owned.

Jointly Owned Item Purchased on Credit In One Partner's Name

James O'Brien and Brian Joyce make the following agreement:

1. James has a credit card with Sears. James and Brian purchased a washer-dryer for $1,000 from Sears using James's credit card.

2. James and Brian intend that the washer-dryer be owned equally and that each pay one-half of the $1,000, plus interest accrued on the credit card bill.

3. Neither James nor Brian want to incur a lot of interest on the purchase. Therefore, they agree to pay $250 per month for four months to pay it off. They acknowledge that the final payment will be more than $250, as it will include interest accumulated on the bill for the previous three months.

4. Each month, Brian will give James $125. James will then directly pay Sears the entire $250 on or before the date it's due.

5. If one person fails to pay his share, the other has the right to make the entire payment and will proportionally own more of the washer-dryer. Thus, if James ends up paying $750 and Brian $250, Brian will own it three-fourths and James, one-fourth.

6. If James or Brian dies, the financial interest in the washer-dryer belonging to the deceased person will go to the survivor, who will be obligated to pay the entire amount still due. [For an expensive item, such as a car, consider adding: "This provision shall be incorporated into James's will and Brian's will."]

7. If James and Brian separate, either may buy out the other's interest in the washer-dryer by paying one-half the fair market value, less any money still owing.

8. If James or Brian can't agree on who will buy the other out or the amount to be paid, the washer-dryer will be sold. Each will receive one-half of the net proceeds from the sale, unless one has paid more than the other, as provided in Clause 5. In that case, each will receive the percentage of the net proceeds corresponding to the percentage of the payments he's made.

9. Any provision in this agreement found to be invalid shall have no effect on the validity of the remaining provisions.

Dated: _____   _____
James O'Brien

Dated: _____   _____
Brian Joyce

⚠️ **Only the partner whose name is on the credit card is legally obligated to pay, even if you have an agreement splitting the cost.** *Thus, Brian doesn't have to pay Sears if James stops paying the bill. Brian has a legal contract with James, but not with Sears. Of course, the store doesn't care who pays the bill. Brian can send the money and the store will credit James's account.*

3. Contracts for Long-Term Couples

Not long ago, we got a letter from a woman asking the following:

My partner and I have been living together, with commingled finances, for some time and only now are drawing up a contract. When we moved in together, right out of college, we couldn't afford the fees for two bank accounts; we could barely afford the relationship, and pooling our resources was the only way to go. I suspect this configuration is fairly common for people our age (early 30s). So how do we draw up a contract when we've gone from no income and quite a few debts to two stable incomes, few or no debts, and some jointly owned property?

Long-term couples who want to draw up a contract must decide one important issue: Do we keep things as is or start all over? In either case, you must acknowledge how it's been—that is, what you've orally or implicitly agreed to over the years—and how you want it to be in the future.

A Simple Contract for Long-Term Couples

Ralph Palme and Hinton Wayne agree as follows:

1. We have been living together for 14 years. We moved in together as college juniors. It has been a continuous relationship since then.

2. We each had very little money and property when we first got together. Ralph had moved here from Sweden and left his belongings behind. He had his clothes and some Swedish albums and books. Hinton furnished the apartment with hand-me-down furniture from his parents. The art that decorated our apartment was movie posters from our friend Cynthia who worked at a retro movie house.

3. Since we have been together, we have pooled all our money and jointly paid all our expenses. Over the years, one of us may have been out of work or in school while the other worked full-time. When we've both been working, our salaries have varied a lot. Sometimes Ralph earns more; sometimes Hinton does.

4. We agree that our financial life is so intertwined that as of this date, everything we have is jointly owned, and all debts are jointly owed. We agree to review all title documents (for the two cars and deposit accounts) and change all title slips to include both names.

5. We recognize that one or the other of us may have a preference for certain things we own. Therefore, we attach three lists to this agreement. List 1 is the property we agree Ralph gets if we split up. List 2 is the same for Hinton. List 3 is the rest of our property.

6. We agree to continue living as we have. Once a year, during the week of our anniversary, we will pull out our lists and add purchases made during the past year to List 1, 2 or 3.

7. We each agree to make a valid will, revocable upon the termination of this agreement, leaving all his property to the other upon death.

8. If we separate, Ralph gets the items on List 1 and Hinton the items on List 2. We will equally divide the items on List 3 by each taking one item in turn, with the first chooser to be selected by flipping a coin.

9. Any provision in this agreement found to be invalid shall have no effect on the validity of the remaining provisions.

_____ _____
Date   Ralph Palme

_____ _____
Date   Hinton Wayne

One couple we know sat down to draft a short agreement like this the summer before their eighth anniversary. They got so depressed at the thought of dividing their property if they split up that they tossed the agreement into the recycling bin before they could complete lists 1 and 2. That was 12 years ago and they're still very happy and very together.

Moral of the story: Sometimes, history and trust is enough. If the thought of writing a contract after years of not having one makes you depressed and you are sure your relationship is in good shape, throw out the paper and go have dinner.

For couples with greater assets and those wanting more formal agreements, here are two longer contracts that will work for you.

Living Together Agreement—Keeping Things Separate

We, _____*Susana Lopez*_____ and _____*Anne Murphy*_____, agree as follows:

1. This contract sets forth our rights and obligations toward each other, which we intend to abide by in the spirit of joy, cooperation and good faith.

2. We agree that any and all property (real, personal and otherwise) owned by either one of us as of the date of this agreement shall remain that person's separate property and cannot be transferred to the other unless done by writing. We have attached a list of our major items of separate property.

3. The income of each person, as well as any accumulations of property from that income, belongs absolutely to the person who earns the money.

4. We shall each keep our own bank accounts, credit accounts, etc., and neither is in any way responsible for the debts of the other.

5. Living expenses, which include groceries, utilities, rent and day-to-day expenses, shall be equally divided.

6. We may from time to time decide to keep a joint checking or savings account for some specific purpose, or to own some property jointly. Any joint ownership shall be reflected in writing or shall be reflected on the ownership document of the property. If we fail to otherwise provide in writing for the disposition of our jointly owned property, should we separate, we agree to divide the jointly held property equally. Such agreements aren't to be interpreted as creating an implication that any other property is jointly owned.

7. Should either of us receive real or personal property by gift or inheritance, the property belongs absolutely to the person receiving the gift or inheritance and cannot be transferred to the other except by writing.

8. We agree that neither of us shall have any rights to, or financial interest in, any separate real property of the other, whether obtained before or after the date of this contract, unless that right or interest is in writing.

9. Either one of us may terminate this contract by giving the other a one-week written notice. In the event either of us is seriously considering leaving or ending the relationship, that person shall take at least a three-day vacation from the relationship. We also agree to at least one counseling session if either one of us requests it.

10. In the event that we separate, all jointly owned property shall be divided equally, and neither of us shall have any claim for post-separation support or for any other money or property from the other.

11. We agree that any dispute arising out of this contract shall be mediated by a third person mutually acceptable to both of us. The mediator's role shall be to help us arrive at our solution, not to impose one on us. If good-faith efforts to arrive at our own solution to all issues in dispute with the help of a mediation prove to be fruitless, either of us may:

   (a) Initiate arbitration by making a written demand for arbitration, defining the dispute and nominating one arbitrator;

   (b) Within five days from receipt of this notice, the other shall nominate a second arbitrator;

   (c) If neither of us accepts the other's nominee, the two nominated arbitrators shall within ten days name a third arbitrator, who shall be the arbitrator;

   (d) Within seven days an arbitration meeting will be held. Each of us may have counsel if we choose, and may present pertinent evidence and witnesses;

   (e) The arbitrator shall make his or her decision within five days after the hearing. The decision shall be in writing and shall be binding upon us;

   (f) If the person to whom the demand for arbitration is directed fails to respond within five days, the other must give an additional five days' written notice of her intent to proceed. If there's no response, the person initiating the arbitration may proceed with the arbitration before the arbitrator she has designated, and her award shall have the same force as if it had been settled by the mutually selected arbitrator.

12. This agreement represents our complete understanding regarding our living together and replaces any and all prior agreements, written or oral. It can be amended, but only in writing, and must be signed by both of us.

13. We agree that if a court finds any portion of this contract to be illegal or otherwise unenforceable, the remainder of the contract is still in full force and effect.

Signed this _____14th_____ day of _____April, 20xx_____

_____Susana Lopez_____   _____Anne Murphy_____
Signature   Signature

[Attach lists of separate property.]

Living Together Agreement—Sharing Most Property

We, _____Daniel Huang_____ and _____Peter Ross_____, agree as follows:

1. This contract sets forth our rights and obligations toward each other, which we intend to abide by in a spirit of joy, cooperation, and good faith.

2. All property (real, personal or otherwise) earned or accumulated prior to this date belongs absolutely to the person who earned or accumulated it and cannot be transferred to the other except in writing. Attached is a list of the major items of property we own separately.

3. All income earned by either of us while we are living together and all property (real, personal or otherwise) accumulated from that income belongs in equal shares to both of us, and should we separate, all accumulated property shall be divided equally, regardless of who is the legal owner or whose name is on the asset's title.

4. Should either of us receive real or personal property by gift or inheritance, the property belongs absolutely to the person receiving the gift or inheritance and cannot be transferred to the other except by writing.

5. We agree that neither of us has any rights to, or financial interest in, any separate real property of the other, whether obtained before or after the date of this contract, unless that right or interest is in writing.

6. Either one of us may terminate this contract by giving the other a one-week written notice. In the event either of us is seriously considering leaving or ending the relationship, that person shall take at least a three-day vacation from the relationship. We also agree to at least one counseling session if either one of us requests it.

7. In the event we separate, all assets or property other than the listed separate property shall be divided equally, and neither of us shall have any claim for support or for any other money or property from the other.

8. We agree that any dispute arising out of this contract shall be mediated by a third person mutually acceptable to both of us. The mediator's role shall be to help us arrive at our solution, not to impose one on us. If good-faith efforts to arrive at our own solution to all issues in dispute with the help of a mediation prove to be fruitless, either of us may:

   (a) Initiate arbitration by making a written demand for arbitration, defining the dispute and nominating one arbitrator;

   (b) Within five days from receipt of this notice, the other shall nominate a second arbitrator;

   (c) If neither of us accepts the other's nominee, the two nominated arbitrators shall within ten days name a third arbitrator, who shall be the arbitrator;

   (d) Within seven days an arbitration meeting will be held. Each of us may have counsel if we choose, and may present pertinent evidence and witnesses;

   (e) The arbitrator shall make his or her decision within five days after the hearing. The decision shall be in writing and shall be binding upon us;

(f) If the person to whom the demand for arbitration is directed fails to respond within five days, the other must give an additional five days' written notice of his intent to proceed. If there's no response, the person initiating the arbitration may proceed with the arbitration before the arbitrator he has designated, and his award shall have the same force as if it had been settled by the mutually selected arbitrator.

9. We agree that any dispute arising out of this contract shall be arbitrated under the terms of this clause as follows:

(a) Initiate arbitration by making a written demand for arbitration, defining the dispute and nominating one arbitrator;

(b) Within five days from receipt of this notice, the other shall nominate a second arbitrator;

(c) If neither of us accepts the other's nominee, then the two nominated arbitrators shall within ten days name a third arbitrator, who shall be the arbitrator;

(d) Within seven days an arbitration meeting will be held. Each of us may have counsel if we choose, and may present evidence and witnesses pertinent;

(e) The arbitrator shall make his or her decision within five days after the hearing. The decision shall be in writing and shall be binding upon us;

(f) If the person to whom the demand for arbitration is directed fails to respond within five days, the other must give an additional five days' written notice of his intent to proceed. If there's no response, the person initiating the arbitration may proceed with the arbitration before the arbitrator he has designated, and his award shall have the same force as if it had been settled by the mutually selected arbitrator.

10. This agreement represents our complete understanding regarding our living together and replaces any and all prior agreements, written or oral. It can be amended, but only in writing, and must be signed by both of us.

11. We agree that if the court finds any portion of this contract to be illegal or otherwise unenforceable, that the remainder of the contract is still in full force and effect.

Signed this _____3rd_____ day of _____October, 20xx_____

___Daniel Huang_____
Signature

___Peter Ross_____
Signature

[Attach lists of separate property.]

4. Contracts for Sharing Household Expenses and Chores

Thousands of gay and lesbian couples find themselves in the same situation as Lynne and Sarah. They are both professionals—Lynne's an ad executive and Sarah works as a designer—who make about the same amount of money. They want to keep their property separate, but want to share household expenses.

Sharing Household Expenses

Lynne Jacobs and Sarah Elderberry agree as follows:

1. We plan to live together indefinitely.

2. We will each maintain our own separate bank and credit accounts.

3. Our earnings and the property we each accumulate will be kept separate, unless we agree to share something jointly.

4. Any item of separate property can become joint property or the separate property of the other only by a written agreement signed by the person whose property is to be reclassified or by putting both names on a title document.

5. We will each be responsible for our own personal expenses. This includes clothing, medical/dental bills and long-distance telephone calls. We will pay household expenses, including rent, food, utilities and cleaning, jointly. We agree to keep receipts for all expenses, and to do an accounting every six months. The person who spends less will pay the other whatever sum is necessary to arrive at a 50-50 split.

6. Lynne generally will food shop and cook. Sarah generally will wash dishes and do general cleaning. We will both maintain the plants and pets.

7. We each agree to make a valid will, revocable upon the termination of this agreement, leaving all her property to the other upon death.

8. Either of us can end this agreement at any time. If we separate, we will equally divide jointly purchased property, and each retain our separate assets. Neither, however, will be obligated to support the other.

9. Any provision in this agreement found to be invalid shall have no effect on the validity of the remaining provisions.

_____   _____
Date   Lynne Jacobs

_____   _____
Date   Sarah Elderberry

5. Contracts for Joint Projects

A joint project agreement can cover building a cabin, refurbishing a boat or any other major project. We include two contracts, although, of course, we don't cover every contingency.

EXAMPLE: Tony and Ray live together. Both are landscape gardeners and share a dream of building a greenhouse and raising orchids on a piece of land they jointly own. They know it's a big job and want to anchor their dream on a strong foundation of good business practice, so they make an agreement reflecting that.

Joint Project Agreement

Tony Freeling and Ray Vivaldi agree as follows:

1. We both want to build a glass and wood greenhouse to house tropical orchids.

2. We each will contribute $9,000 towards the purchase of construction materials. The money will be kept in a joint bank account and both of our signatures will be required on checks.

3. We each will work at least 40 hours per month on building the greenhouse.

4. We will keep records of all hours worked and money spent for materials.

5. If we separate, Ray will have the opportunity to buy Tony's share for an amount equal to Tony's actual cash investment plus $15 per hour for the time he has worked on building the greenhouse. [If Tony was a professional carpenter and Ray was not, it may be fairer for Ray to contribute more money (Clause 2) or for Tony's hourly salary to be greater.]

6. At separation, if Ray decides not to buy Tony's share under the terms of Clause 5, Tony will have the opportunity to buy Ray's share on the same terms.

7. If neither of us elect to purchase the other's share of the greenhouse, we will sell it and equally divide the proceeds.

8. If either of us fails to work on the greenhouse 40 hours per month for three consecutive months, the other may buy out his share under the terms set out in Clauses 5 and 6.

9. If either of us dies, the other becomes sole owner of the greenhouse. If either of us makes a will, this provision will be incorporated into that will.

10. Any provision in this agreement found to be invalid shall have no effect on the validity of the remaining provisions.

_____ _____
Date   Tony Freeling

_____ _____
Date   Ray Vivaldi

Tony and Ray's joint project augmented their home. Other couples use a joint project agreement to cover professional endeavors.

EXAMPLE: Patti and Maria's shared dream is to own and run a bakery—supporting themselves through their mutual love of scones and croissants. They know the odds are against any small business succeeding and that they'll have to work extremely hard to make their dream a reality. They want to protect their enterprise if they separate, or if one loses interest but the other wants to continue. They face another challenge—Patti has more cash to invest initially, but they eventually want to own the business equally.

Joint Project Agreement

Patti Valdez and Maria Ness agree as follows:

1. We desire and intend to jointly own and operate a bakery in San Francisco, California (at a rented location not yet ascertained).

2. Patti will contribute $75,000 and Maria $25,000 toward the working capital of the business.

3. We both will work diligently in our bakery business, and it will be the principal business endeavor of each.

4. Initially, Patti will own 3/4 of the business and Maria 1/4. Each of us will receive pay of $700 a week for her work in the bakery. Any profits beyond salaries and operating expenses will be paid to Patti, until she receives $50,000 plus interest at 10% per year on her excess contribution of $50,000. Once Patti receives the $50,000 plus interest, we will co-own the business equally, and divide all profits equally beyond salaries and operating expenses. If we break up prior to full repayment of Patti's excess contribution, the ownership shares will be adjusted pro rata.

5. If either of us decides she no longer wants to operate the bakery, the person wishing to continue may purchase the other's interest in the bakery as set out under Paragraph 7.

6. If we separate and are unable to work together, but both want to continue the bakery under sole ownership, we will ask someone to flip a coin; the winner will have the right to purchase the loser's interest as provided in Paragraph 7. Likewise, if we separate and only one of us wishes to maintain the bakery, that person has the right to purchase the other's interest as provided in Paragraph 7.

7. If for any reason one of us wants to purchase the other's interest in the business, she will pay the fair market value of the other's share. If we cannot agree on the fair market value, we agree to accept the fair market value as determined by Bill's Commercial Real Estate Appraisers.

8. If either of us dies, the other will become the sole owner of the bakery. We agree to each make a will containing this provision.

9. Any provision in this agreement found to be invalid shall have no effect on the validity of the remaining provisions.

_____   _____

Date   Patti Valdez

_____   _____

Date   Maria Ness

Help with starting a small business. *If you and your lover are opening a business together, you will be investing a great deal of time—and money. Nolo has excellent resources to educate you on all the major issues you should consider before jumping into this venture.* The Small Business Start-Up Kit, *by Peri Pakroo, gives you the information you need to get your small business off the ground. If you choose to organize your business as a partnership, check out* The Partnership Book, *by Denis Clifford and Ralph Warner. You can also look for small business information on our website, at www.nolo.comcategory/sb_home.html.*

6. Contracts to Give a Partner "Time Off"

Often, when both partners work outside the home, one wants to take time off to study art, travel, have a child or just stay home. The challenge is working out the details so that the person who continues to earn a living doesn't get resentful and the person taking time off doesn't start feeling guilty. One option is to alternate earning an income and taking time off; that way, each partner takes time to financially support the couple. Another possibility is for the person working to lend money to the one taking time off. Or, if the person taking time off will be raising a child, clearly both partners are contributing to the relationship and no "equal time off" or loan is needed. No matter what you arrange, you must specify how much time equals how much money, and, if appropriate, set a method of repayment.

Below is a "time-off" agreement for a couple who are both artists, but need to hold regular jobs to pay the bills.

EXAMPLE: Martha and Lianne have lived together on and off for three years. Martha is a poet and Lianne an illustrator, but both have other part-time jobs to make ends meet. They recently moved in together, and decided to "trade" working. Each will work full time at her art, as they take turns supporting each other. This way, they can be creative while also paying their rent and groceries.

Allowing One Person Time Off

Martha Rutherford and Lianne Wu agree as follows:

1. Each of us will retain whatever property we currently own as our separate property (lists are attached to this contract). All income stemming from the earnings of either of us while we live together, including income from our artistic pursuits, will be jointly owned and kept in joint bank accounts. Any property purchased with this income will be jointly owned and any debts will be jointly owed.

2. We will each work at full-time jobs for alternating six-month periods for the duration of this agreement. Lianne will work the first six-month period and then it will be Martha's turn.

3. The person employed will be responsible for all personal and household expenses for both of us.

4. If we separate during a year—that is, before each person has supported the other for six months—the support obligation will continue for the remainder of the year in an amount roughly equal to that previously contributed by the other partner.

5. If one of us wants to end the living arrangement, we agree to participate in mediation sessions with a mutually acceptable third person. If, after a minimum of three sessions, one of us still wants to separate, we will. Each one of us will take her separate property (property owned prior to living together), and we will equally divide all joint property (property acquired while living together). No financial or other responsibilities will continue between us after we separate, except as set out in Clause 4.

6. Any provision in this agreement found to be invalid shall have no effect on the validity of the remaining provisions.

_____   _____
Date   Martha Rutherford

_____   _____
Date   Lianne Wu

7. Contracts for People in School

It's common for one partner to help the other with educational expenses or support while he or she's in school. This is a situation for a written agreement.

EXAMPLE: Sam supports George while he's in plumber's school. Sam expects their financial lives to improve once George graduates. If George leaves Sam just after graduating, Sam is likely to feel that George owes him something. A court might agree, but the couple doesn't want to leave it to a court to decide. So they define their expectations in a written agreement.

Educational Support

Sam Adaba and George Fujimoto make the following agreement:

1. Each wants to further his education, and so they will take turns going to school. Sam has already started school to learn plumbing, and his schooling is shorter than George's, so he will go first. George will pay Sam's educational expenses and support for them both for the next 18 months. After 18 months, Sam will assume these responsibilities for two years while George finishes his accountant's training. If their relationship dissolves during the first three and one-half years, the financial responsibilities won't be affected.

   Specifically, if Sam and George separate during the first 18 months, George will continue to pay Sam's tuition and will pay Sam $5,000 per year for living expenses. At the end of the 18 months, Sam will pay George's tuition, and his living expenses at $5,000 per year, for two years. If they separate after George starts school, Sam will pay George's remaining tuition up to two full years in accounting school and pay him $5,000 a year for living expenses. Expenses will be paid in 12 equal monthly installments on the first day of each month.

2. All property owned by Sam or George before the date of this contract remains his separate property and can't be transferred to the other except by a written agreement.

3. During the first three and one-half years, all income and property accumulated with that income, except gifts and inheritances, will be jointly owned. When both Sam and George finish school, they will make a list of all jointly accumulated property. That property will be divided equally if they separate. Thereafter, each person's earnings will be his separate property and neither will have any right in the property of the other. If they separate before the end of three and one-half years, all property accumulated since the beginning of this agreement

   will be divided according to the fraction of the time each provided support. (For example, if Sam supports George for 18 months and George supports Sam for 12, Sam is entitled to three-fifths of the property.)

4. Any provision in this agreement found to be invalid shall have no effect on the validity of the remaining provisions.

_____   _____
Date   Sam Adaba

_____   _____
Date   George Fujimoto

8. Contracts for Work Done Around the House

In some relationships, one person works outside the home while the other cooks, cleans, shops and otherwise takes care of the place. This sort of labor division can raise questions, such as whether the homemaker should be compensated, especially if there are major tasks or renovation work to be done.

More frequently, both partners work outside the home, but one also makes significant improvements to the home, while the other idles in the sauna. Is it fair that the person who does the extra work should receive nothing for her labor? Only you can answer these questions, and no two answers will be the same. But remember one thing—these situations are likely to lead to misunderstandings unless you discuss them openly, and write down your agreement.

The worst thing you can do if one person contributes all the money or does all the work around the house is ignore it. First, a person with money also has power and may be the only legal owner of the property, and relationships rarely prosper when one person has too much of anything. Second, a person who does all the work around the house tends to feel resentful toward the other, especially if he is not a full legal owner.

Here are some suggestions. A person who spends all weekend fixing up a jointly owned house or a home solely owned by the other partner can be paid an agreed-upon hourly rate, with the compensation either paid in cash by the other or added to the carpenter's equity in the house. A stay-at-home mate can be given a weekly salary or can trade services (you fix the car while your lover does the laundry). You should also think about the homemaker's future if you split up. You can agree on a period of support payments for the home-maker, thereby creating your own alimony-like arrangement by contract, and such an agreement generally will be legally valid.

Make sure you give some thought to the tax implications of your arrangements, however. Giving your partner more than $10,000 per year can trigger a gift tax obligation (see Chapter 5), and paying "wages" to a lover for domestic services can trigger Social Security and income tax withholding obligations.

Compensating a Homemaker

Sandi Potter and Carole Samworthe agree that as long as they live together:

1. Sandi will work full-time (at least 40 hours a week).

2. Carole will work in the home, taking care of her daughter, Judy, and performing the domestic chores, including cleaning, laundry, cooking and yard work. Sandi will contribute an additional $200 a week to Carole's personal expenses [or will pay Carole $200 per week] for her services. This payment will be adjusted from time to time to reflect changes in the cost of living.

3. Sandi will also provide reasonable amounts of money each month for food, clothing, shelter and recreation for the entire family as long as they live together. This payment will be adjusted from time to time to reflect changes in the cost of living. Sandi, however, assumes no obligation to support Carole or Judy upon termination of this agreement.

4. [If Carole is treated as Sandi's employee] Sandi, as Carole's "employer," will make Social Security payments for her and will obtain medical insurance for her and Judy.

5. All property purchased or accumulated by either Carole or Sandi will be owned by the person purchasing or accumulating it. The property cannot be transferred from one person to the other except by a written agreement. The house will be provided by Sandi and will be owned solely by her.

6. Either Sandi or Carole can end this agreement by giving the other two months' written notice. If Sandi and Carole separate, Sandi will pay Carole severance pay at the rate of two months for every year the agreement has been in effect. Sandi's agreement to pay this money is part of the consideration necessary to get Carole to agree to this contract. This money will be paid in a lump sum at the time of separation. Neither Carole nor Sandi will have any other financial obligation to the other upon separation.

7. Any provision in this agreement found to be invalid shall have no effect on the validity of the remaining provisions.

_____   _____
Date   Sandi Potter

_____   _____
Date   Carole Samworthe

E. Modifying Your Agreement

Modifications of a written living together contract should always be in writing. This is because ancient, but still applicable, legal doctrines usually make oral modifications of a written contract invalid. In addition, our contracts expressly state that any modifications must be in writing. A modification can simply state that you agree to change your contract, and then set out the change. Date and sign all modifications. But if you're making really major changes, tear up the old agreement and start over.

⚠ **Beware the tax man!** _The government's rules about money often create serious problems for same-sex couples. Transfers of property or debt can be construed as taxable income or as legal gifts, and if the amount is sufficiently high, this can trigger a serious gift tax liability. And if one of you is receiving government benefits or alimony from a prior marriage, the legal implications can be even more complicated. If you are contemplating a transfer of more than $10,000 per year in assets (for example, where you put your lover's name on a property title without requiring him to pay for his ownership interest) or debts (for example, when you "lend" your partner $15,000 but don't ever collect on the debt), we strongly encourage you to speak with an accountant who know the rules for unmarried couples._ ∎

Buying a Home Together (and Other Real Estate Ventures)

To Freud, a home symbolized motherhood. For E. M. Forster, in *Howard's End,* it was a sign of stability and the best of the old order. Others have likened a home to a castle and valued it as a haven of peace and refuge. One way or another, home ownership has long been an important part of our culture. Indeed, it's probably fair to say that if you dream of purchasing a home, you dream along with much of America. And for those of us who are not allowed to legally marry, owning a home together can be the ultimate symbol of our coupledness.

Beyond the emotional urges, there are many practical reasons to own a home—a hedge against rent increases and an unstable economy, avoiding the powerlessness of being a tenant and gaining the tax deductibility of mortgage interest. In addition, owning a home offers a lesbian or gay couple a valuable degree of freedom and privacy from the sometimes hostile intrusions of the world.

Your Home as Investment and Tax Shelter

There are many financial benefits to owning a home, especially in times of rapid appreciation. With any luck your investment will go up in value—but remember, selling a home can itself be expensive and prices can go down as well as up. You can deduct from your taxable income all interest you pay on your mortgage, and all your property taxes. By comparison, renters get no such deductions, even if, as is usual, their rent helps pay the landlord's taxes and mortgage interest payments, and renters never acquire any equity in their residence.

Homeowners qualify for another tax advantage. If you sell your home and have lived there two of the prior five years, you are allowed to reap any profits (up to $250,000 per owner) without paying any federal taxes on the sale, ever—and most states offer a parallel exemption from state taxes. This means you can keep buying up more expensive properties and avoid paying taxes on your accumulated profits while you're doing it. Gays and straights alike can take advantage of this exemption, regardless of their marital status.

At the same time, home ownership has some very real drawbacks. When the boiler explodes, you may pine for the days when you could just call your landlord. You might recall Thoreau, who noted that most people didn't own their houses; their houses owned them. And if the property declines in value, you can lose all or part of your down payment. Still, despite the drawbacks, it is your home. It can be fun to tear down walls, plant your own trees, paint an ivy decoration across the dining room walls or even fix the boiler. Most Americans agree with Mark Twain, who advised, "Buy land. They aren't making any more of it."

Buying and fixing up a home with a lover also can be a wonderful foundation for a relationship, both spiritually and economically. Of course, it can be damn scary too. The bulk of this chapter suggests ways to handle the practical aspects of buying a home. Even if you skipped Chapter 6 on living together contracts, you definitely will need a contract regarding the ownership of a house. And recognizing what continues to be a trend in the lesbian and gay community, some of these contracts are for friends, with or without lovers, who buy together.

Before you can pin down your agreement, you have to find the house, arrange for financing and understand the ways in which you can hold title to the property. Let's begin with these first steps.

A. Finding a House

Given your needs, tastes and finances, you probably already have a good idea of the type of house you want to buy. Indeed, if you sit quietly for a few moments, shut your eyes and let your imagination do the walking, you can probably conjure up an image of the house, or perhaps if you're a flexible sort, several houses that you would dearly love to call home.

We have no advice to give you on what type of home to look for. Some folks love living on a dusty road in outer suburbia; others want the convenience of living in a townhouse in a major city. Many people enjoy fixing a place up while others insist on move-in condition. Some crave a view, while others can live with almost no light.

But we do have something to say about buying a house you'll be happy with. You need an organized house-buying method to translate your dream into reality. This is particularly true in high-priced markets (often urban areas) where most buyers face an affordability gap between the house they'd like to buy and the one they can afford. Without an organized approach, there is a good chance you'll be talked into compromising on the wrong house by friends, relatives, a real estate agent or even yourself.

"Not me, I know my own mind," you say. "Nonsense," we reply. In today's market, almost everyone must trim their desires to fit their pocketbook and it's easy to buy the wrong house in the wrong

location. So easy, in fact, that every day many confident and knowledgeable people become so anxious and disoriented in the process of searching for a house that they purchase one they later come to regret buying, sometimes bitterly.

Here is our method to all but ensure that you buy a house you'll enjoy living in, even if it's substantially more modest than your dream house:

- Firmly establish your priorities before you look at a house.
- Insist that any house you offer to buy meets at least your most important priorities.
- Do this even if, in buying a house which meets your priorities, you must compromise in other areas and purchase a house less desirable than you really want.

The reason this method works well should be obvious. If your priorities are clearly set in advance, you're likely to compromise on less important features. If they aren't, you may become so disoriented by the house purchase process that you buy a house that lacks the basic features that motivated you to buy in the first place.

Lesbian and gay couples usually have no special problems in finding a house to buy. Be aware, however, that some communities (or neighborhoods) have adopted zoning ordinances prohibiting groups of unrelated people from living together, and the U.S. Supreme Court has upheld these ordinances. Most of these laws are aimed at barring groups, foster families, shelters or boarding houses, and a very few prohibit two unrelated adults from living together. But some of these laws have been used to harass lesbians and gays who lived together, just as they have been used to discriminate against unmarried heterosexual couples. Before you buy, make sure the town—or neighborhood—isn't zoned only for people related by "blood, marriage or adoption." If it is, you may need to be prepared to make a challenge to this remaining vestige of homophobia.

Also, occasionally a seller may hesitate to sell to you because he thinks you are immoral or even criminal. We've never heard of anyone ultimately refusing to sell to a lesbian or gay couple, however;

the god Mammon appears to be stronger than the god Discrimination. But be sensible and strategic if your preferred neighborhood has been hostile to gay buyers.

The most common way to find a home is to use an agent, broker or realtor. (We use the term agent for simplicity.) Again, you may encounter an agent who refuses to work with a lesbian or gay couple, although we're not aware of anyone this has happened to. To avoid it, you have two choices: Look for a gay or gay-friendly agent. (Ask your gay home-owning friends who they used.) Or buy on your own, without an agent. With the latter, in effect you are using the seller's agent—although the seller rarely lowers the price to reflect that fact.

Indeed, you may well be tempted to proceed on your own. But bear in mind that buying real estate takes a lot of work and patience, and involves understanding much strange jargon. In some places, using an agent is virtually a necessity. It's often easier to let someone knowledgeable do the work. If you decide to use an agent, initially you are not obligated to work with just one. Shop around. Eventually, you may select one to work with, and if you do, at least in theory, you get a chance at the "hottest" deals—the ones the agent would otherwise save for his best customers.

Just as you (the buyers) don't have to use an agent, neither does the seller. A small but significant number of people sell their homes this way. You can find homes sold by owners by checking newspaper ads or driving around and looking for "for sale by owner" or "FSBO" (pronounced fizzbo) signs. You can also check out these websites: http://www.forsalebyowner.com or http://www.salebyowner.com. There are several books that explain the ins and outs of buying or selling a home yourself, including *How to Buy a House in California,* by Ralph Warner, Ira Serkes and George Devine (Nolo), and *For Sale by Owner,* by George Devine (Nolo), for those who live in California.

Working With an Agent

In most states, agents assist with all aspects of the purchase. In addition to finding homes, they can give you advice on prices, school districts, transportation, demographics and economic trends in the area (whether property values are going up or down). An agent should also help you find the experts you need—such as a termite inspector, a roofer or a soil engineer—and assist with arranging financing and the closing.

An agent's commission is a percentage of the price of the home, and is paid by the seller. Because the agent isn't being paid on an hourly basis, take your time and ask all the questions you want. A common commission is 6%, but it's supposedly negotiable. You may find commission competition in some urban areas, and a seller may find someone who'll do a good job and charge less. After all, 6% can be a large chunk of money. Because the seller pays the commission, however, the buyer won't save much unless the seller's willing to pass along some of the savings.

Technically speaking, agents who share in the commission paid by the seller primarily represent the seller. In most states, however, your agent represents your interest as well. When it comes to the negotiations, however, quite a gap can develop between this legal truth and the marketplace reality. An agent doesn't get a commission until a sale is consummated; it's therefore in her interest to consummate the deal. This may not be in your interest at all, so be careful you're not talked into a house you don't want. If you don't trust your agent's actions, switch agents.

B. How Much House Can You Afford?

Many prospective home buyers face an affordability problem when it comes to buying the house they'd really like to live in. This is still true, even though mortgage interest rates are at comparatively reasonable levels.

Against this somber background, it's essential to determine how much you can afford to pay before you look for a house. Many people don't understand how institutional lenders (banks, savings and loans, credit unions) determine how much money they'll lend to you. If you don't do the calculations ahead of time, or talk to a loan broker, you may enter into a home purchase contract and then not qualify for the necessary loan. As part of this initial evaluation, you must also decide whether both of you or just one of you will be owners from the outset.

Let's start with the basics. As a broad generalization, most people can afford to purchase a house worth about three times their total (gross) annual income, assuming a 20% down payment and a moderate amount of other long-term debts. With no other debts, most people can afford a house worth up to four times their annual income.

A much more accurate way to determine how much house you can afford is to compare your monthly carrying costs (monthly payments of mortgage principal and interest, insurance and property taxes) plus your monthly payments on other long-term debts, to your gross (total) monthly income. This is called the "debt-to-income ratio." Lenders normally want you to make all monthly payments with 28%–38% of your monthly income. You can qualify near the bottom or the top of this range depending on the amount of your down payment, the interest rate on the type of mortgage you want, your credit history, the amount of your other long-term debts, your employment stability and prospects, the lender's philosophy and the money supply in the general economy. In some cities, there are special subsidies to help first-time home buyers, often with the down payment or mortgage.

Generally, the greater your other debts, the lower the percentage of your income lenders will assume you have available to spend each month on housing. Conversely, if you have no long-term debts, a great credit history and will make a larger than normal down payment, a lender may approve carrying costs that exceed 38% of your monthly income—sometimes as high as 40% or 42%. In either case, these rules aren't absolute.

Your Credit Score Is Important When Applying for a Home Loan

When deciding whether to approve your home loan application, most lenders will consider your credit score. Credit scores are numerical calculations that are supposed to indicate the risk that you will default on your payments. High credit scores indicate less risk and low scores indicate potential problems.

Factors which many companies use when generating credit scores include:

- Your payment history.
- Amounts you owe on credit accounts.
- Length of your credit history. In general, a longer credit history increases the score.
- Your new credit. It helps to have an established credit history without too many new accounts. Opening several accounts in a short period of time can represent greater risk.
- Types of credit. Credit scorers look for a "healthy mix" of different types of credit.

Although credit bureaus are not required to disclose your score to you, the nation's biggest credit scoring company, Fair, Isaac and Company, recently made credit scores available to consumers for a fee of $12.95. To get your Fair, Isaac credit score, visit http://www.equifax.com, http://www.myfico.com or http://www.scorepower.com. And if you live in California, you're in luck. A new California law requires that mortgage lenders disclose credit scores to consumers shopping for a mortgage.

If you do get your credit score, and it seems lower than it should be, there may be a mistake on your credit report. (See Chapter 2, Section D, for information on how to get a copy of your credit report and correct errors, if necessary.)

To keep up on credit scoring developments, visit http://www.creditscoring.com, a private website devoted to credit scoring.

1. Prepare a Financial Statement

The first step to determine the purchase price you can afford is to thoroughly prepare a list of your monthly incomes and your monthly expenses.

Total monthly gross income. List your gross monthly income from all sources. Gross income is total income before withholdings are deducted. Include income from:

- employment—your base salary or wages plus any bonuses, tips, commissions or overtime you regularly receive
- public benefits
- dividends from stocks, bonds and similar investments
- freelance income, self-employment and hobbies, and
- royalties and rents.

Total monthly deductions. Total up all required monthly deductions from your income (such as taxes and Social Security deducted from your paycheck). Don't include money deducted to pay credit unions, child support or other debts. If you deliberately have more money than necessary subtracted from federal or state income tax by underclaiming deductions, ask your employer what amount you are obligated to pay.

Total monthly net income. Subtract your total monthly deductions from your total monthly gross income to arrive at your net income.

Total monthly expenses. List and total up what you spend each month on the following:

- child care
- clothing
- current educational costs
- food—include eating at restaurants, as well as at home
- insurance—auto, life, medical, disability
- medical expenses not covered by insurance
- personal expenses—include costs for personal care (haircuts, shoe repairs and toiletries) and fun (attending movies and theater, renting videos, buying CDs, books and lottery tickets, subscribing to newspapers and magazines)
- installment payments—student loans, car payments, child support, alimony, personal loans, credit cards and any others
- taxes
- transportation
- utilities
- other—such as regular charitable or religious donations and savings deposits.

2. How Much Down Payment Will You Make?

Unless you're eligible for a government-subsidized mortgage that has low or—in the case of the Veterans Administration—no down payment, you'll probably need to put down 10%–25% of the cost of the house to qualify for a loan. Also, you'll have to pay the closing costs, an additional 2%–5% of the cost of the home. Some banks, however, will make mortgage loans with only 5% down, although the monthly interest rate may be higher than if you had put 10% or 20% down.

Generally speaking, the larger the percentage of the total price of a house you can put down, the easier it will be for you to qualify for a mortgage. This is because larger down payments mean less money due each month to pay off your mortgage. The monthly mortgage payment (plus taxes and insurance) is the major factor in determining the purchase price of the house you can afford.

Total up the money you have for a down payment and then multiply this number first by five and then by ten. These figures represent the very broad price range of house prices you can likely afford, based on your ability to make a down payment. Of course, you must be able to afford the monthly mortgage, interest and property tax payments too. If your income is relatively low, you'll have to increase your down payment to 25%–30% or even more of the price of a house to bring down the monthly payments.

3. Estimate the Mortgage Interest Rate You'll Likely Pay

Because different mortgage types carry different interest rates, start by deciding the mortgage type you want. For a reading of the market's direction, check the mortgage interest rate round-up published in the real estate sections of many Sunday newspapers.

In general, adjustable rate mortgages (ARMs) have slightly lower initial interest rates and payment requirements than do fixed rate loans, and are therefore more affordable than fixed rate loans. This isn't saying they're better, however. Before selecting an ARM, compare interest rates by looking at the ARM's annual percentage rate (APR), not just its introductory rate. (APR is an estimate of the credit cost over the entire life of the loan. APR comparisons can sometimes be deceptive.)

4. Calculate How Much House You Can Afford

Now that you have a pretty good idea of the size of your down payment and the interest rate you expect to pay, you can calculate how much house you can afford.

Step 1. Estimate the price you think a house with your priorities will cost.

Step 2. Estimate the likely mortgage interest rate you'll end up paying. If you're eligible for a government-subsidized mortgage, be sure to use those rates.

Step 3. Find your mortgage interest and principal payment factors per $1,000 over the length of the loan (30 years is most common) on the chart on page 7/8.

Monthly Payments on a $100,000 Fixed Rate Mortgage

Interest rate (%) ($)	15-year period monthly payment ($)	Total payments ($)	30-year period monthly payment ($)	Total payments
6.5	871.11	156,799	632.07	227,544
7.0	898.83	161,789	665.30	239,509
7.5	927.01	166,862	699.21	251,717
8.0	955.65	172,017	733.76	264,155
8.5	984.74	177,253	768.91	276,809
9.0	1,014.27	182,569	804.62	298,664
9.5	1,044.22	187,960	840.85	302,708
10.0	1,074.61	193,430	877.57	315,926
10.5	1,105.40	198,972	914.74	329,306
11.0	1,136.60	204,588	952.32	342,836
11.5	1,168.19	210,274	990.29	356,505
12.0	1,200.17	216,031	1,028.61	370,301
12.5	1,232.52	221,854	1,067.26	384,214
13.0	1,265.24	227,743	1,106.20	398,232
14.0	1,331.74	239,713	1,184.87	426,554

Step 4. Subtract the down payment you want to make from your estimated purchase price. The result is the amount you'll need to borrow.

Step 5. Multiply the factor from the chart below by the number of thousands you'll need to borrow. The result is your monthly principal and interest payment.

Here's how to put the first five steps together.

EXAMPLE: Bill and Mark estimate the house they want to buy will cost $200,000. A 20% down payment of $40,000 leaves them with a $160,000 mortgage loan. They plan to finance with an adjustable rate mortgage (ARM), which they believe they can get at an interest rate of 6%. The monthly factor per $1,000 for a 30-year loan at

6% rate is 6. So their monthly payments will begin at (because it's adjustable) 160 x 6, or $960.

Step 6. To get the total carrying costs for the mortgage loan, you must add the estimated monthly costs of homeowner's insurance and property taxes. Very roughly, homeowner's insurance costs about $400 per $100,000 of house value. On a $200,000 house, expect to pay $800 per year or $67 per month.

Step 7. Property taxes are initially based on the new assessed value (market price) of the house as of the date of transfer of title. They vary state to state and even county to county, so use 1% of the market value as an estimated annual tax. (For an exact number, call the tax assessor in the county in which you're looking to buy.) On a $200,000 house, taxes would be about $2,000 per year or $167 per month.

Mortgage Principal and Interest Payment Factors (Per $1,000)

Interest rates	15-year mortgage	20-year mortgage	25-year mortgage	30-year mortgage
5.00	7.91	6.60	5.85	5.37
5.25	8.04	6.74	5.99	5.52
5.50	8.17	6.88	6.14	5.68
5.75	8.30	7.02	6.29	5.84
6.00	8.44	7.16	6.44	6.00
6.25	8.57	7.31	6.60	6.16
6.50	8.71	7.46	6.75	6.32
6.75	8.85	7.60	6.91	6.49
7.00	8.99	7.75	7.07	6.65
7.25	9.13	7.90	7.23	6.82
7.50	9.27	8.06	7.39	6.99
7.75	9.41	8.21	7.55	7.16
8.00	9.56	8.36	7.72	7.34
8.25	9.70	8.52	7.88	7.51
8.50	9.85	8.68	8.05	7.69
8.75	9.99	8.84	8.22	7.87
9.00	10.14	9.00	8.39	8.05
9.25	10.29	9.16	8.56	8.23
9.50	10.44	9.32	8.74	8.41
9.75	10.59	9.49	8.91	8.59
10.00	10.75	9.65	9.09	8.78

Step 8. Now total up your mortgage/interest payment, insurance and taxes. These are your monthly carrying costs.

Step 9. Total up the monthly payments on your long-term debts and add this number to the monthly carrying costs you arrived at in Step 8. Then, divide that total by a number between .28 and .38, depending on your debt level (the fewer your debts, the higher number to divide by), to determine the monthly income needed to qualify.

C. Proceeding With Your Purchase

Once you find the house you want to buy, you will need to take care of a few details before you actually buy it.

1. Inspections

Any contract to purchase a home should allow you a few weeks to make all necessary inspections. A buyer usually pays for inspections, but it may be possible to negotiate with the seller and have her pay a portion. These routinely include termite, electrical and plumbing, and a roof inspection. In addition, you may want a soil engineer to check the foundation, or a general contractor to do a full inspection of the house. Your purchase contract should be contingent upon these experts reporting

that the house either is in good condition or can be repaired for a reasonable price, and you may want to negotiate for a price reduction if the repairs will be extensive.

2. Financing That White Picket Fence

After you've conducted the inspections and reached a firm agreement on price and terms, you will have to come up with the money. Usually, your obligation to buy is contingent on your finding financing for a specific amount at a specific interest rate. Obviously, you don't want to sign a contract to purchase a home and then not be able to find a loan you can afford.

Few of us can pay all cash for a house. We borrow money from a lending institution, family member, the seller or a loan shark, and accept whatever conditions the lenders impose. Most often you'll borrow from a bank. In exchange, the bank will require you to sign a note promising to repay the money plus a healthy interest. Your promise to pay, standing alone, however, won't be sufficient security for the bank; it will also require you to sign a document giving it the power to foreclose on the house if you default on your payments. This document is normally called a mortgage or a deed of trust.

In the distant past, many lenders refused to lend to lesbian and gay couples. Same-sex couples were considered immoral or unstable, no matter what their financial worth. Throughout the 1970s and easy-credit 1980s, times changed. Banks just looked at both persons' incomes. If the money was there, so came the loan, regardless of your sleeping arrangement.

Some lenders admit that they view lesbian and gay relationships as inherently unstable and therefore consider it too risky to lend to lesbian and gay couples. Unfortunately, this kind of discrimination is legal. You will need to present yourselves as sophisticated buyers. Do your homework. Know the interest rates from several other lenders before you walk in the door. Get familiar with fixed rate loans, adjustable rate mortgages, special 15-year mortgages, points, closing costs and the rest. Provide information showing that you're both on your jobs for the long haul (get letters from your supervisors) and are up for a promotion or a raise. And then be persistent. A hard-working loan broker might be very helpful.

To the extent it's possible, try to be creative in your financing. You may be able to "assume" a seller's loan. Or, she may be willing to finance any portion of the purchase. If she doesn't need all the money at once, she might give you a second mortgage.

EXAMPLE: Wendy and Alice love a home selling for $180,000. Their savings, borrowing from parents and friends total $36,000. They need $144,000 more (plus $9,000 for closing costs). The seller has owned the home for a few years and has a $90,000 mortgage at 8% interest. Here are several possible methods of financing their purchase:

Plan A
- $36,000 down payment
- $144,000 at current bank interest rates.

Plan B
- $36,000 down payment
- $90,000 by assuming the seller's old mortgage at 8%

- $54,000 loan from the seller including interest at 10%, with a final (balloon) payment for whatever balance is due in seven years. (The monthly interest payment rate and the time of the balloon payment will be negotiable.)

Plan C
- To make it more attractive to the seller, they offer $2,000 above the sales price
- $36,000 cash down
- $90,000 by assuming the seller's old mortgage at 8%
- $56,000 loan from seller including interest at 10%, with a final (balloon) payment for whatever balance is due in seven years.

3. Escrow and Closing Costs

In buying and selling a house, paperwork and money must eventually change hands. The practice is for the buyers to deliver their money and the sellers to deliver the house deed to a third person, called an escrow holder. The escrow holder hangs on to everything until all inspections are complete, the papers are signed and financing is arranged. Then, "escrow closes," the deed is recorded with the county, the buyers receive the deed establishing that they now own the house and the seller gets the money.

Closing Costs and Loan Fees

Closing costs and loan fees can add up to 5% to your mortgage. Some fees are paid to the bank when you apply for the loan, but most are paid the day you close escrow. Not all lenders and escrow holders require the same fees (some are waived as part of special offers). When escrow closes, you'll receive a statement with an itemized list of the closing costs.

Typical closing costs and loan fees are:

Application fee: Loan application fees (typically $350–$400) cover the lender's cost of processing your loan.

Appraisal fees: Charged by an appraiser hired by the lender to appraise the property to be sure it's worth what you've agreed to pay. They usually run between $275 and $300 for a regular-sized single-family home, and somewhat more for a very large, or multiple-unit building.

Assumption fee: Typically 1% of the loan balance to assume the seller's existing ARM; to assume an FHA or VA loan, the fee will range from $50 to $100.

Credit report: Can cost up to $75 to check each partner's credit. While standard credit checks cost $5–$15, for home loans lenders check two credit reporting agencies' files and the county records for judgment and tax liens.

Escrow company fees: An escrow company that is not a title insurance company may charge a nominal fee for doing the escrow work.

Garbage fees: Real estate business slang for a number of small fees, including notary, courier and filing fees, which typically run from $150 to $250.

Loan fees: This includes points (one point is 1% of the loan principal), a fee the bank charges you for the privilege of making a loan, and an additional fee, usually between $100 and $450. Lenders also often charge $150 to $250 to complete the loan paperwork.

Physical inspection reports: May add several hundred dollars or more, depending on how many are requested.

Prepaid homeowner's insurance: Amount as required by lender; depends on the house's value, level of coverage and location of the house.

Prepaid interest on the loan: You'll be asked to pay per diem interest in advance, from the date your loan is funded to the end of that month. The maximum you'll be charged is 30 days of interest.

Prepaid property taxes: Depends on tax assessment; covers the time period between closing and your first monthly mortgage payment.

Private mortgage insurance: This insurance protects the lender in the event of a foreclosure, in case the property is worth less than what you paid for it. For a loan with less than 10% down, the total PMI you will pay is about 1.6%–2% of the loan. In the first year, you'll pay approximately .5% of the total loan. For each year you renew your PMI policy, you'll pay about .35% of the outstanding loan. PMI on FHA loans costs 3.8% of the loan. Most lenders require the first few payments to be made up front.

Recording and filing fees: The escrow holder will charge about $100 for drawing up, reviewing and recording the deed of trust and other legal documents. The total escrow and title fees can amount to .5% of the loan.

Survey fee: May be needed to show plot measurements if house has easements or is in a rural location; a survey will run as much as $500 or more.

Tax service fee: Issued to notify the lender if you default on your property taxes; usually costs about $75 to $80.

Title search and title insurance: Not all buyers must pay all of the title costs. Most lenders require title insurance for the face amount of their mortgage or for the value of their loan. Title insurance is a one-time premium which costs about .075% of the cost of your house. The title search confirms that the seller of the property is really the legal owner.

Transfer tax: Tax assessed by the county when the property changes hands. May be split with seller, and costs about $.55 per $1,000 of value transferred. Many cities also charge transfer tax; it varies city to city, but can be as much as 1.5% of the purchase price.

In some states, a lawyer must handle the real estate closing. Title companies and real estate agents cannot conduct closings, or even give their clients advice about them, as that would be practicing law without a license. In many other states, such as California, attorneys are not typically involved in residential property sales, and a title or escrow company handles the entire closing process.

D. Taking Title to Your New Home

When you buy your home with your partner, you must decide how you will own the property, or in real estate talk, how to "take title." This decision has huge consequences, especially on estate planning issues. You have three choices:

- only one person holds title
- both of you hold title as "joint tenants"
- both of you hold title as "tenants in common."

1. In One Person's Name

This means that absent a contract to the contrary, only the person named in the deed owns the house. It isn't wise to put only one name on the deed unless in truth only one of you owns the house. Sometimes, a couple who jointly owns a home is tempted to put only one name on the deed to save on taxes or avoid one partner's creditors. The tax savings are attractive if one of your incomes is very high and the other's is very low; the high-income person takes all the house tax deductions. But in general, this is a bad strategy. Although you might fool a few creditors, there are real risks to this.

If the person on the deed (and therefore the presumed sole owner) sells the house and pockets the money, or dies without making provisions, the other person may be out of luck. Sure, she can sue to recover her portion of the property. But a lawsuit to recover your share might be difficult, or even impossible. In any case, it's absurd to risk a lawsuit. If more than one person is buying the property, all owners should normally be named on the deed. If

you are not planning to do this, have a lawyer draft a contract clearly spelling out the interests and rights of both owners, and verify that such a contract is valid in your state. If it isn't, the one not on the title may be considered a creditor, not a co-owner.

2. Joint Tenancy

Joint tenancy means you share property ownership equally, and that each of you has the right to use the entire property. Joint tenancy also comes with something called the "right of survivorship." In fact, the deed sometimes reads "joint tenancy with right of survivorship." This means that if one joint tenant dies, the other one automatically receives the deceased person's share, even if there's a will to the contrary. And when joint tenancy property passes to the other joint tenant at death, there's no need for any probate proceedings.

Another feature of joint tenancy is that if one joint tenant sells his or her share or transfers it to a living trust, the sale or transfer ends the joint tenancy. The new owner (or the trust) and the other original owner become tenants-in-common (see below). Each joint tenant has the right to sell his or her interest, regardless of whether the other joint tenants agree with, or are even aware of, the sale.

Joint tenancy can't be used if a house is owned in unequal shares. It's appropriate only when each joint tenant owns the same portion. This means that you and your lover could put a house you owned 50-50 in joint tenancy or that three people could have joint tenancy with each owning one-third of a property. If you own 65% of a house, however, and your lover owns 35%, joint tenancy won't work. Finally, joint tenancy can create some serious adverse tax consequences for high-asset couples. If that's a concern for you, see a tax specialist before making a final decision.

Even if you are equal owners taking title as joint tenants, you can still provide compensation if one of you contributed more to the down payment. But in order to avoid undermining the basic framework of joint tenancy—which is inherently 50-50—set a dollar value for reimbursement rather than adjusting ownership percentages.

EXAMPLE: Tom and Liam decide to buy a house together; they want to own it equally as joint tenants and pay the monthly expenses equally, but they've kept their savings separate so far and they've each saved different amounts. Tom is going to contribute $10,000 towards the $40,000 down payment and Liam is going to contribute $30,000. They've decided to honor their unequal contributions by Tom committing to pay Liam $10,000 (so that they each will have contributed an equal $20,000), either over time as Tom can afford it, or out of Tom's share of the proceeds of the sale if and when they sell the house.

Tom and Liam should put this commitment in writing as part of their co-ownership agreement. They will own the property equally as joint tenants, but Tom will have a debt to Liam.

3.　Tenants-in-Common

Tenancy-in-common is the other way to hold title when there's more than one owner. The major difference between joint tenancy and tenancy-in-common is that tenancy-in-common has no right of survivorship. This means that when a tenant-in-common dies, her share of property is left to whomever she specified in a will, or if there's no will, by the process of "intestate succession." (See Chapter 5.)

Also, and of particular importance in many lesbian or gay real estate ventures, tenants-in-common can own property in unequal shares—one person can own 80% of the property, another 15% and a third 5%. All are listed on the deed as tenants-in-common. You can specify the precise percentages on the deed, for example, "The owners named are tenants-in-common; Sappho has a one-third interest and Joan of Arc two-thirds." More commonly, you can simply list all owners' names on the deed and set out the shares in a separate written agreement. Especially if shares are unequal, it's important to prepare a contract.

4. Changing Title

If you take title in one format and later jointly agree you want to change it to another, you can change the title; you need only record a new deed. For in-

stance, if you want to start as tenants-in-common and later change to joint tenants, make and record a deed granting the property "from Sappho and Joan of Arc as Tenants-in-Common, to Sappho and Joan of Arc as Joint Tenants." If you add a new person, the IRS will call it either a sale or a gift and tax you accordingly, which can be expensive.

E.　Contracts for People Buying or Owning Homes Together

A house is a major economic asset. It's foolish to avoid or postpone clearly defining your mutual expectations and obligations, especially if your contributions are unequal. In this section, we discuss ways to handle joint ownership problems and give sample contracts to cover the most common situations.

In the previous chapter of this book, we suggested that you prepare a broad living together contract. Even if you don't take that advice, you should prepare a contract if you plan to jointly own a home or if one of you is making significant contributions to the other one's home. As you'll see, most of the samples we give are simple and uncomplicated. We have found that the people who most often resist contracts are those who don't have a solid agreement in the first place. If this is your situation, sit down immediately and have a long, honest talk.

Although we recommend simple, uncomplicated contracts, some complicated home ownership arrangements will require complicated contracts. If this is your situation, you may want to have your agreement checked by a lawyer familiar with real estate and sympathetic to lesbian and gay couples. This doesn't mean you should take a full wallet and a basketful of problems to the lawyer. Do as much work as possible yourself and use the lawyer to help you with particular problem areas, or to check the entire agreement when you're finished.

1.　Agreement for Equal Ownership

Let's start with a sample agreement between two people who contribute equal amounts of money for the down payment and intend to share all costs and eventual profits equally.

In this contract, Michael and Hadrian take title as joint tenants. As we discussed above, this means that if either dies, the survivor would automatically get the other's share. If Michael and Hadrian took title as tenants-in-common and one died, his heirs, or whomever he has designated in his will, would inherit his half of the property. Taking title in joint tenancy is common with long-term couples who don't want to hassle with probate, or with setting up a living trust.

Michael and Hadrian also wanted to make sure Michael's mother received credit for the $20,000 she gave him for the down payment if he died while she was still alive. So they had to work that into their agreement.

Contract for Equal Ownership

Michael Angelo and Hadrian Rifkin make the following agreement to jointly purchase a house that they will live in. They agree that:

1. They will buy a house at 423 Bliss Street, Chicago, Illinois, for $180,000.

2. They will take title as joint tenants.

3. They will each contribute $20,000 to the down payment and closing costs and will each pay one-half of the monthly mortgage and insurance costs, as well as one-half of the property taxes and costs for repairs that both agree are needed.

4. If either Michael or Hadrian want to end the relationship and living arrangement, and if both men want to keep the house, a friend will be asked to flip a coin within 60 days of the decision to separate. [For information on mediation as an alternative method of resolving this dispute, see Chapter 6.] The winner of the coin toss will be entitled to purchase the house from the loser, provided that the winner pays the loser the fair market value (see Clause 5) of his share and refinances the property in his name alone within 90 days. When payment is made, Michael and Hadrian will deed the house to the person retaining it in his name alone. If payment isn't made within 90 days, the other owner will have a similar 90-day period to buy the house. If neither makes the purchase or if neither person wants to buy the house, it will be sold and the profits divided equally.

5. If Michael and Hadrian cannot agree on the fair market value of the house, this value will be determined by an appraisal conducted by Sheila Lim, the real estate agent they used when they bought the house, or an appraiser appointed by her successor.

6. Michael and Hadrian agree to maintain life insurance policies for at least $100,000, naming the other as beneficiary. If Michael dies while his mother is alive, Hadrian agrees to pay her $20,000 out of the proceeds of Michael's life insurance policy.

7. If either Michael or Hadrian must make a payment of mortgage, taxes or insurance for the other, who is either unable or unwilling to make the payment, that payment will be treated as a loan to be paid back within six months, including 10% interest per year.

8. This contract is binding on our heirs and our estates.

Date   Michael Angelo

Date   Hadrian Rifkin

2. Owning a House in Unequal Shares

If each person puts up the same amount for the down payment, pays equal shares of the mortgage and other expenses and contributes equally to fix-up fees, each person would have an equal share of the ownership. It's common, however, for joint purchasers to contribute unequally. One person may have more money for the down payment. Another person may be able to afford larger monthly payments than the other, or has skills (such as carpentry) and can renovate the house while the other sits by, beer in hand, and kibbitzes.

Below are sample contracts for unequal ownership. Some factors to consider are easily expressed in cash (making comparisons simple), while other factors are almost impossible to evaluate financially. For example, work on the house can be given a cash value by establishing an hourly wage and multiplying it by the number of hours worked. But what value do you assign to someone's ability to borrow the down payment from his parents—especially in a society structured to reward the owners of capital? We don't mean to suggest that you must arrive at a mathematically exact determination—as you'll see, we suggest that it's enough to decide on rough values that satisfy you both.

a. Two-Thirds/One-Third Ownership

Tina and Barb purchased a home. Tina had more capital, so she made two-thirds of the down payment and owns two-thirds of the house. To keep things simple, Tina will pay two-thirds of the mortgage, taxes and insurance.

Here's their contract:

Contract for Ownership and Payments Split 2/3–1/3

We, Tina Foote and Barb Bibbige, enter into this contract and agree as follows:

1. Property: We will purchase the house at 451 Morton Street, in Upper Montclair, New Jersey.

2. Contributions: We will contribute the following money to the down payment:

    Tina $20,000
    Barb $10,000

3. Ownership: We will own the property as tenants-in-common with the following shares:

    Tina 2/3
    Barb 1/3

4. Expenses and Mortgage: All expenses, including mortgage, taxes, insurance and major repairs on the house, will be paid as follows:

    Tina 2/3
    Barb 1/3

    Utilities and minor repairs (under $500) will be split equally, reflecting the fact that we equally occupy the property.

5. Division Upon Sale: In the event the house is sold, the initial contributions ($20,000 to Tina and $10,000 to Barb) will be paid back first; the remainder of the proceeds will be divided two-thirds to Tina and one-third to Barb. If the property has dropped in value, the proceeds will be divided two-thirds to Tina and one-third to Barb.

6. Contingencies:

    a. We agree to hold the house for three years unless we mutually agree otherwise. After three years, either person may request the house be sold. The person who doesn't want to sell has the right of first refusal; that is, she has the right to purchase the house at the agreed-upon price, and must state in writing that she will exercise this right within two weeks of the setting of the price. She has 60 days to complete the purchase, or the right lapses. If we can't agree on a price, we will jointly select an appraiser to set the price.

    b. If one owner moves out of the house before it's sold, she will remain responsible for her share of the mortgage, taxes, insurance and repairs. She may rent her quarters with the approval (which won't be unreasonably withheld) of the other. The person who stays in the house has the first right to rent the quarters herself or assume the cost if she so chooses.

    c. If Tina and Barb decide to separate and both want to keep the house, they will try to reach a satisfactory arrangement. If by the end of two weeks they can't, they will ask a friend to flip a coin. The winner has the right to purchase the loser's share provided the winner pays the loser her fair market value within 90 days of the toss. We will use an appraiser to set the value.

    d. If either Tina or Barb dies, the other, if she hasn't been left the deceased person's share, has the right to purchase that share from the deceased's estate within six months. The value of the share will be determined as set out above.

7. Binding: This agreement is binding on us and our heirs, executors, administrators, successors and assigns.

8. Mediation: [For information on mediation as an alternative method of resolving this dispute, see Chapter 6.]

_____   _____
Date   Tina Foote

_____   _____
Date   Barb Bibbige

b. Unequal Ownership Turns Into Equal Ownership

For the next example, let's fantasize that we're drawing up a contract for Gertrude and Alice. Gertrude can sell some valuable antiques and come up with the full $50,000 down payment for a little cottage with a mansard roof. Alice can pay one-half the monthly mortgage, insurance and maintenance costs, but has no money for the down payment. They eventually want to equally own the home, but also want to fairly account for Gertrude's down payment.

Gertrude could make a gift of one-half of the down payment to Alice, but she'd be liable for a gift tax and doesn't feel quite that generous. We suggest that Gertrude call one-half of the down payment a loan to Alice that can either be paid back in monthly installments or deferred until the house is sold. If this is done, they should write a contract similar to Michael and Hadrian's, indicating a 50-50 ownership. They should also execute a promissory note providing a record of the loan. And it's good news for Gertrude. If she records the note, turning it into a secured mortgage, she can deduct the interest received on her tax return.

Promissory Note for Down Payment Money

I, Alice B. Toklas, acknowledge receipt of a loan of $25,000 from Gertrude Stein, to be used as my share of the down payment for our house located at 10 Rue de There, Oakland, California. I agree to pay this sum back, plus interest, at the rate of 10% per year, by making monthly payments of $_____, all due in seven years. [Or: I agree to pay the entire loan and interest at 10% per year when and if the house is sold.]

I agree that if the loan and all interest due hasn't been repaid when the house is sold, the remaining balance owed will be paid to Gertrude out of my share of the proceeds from that sale.

_____ _____
Date   Alice B. Toklas

c. One Person Buys the House and the Other Fixes It Up

Sometimes, one person contributes a greater portion, or even all, of the down payment, and the other contributes labor and/or materials to fix a place up. When this occurs, we have a strong bias for a simple contract. If special circumstances require more complex details, have a lawyer review your agreement.

Stephan, Bob and Lyn decide to purchase a graceful but dilapidated Victorian. Stephan and Bob can put up the cash for the down payment and Lyn the expertise and time to fix it up. They can each afford to pay one-third of the monthly expenses. Like Gertrude and Alice, they want to own the place in equal shares and need guidance only on how to do it. Because Stephan and Bob are each going to contribute $17,000 to the down payment, they agree that Lyn should contribute $17,000 worth of materials and labor (at $20 an hour) to fix up the house.

Agreement to Contribute Cash and Labor

We, Stephan, Bob and Lyn, agree as follows:

1. We will purchase the house at 225 Peaches Street, Atlanta, Georgia, for $200,000 and will own the house equally as tenants-in-common.

2. Stephan and Bob will each contribute $17,000 to be used as the down payment.

3. Lyn will contribute $11,000 for materials over the next seven months and 300 hours of labor (valued at $20 per hour) making a total contribution of $17,000, toward fixing up the house.

4. If we all agree that more labor or materials are needed to fix up the house, the materials will be paid equally by Lyn, Bob and Stephan, and Lyn (or Bob or Stephan if they work) will be credited $20 an hour unless all three work an equal number of hours.

5. All monthly expenses will be shared equally.

6. This contract may be amended in writing at any time by unanimous consent.

_____   _____
Date   Stephan Valery

_____   _____
Date   Bob Bisell

_____   _____
Date   Lyn Rosenthal

It's easy to determine ownership interests based on the contributions made (or promised) at the time the contact is drafted. It's possible, however, to provide for ownership shares that will fluctuate over time. Obviously, doing this can get complicated. If Stephan, Bob and Lyn want to vary their shares, with Stephan and Bob owning the place to start with and Lyn's share growing as he contributes labor and materials, they could append to their contract a sheet showing all contributions. Such a sheet might look like this when Lyn finished his work:

Sheet 1—Capital Contributions

Nature of Contribution	Date	Value	Contributed by: Stephan	Bob	Lyn
Cash	1/29	$34,000	$17,000	$17,000	
Paint, Roof Supplies	3/10	4,000			$4,000
Wood	3/12	3,500			3,500
Floor Supplies	3/12	3,500			3,500
Labor	3/13–6/15	6,000			6,000
Cash: Hot Tub	7/20	1,500	500	500	500
Totals		$52,500	$17,500	$17,500	$17,500

We cannot overemphasize that the best contracts are simple contracts. For example, round ownership interests off (e.g., 25% and 75%, not 26.328% and 73.672%). Why? Because trying to achieve absolute accuracy—even if such a thing were possible—is usually more trouble than it's worth. If one person puts up a little extra cash or labor, or forks out more money in an emergency, consider the extra contribution a loan to be paid back, either when the house is sold or by the other owner making a similar extra contribution, rather than redrafting the basic agreement. As long as any promissory notes are paid off before the house is sold, this approach is safe and simple.

d. Complicated Contribution Contracts

Our friends Rosemary and Glenna decided that a very detailed contract would be fairer than a rough, general division. Rosemary is a carpenter by trade, and she and Glenna agreed that her carpentry work should be valued at a higher hourly rate than the ordinary labor of either. Here's the contract they drew up. We believe it's more cumbersome than most people need, but for those of you with very tidy minds, we've seen it work very well in several instances.

Detailed Property Agreement

Glenna O'Brien and Rosemary Avila agree as follows:

1. That they will buy the house at 15 Snake Hill Road, Cold Springs Harbor, N.Y., for a total price of $300,000. The initial investment (down payment and closing costs) of $24,987.07, will be contributed by Rosemary. The title to the house will be recorded as Rosemary Avila and Glenna O'Brien as tenants-in-common.

2. They will each pay one-half of the monthly mortgage, tax and homeowner's insurance payments, and will each be responsible for one-half of any costs necessary for maintenance and repairs.

3. They will contribute labor and materials to improve the house. Rosemary's labor—doing skilled carpentry—will be valued at $24 per hour and both Glenna and Rosemary's labor making other house repairs will be valued at $10 per hour; these rates may be raised in the future if both agree. Materials will be valued at their actual cost.

4. They will maintain a ledger marked "Exhibit I - 15 Snake Hill Road Home Owner's Record." This ledger is considered a part of this contract. They will record the following information in the Home Owner's Record:

   a. The $24,987.07 initial contribution made to purchase the house by Rosemary.

   b. Their monthly payments for the mortgage, property taxes and homeowner's insurance.

   c. Rosemary's labor as a carpenter on home improvements valued as stated in clause 3.

   d. Their labor on noncarpentry home improvements valued as stated in clause 3.

   e. All money that they pay for supplies and materials necessary for home improvements.

   f. Any other money that either spends for improvements as long as the expenditure has been approved in advance by the other.

5. Their ownership shares of the house are determined as follows:

   a. The dollar value of all contributions made by either will be separately totaled, using the figures set out in the 15 Snake Hill Road Home Owner's Record.

   b. They may add interest to their investment totals in any amount with the value of those additional contributions increased by 5% per year simple interest. Simple interest will be calculated twice a year (January 1 and July 1), with the interest being added to each person's total investment as of that date.

   c. The total equity interest in the house will be computed by subtracting all mortgages and encumbrances outstanding from the fair market value as of the date of the computation. If they can't agree on the fair market value, each will have the house appraised by choosing a licensed real estate agent familiar with their neighborhood to estimate the market value. The average of the two estimates will be deemed the fair market value of the house.

   d. A fraction will be created. The numerator will be the larger share (as computed in (5a) and (5b), above) and the denominator will be the total amount of both owner's shares. This fraction represents the total equity in the house of the person with the larger share. The person with the smaller share will compute her share by either subtracting the larger share from the number "1," or by also forming a fraction using the steps outlined above.

6. If either does not pay her share of the mortgage, taxes or insurance in a timely manner, the other person may make the payment, and that payment will be treated as a loan to be paid back as soon as possible, but not later than six months, plus interest at the rate of 5% per annum.

7. Either person can terminate this agreement at any time. If this occurs, and both women want to remain in the house and can afford to buy the other out in 90 days, a third party will flip a coin to determine who keeps the house. If only one person wants the house, she will pay the other her share within 90 days. If the person who wants to keep the house is unable to pay the other within 90 days, the other owner will have a similar 90-day opportunity. If neither elects to or is able to purchase the house, the house will be sold and the proceeds divided according to the shares established under clause (5d).

8. [For information on mediation and arbitration as alternative methods of resolving disputes, see Chapter 6.]

_____   _____
Date   Glenna O'Brien

_____   _____
Date   Rosemary Avila

3. When Not All Owners Live in the House

If only some owners live in the house (as often happens when a group invests), those living in the house usually contribute more to the property as a kind of fair rental value to the "partnership"—the group of owners. If this rent doesn't cover the monthly expenses, then each owner (including those living in the house) must pay his or her share of the difference. If the rent exceeds the monthly expenses, the extra payments should be deposited into a bank account and divided among the owners, in proportion to ownership shares, once a year. The amount paid as fair rental value should be adjusted every year or two.

There are other considerations. Those living in the home want low rent-based costs and will resist sale of the house. It is their home, not just an investment. The outside investors might want high rent-based payments, low maintenance and sale for peak profit. Expectations can differ considerably concerning the quality of maintenance and improvement. What happens, for example, when the occupants want to put in a hot tub costing $1,500, of no immediate benefit (but perhaps an expense) to the investors? The potential conflict should be addressed in advance in a contract.

Other issues to put in the contract include:

- The set period of time after the purchase in which the house will be sold or the non-occupant investors may withdraw their money and profit.
- The fair rent-based payments to be paid by the occupants. Rental value should be based on a comparable rental market analysis, and not simply on the total of all ordinary monthly payments for mortgages, insurance and taxes, plus something extra for minor repairs. The rental value ought to be adjusted every year or two.
- An understanding that the occupants may improve the premises, but that purely decorative improvements are at their own expense. Necessary improvements and major repairs are usually charged to the entire "partnership."
- The right of the occupant-owners to buy out the nonoccupant-owners at a specific time for the net fair market value. Net fair market value means that expenses such as termite clearances, a broker's fee and loan prepayment penalties are subtracted from the appraised value.

Let's assume that Violet Clarke and Teresa Conroy are lovers who want to buy a little island of peace. Their friend Melanie Stuart has some money, is looking for an investment and wants to help. Their contract is simple and to the point. If Melanie's lover, Janet, wanted to help out too, this contract could easily be modified to provide for four owners.

Contract When One Owner Does Not Live on the Premises

We, Violet Clarke, Teresa Conroy and Melanie Stuart agree as follows:

1. We agree to purchase the home known as 21 Island Retreat.

2. We will contribute the following money for the down payment:

Melanie	$10,000
Violet	$5,000
Teresa	$5,000

3. We will own the property in the following proportions: Melanie—50%, Violet—25% and Teresa—25%. If we sell the house, each person will be repaid her initial contribution or a pro rata share if the property has declined in value; then the remaining profit or loss will be divided: Melanie—50%, Violet—25% and Teresa—25%.

4. Violet and Teresa will live on the property and will contribute $750 per month for the first two years. At the end of two years, we will decide what is a fair rent-based contribution, taking into consideration that Violet and Teresa do all the work necessary to maintain and manage the property.

5. Mortgage payments, insurance and taxes total $695 per month. These expenses will be paid from Violet and Teresa's contribution. Violet and Teresa will be responsible for all maintenance and repair costs.

6. We will sell the house within five years unless we unanimously agree in writing to keep it longer. If at any time after two years and before five years Violet and Teresa desire to purchase Melanie's share, they may do so at the fair market value of Melanie's interest.

7. Mediation—Arbitration clause. (See Chapter 6, Section C.3.)

8. Moving-on clause. (See Section E.5, below.)

9. If one of us isn't able to make a timely payment, then either one or both of the other women may make the payment, and the payment will be considered a loan at 10% interest to be paid back within six months.

10. If any one of us dies and doesn't leave her share to the other owners, the survivors have the right to purchase that share from her estate. The value of that share will be the initial down payment plus an increase of 3% per year (simple interest). The surviving owners may buy this share with no down payment and pay the estate over a ten-year period, including interest of 10% per year on the share.

11. This agreement is binding on our heirs, executors, administrators, successors and assigns.

_____   _____
Date   Violet Clarke

_____   _____
Date   Teresa Conroy

_____   _____
Date   Melanie Stuart

Another example of group ownership is provided by Sarah, Guy and Millet. They bought a duplex together with the understanding that Sarah and her children would live in one half and Guy would live in the other half. Millet joined the venture to invest some money and aid her friends. Here's their contract:

Another Contract (When Not Everyone Lives on the Premises)

We, Sarah Wren, Guy Wright and Millet Victor, on _____, 20__, agree to enter into a joint venture as follows:

1. Purpose: The purpose of the joint venture is to purchase the property known as 1 Lake Front, Jefferson, Iowa.

2. Duration: The joint venture will commence this day and will continue until dissolved by mutual agreement or sale of the property.

3. Contributions: The parties will make the following contributions, which will be known as their Capital Contribution:

Guy Wright	$20,000
Sarah Wren	$12,000
Millet Victor	$8,000

4. Responsibility for Loans: In addition to the Capital Contribution, the parties agree to be responsible for the loans and mortgages as follows:

   a. Sarah will be responsible for 50% of all payments due to The Jean Mortgage Company.

   b. Guy will be responsible for 50% of all mortgage payments due to The Jean Mortgage Company.

   c. Millet will have no additional responsibility beyond her initial capital contribution.

5. Mortgages: If at any time Sarah or Guy cannot make her or his half of a mortgage payment in a timely manner, one or both of the other parties, at their option, may make the payment in order to keep the property from being foreclosed. The person(s) making the payment will be repaid within six months, with 10% annual interest.

6. Rights and Duties of the Parties: Guy has the right to live in the upper unit of the building or to rent it out at whatever rate he may choose. If he rents it out, he remains responsible for 50% of The Jean Mortgage Company payment, and, in either case, he's responsible for all repairs and maintenance of the upper unit.

   Sarah has the right to live in the lower unit of the building or to rent it out in whole or part at whatever rate she may choose. If she rents it out, she remains responsible for 50% of The Jean Mortgage Company payment, and, in either case, she's responsible for all repairs and maintenance of the lower unit.

   Millet isn't responsible for any payments beyond her initial Capital Contribution.

7. Repairs: Either Guy or Sarah may need to make extensive repairs to the building. The cost of major repairs (like the roof or boiler) will be divided evenly between them. If either wants to improve her or his unit, either may do so under the following rule:

   • Any repairs or additions costing more than one thousand dollars ($1,000) will be considered a capital investment, credited to the party's Capital Account and paid back upon sale of the building.

   • Repairs or additions above $1,000 must be approved by Sarah, Guy and Millet in writing if they are to be paid back.

8. Forced Payments: If Guy or Sarah can't make a payment in a timely manner, then the other may make that payment for them, and the payment will be considered a loan at the highest interest rate allowed by law, to be paid back in six months.

9. Shares: Sarah will own 30% of the property, Guy will own 50% and Millet will own 20%.

10. Profit and Loss: Upon the sale of the building, the respective capital investments, reflected by the Capital Account, will first be returned to the parties. The remaining profit or loss will be distributed as follows: Sarah 30%; Guy 50%; Millet 20%.

11. Regular books will be kept that are open to inspection by all parties upon reasonable notice.

12. Time: Sarah, Guy and Millet agree to hold the property for five years; no sale or encumbrance will be made without unanimous consent. At the end of five years, any one of the parties may request a sale of her or his share by giving four months written notice.

13. Election to Keep Building or Sell: If the venture is dissolved due to the death, withdrawal or other act of any party before the expiration of the five years, the remaining parties may continue to own the building. If the remaining owners so elect, they will have the right to purchase the interest of the other person in the building by paying to such person, or the legal representatives of such person, the value of such interest as follows:

    Appointment of Appraisers. The parties desiring to continue ownership will appoint one appraiser; the withdrawing person or the legal representative of a deceased or incapacitated person will appoint a second appraiser. The appraisers will determine the value of the assets and liabilities of the venture, and the parties desiring to continue ownership will pay to the other, or the representative, his or her capital investment plus the share (as set out in clause 9 above) of the gain or loss of the venture. The withdrawing person or the legal representative will execute the documents necessary to convey such person's interest in the venture to the other parties.

    Additional Appraiser in Event of Disagreement. In the event the appraisers cannot agree on the value of the venture within 15 days after their appointment, they will designate an additional appraiser whose appraisal will be binding on all parties. If any selected appraiser becomes unable or unwilling to serve, the person(s) originally selecting him or her shall appoint a substitute. In the event the two appraisers first appointed cannot agree on a third appraiser, such appraiser will be appointed by the director of the _____ (e.g., local gay rights organization).

    Rights and Obligations of Continuing Parties. The parties continuing the venture will assume all of the existing obligations and will indemnify the withdrawing party against all liability.

14. Dissolution: In the event that all parties agree to dissolve the venture, the building will be sold, the debts paid and the surplus divided among the parties in accordance with their interests as set out in clause 9.

15. Amendments: This agreement may be amended at any time in writing by unanimous agreement.

_____   _____
Date   Sarah Wren

_____   _____
Date   Guy Wright

_____   _____
Date   Millet Victor

In the last two contracts, the owners agreed that the persons not living in the house shouldn't be responsible for maintenance and repairs. Often, the nonoccupant wants to limit her or his liability. A simple method for this is clause 4c, above, in Sarah, Guy and Millet's contract, where Millet isn't obligated to make any payments beyond her initial capital contribution.

Although this is binding between the three partners, if a new roof is added, and Sarah and Guy fail to pay the roofer, the roofer could sue Millet. To insure that Millet wouldn't have to pay the roofer, or face any other liability on the basis of another partner's acts, they could form a limited partnership.

A limited partnership is a special type of legal animal. Specific state laws and registration procedures must be followed to create a valid limited partnership. Each investor is called a "partner." The ones with limited liability are called "limited partners." The partners fully liable are called "general partners." A disadvantage is that a limited partnership is a legal entity of its own, and, requires a tax number and a tax accounting each year. Another disadvantage is that limited partners cannot claim some of the tax deductions general partners can claim. This may be reason enough not to form a limited partnership. But a limited partnership is an excellent idea if one investor (who cannot have a management role) wants to fully protect herself or himself. The limited partner is liable only for the money she has invested; she's not liable for anything beyond that. To learn more about limited partnerships, see *The Partnership Book*, by Ralph Warner and Denis Clifford (Nolo).

4. When You Move Into a Home Owned by Your Lover

Nate fell in love with Alan and wanted to move in with him. Alan agreed, asking Nate to share the monthly house payments, property taxes, fire insurance and utilities. Nate agreed, "but only if I somehow get to own part of the house." Alan, in the rush of first love, murmured he'd be willing to give Nate half of everything. But he later had some second thoughts and realized he wanted to take things a little slower.

Should You Just Add Your Lover's Name to the Deed?

Like Alan, some lesbians and gay men who own their own houses are tempted to put the deed into joint tenancy with their lovers when their lovers move in. This assures that the lover will get the house if the original owner dies.

But it's not always wise. By putting the house in joint tenancy, you in effect have just made a gift of one-half of it to your lover. Not only might you owe gift taxes or reduce your exemption from inheritance taxes, but if you later split up, you will have no right to have the house deeded back to you. It makes more sense for you to keep the house in your name and make a will or living trust leaving the house to your lover. Then, if you split up, you can change the will or trust.

The other option is for the lover to buy into the house by paying a share of the mortgage payments. Take a look at Nate and Alan's agreement.

Alan's house is worth $220,000; his existing mortgage is $120,000, and so his equity is $100,000. After careful thought, Alan told Nate that if he paid one-half of all the monthly payments and contributed to the ongoing repair costs, it would be fair to turn over some of the equity in the house to him. But Alan still had two serious questions.

- "I already have a $100,000 equity in the house; how can Nate ever hope to accumulate anything more than a negligible share?"
- "I agree it's fair for Nate to have some equity in the house, but how can we work out the details?"

We offered four solutions.

1. The simplest was for Nate to forget buying part of the house and instead pay Alan monthly

rent. With this alternative, Nate's rent should be considerably less than one-half the mortgage, tax and insurance because Nate would be getting no equity. A fair rent could be determined by ascertaining the rent for a portion of similar homes in the neighborhood. Alan might also agree that if the relationship faltered, he'd pay Nate's relocation costs.

2. Another easy solution would be for Nate to take out a loan or dip into savings to pay Alan $50,000. This is one-half of Alan's equity in the house and Alan could then deed the house to himself and Nate as either "joint tenants" or "tenants-in-common." Nate stood up and emptied his pockets. He had $68, some change and a Swiss army knife, which he said was a significant part of his net worth. Borrowing $50,000 was totally unrealistic.

3. Next we offered a less simple suggestion. The two men could sign a contract where Nate agreed to pay one-half (or all, or any other fraction) of the monthly mortgage, tax and insurance in exchange for a share of the equity in the house equal to the percentage his total principal payments plus capital investment bear to the total amount of money in-vested in the house by both men, with Alan starting out with credit for the $100,000 in equity to date. Sounds complicated? Well, it's really not that difficult to understand.

After one year of principal payments and improvement totalling $7,000 each, Alan would own ($107,000/$114,000) x 100 or 94% and Nate, ($7,000/$114,000) x 100 or 6%.

4. Our final suggestion was that Alan sell Nate one-half of the house—or some other specified percentage—either at the present fair market value or at some discounted amount, and take a promissory note for the payment with a favorable interest rate. Remember that there is no law against being generous to your partner when setting the buy-in price and interest rate, although the IRS can treat your generosity as a taxable gift if you set the price and interest rate extremely low. The note would be paid in full when the house was sold or refinanced. This method is generous to Nate because he'd be getting the advantage of ownership (tax advantages and market-caused value increases) with no money down. But the simplicity appealed to both, and that's what they did. Here's the agreement they prepared:

Selling a Share of Your House to Your Lover

We, Alan Zoloff and Nate Nichols, agree as follows:

1. Alan now owns the house at 1919 Church Street, Seattle, Washington, subject to a mortgage for $120,000.

2. The present value of the home is $220,000.

3. Alan hereby sells one-half of the home to Nate for $110,000 and retains a one-half interest in the house, also valued at $110,000.

4. The $110,000 will be paid by Nate as follows:

    * $60,000: Nate agrees to assume responsibility for one-half of the $120,000 mortgage and to pay one-half of the monthly mortgage payments.

    * $50,000: Nate will sign a note to Alan for $50,000 plus 5% (simple) interest per year to be paid in full when the house is sold. If Nate so chooses, he can pay any amount in principal or interest at any time, thereby reducing the amount of his debt.

5. All other costs for the home, including taxes, insurance, utilities, repairs and maintenance will be divided evenly.

6. When the house is sold, after all other costs are paid, the remaining proceeds will be divided evenly between Nate and Alan. Nate will pay Alan all sums due to Alan out of Nate's share. If Nate's share is less than what he owes Alan, the debt will be forgiven.

[Other clauses, such as including separation provisions, arbitration clauses, and the like should be included.]

_____   _____
Date   Alan Zoloff

_____   _____
Date   Nate Nichols

5. Moving On

Relationships can end. Planning for this in advance is always wise. If you don't, and a person wants to move and sell her share, the household could be forced to sell and move out. Problems can also develop for the person wanting to move. If she's required by the agreement to continue to pay some expenses after moving out because she can't find a buyer, she may become a prisoner in the house and quite bitter. While the details of separating are covered in Chapter 9, now is the time to do some preventive planning.

Here's a clause to cover the contingency of one person moving on. Include it in the original contract, as an amendment to the original contract, or as its own "moving on" contract.

Sample Moving On Clause

If one owner moves out of the house, he remains responsible for his share of the mortgage, taxes and insurance. He may rent his quarters with the approval (which won't be unreasonably withheld) of the rest of the household. The remaining owners have the first right to rent the quarters themselves or assume the cost if they so choose at a fair market value. The remainder of the house owners must rent the quarters themselves or assume the cost if they reject at least three people the owner moving out proposes as renters.

At the end of two years following the owner's moving out, that owner will have the right to sell his share to the remaining owners or to a new person completely, subject to the approval (which won't be unreasonably withheld) of the remaining owners.

Heterosexual Marriages: The Aftermath

Many lesbians and gay men have been married and become parents. These marriages often end dramatically—sometimes with bitterness, sometimes with real understanding. We have no statistics on the number of lesbians and gay men who have married and divorced, but the number is certainly large. The great variety of experiences makes it hard to generalize about lesbians, gay men and their heterosexual marriages.

The development of a lesbian or gay identity and the emotional consequence that "coming out" can have for spouses and children have been rich subjects for contemporary novelists. But, as is often the case, writers are hardly two exclamation points and a question mark ahead of lawyers, and many lesbians and gay men have watched their dreams of a new and free life unravel in courtrooms. Even people who have not been dragged into the legal arena realistically fear the possibility. We're regularly asked questions like these:

- Can my ex-husband get custody of the children if he learns I am a lesbian?
- My ex-wife says I can't have my lover with me when I take our boy for a weekend. Does she have that power?
- Is it okay to live with my new lover while I am getting divorced?
- My husband knows I am a lesbian. What should I tell my lawyer—and the judge?
- Will my being gay make a difference when it comes to dividing property or deciding on alimony?
- Can I just take the kids and move from this crazy place?

The purpose of this chapter is to discuss what happens legally when a marriage breaks up and one spouse is lesbian or gay. The rules governing divorce, child support, alimony, custody and property division are the same for gays and lesbians as for straights, but it is essential to examine them from a lesbian and gay perspective. Our goal is to help you to understand the legal risks and consequences of your actions so you can effectively enforce your rights.

A. A Good Divorce—As Precious As a Good Marriage

Egos are commonly bruised when a couple splits up, but when the split occurs because one partner has a new sexual identity, bruises can quickly turn into fractures. We don't have any magic formula to dispense with the pain and anger, but we do know three ingredients that are bound to help.

- Be as sensitive as possible to the feelings and needs of your (ex) mate.
- Avoid going to court if at all possible.
- Even if you're sure that avoiding court is hopeless, try again and keep trying.

Even if you're not in a mood to be sensitive, do your utmost to stay out of court. A court battle is almost certain to be emotionally draining, costly and unpredictable, even if you're lucky enough to appear before a nonhomophobic judge—which, it doesn't take a genius to know, is no sure thing.

Arguing over the kids (who gets custody and who pays child support), the property and the debts is almost always part of ending a marriage. It is not, however, sufficient reason to hire an attorney and run off to court. Most people simply need to argue as they separate. Even if you have nothing major to argue about, you may still argue about who gets the couch or the antique lamp. When a newly identified lesbian or gay spouse ends a marriage, there's ready focus for the other spouse's pain.

If you have real disputes about money and property, fighting about them in court only decreases what's left to divide. Seeing a therapist, involving yourself with a gay, lesbian or bisexual support group, engaging in mediation or arbitration or even moving ten miles away can be more effective ways of handling serious disputes than battling them out in court.

Compromise does not require capitulation. Leaving a marriage and giving up everything—especially custody of or visitation with your children—is rash and unwise, regardless of the reason. The joy of moving on, the fear of public disclosure of your sexual orientation or the desire to be rid of the past is no reason to stop parenting your children or give up your share of the property you accumulated while married. You don't want to spend months or years trying to obtain custody, support or property that you impulsively abandoned. Getting out of a heterosexual relationship shouldn't require that much drama.

1. Getting a Divorce

The fact that you are lesbian or gay may not be significant in obtaining a divorce. In every state, a divorce based on either separation or "no fault" is available. In a no-fault divorce, a spouse simply alleges "an irretrievable breakdown of the marriage," "incompatibility" or "irreconcilable differences." A separation-based divorce requires that the spouses live apart for six months to a few years before divorcing.

States have adopted separation-based and no-fault divorces in recognition of the fact that a courtroom is not the place to review what happened in a marriage, and that it is both wasteful and degrading for spouses to allege and prove petty wrongs, un-

fulfilled expectations or betrayals. This isn't to deny that moral wrongs may have been committed—only that the courts have sensibly left them to be worked out by other forces. All that is legally important is that the marriage no longer works and at least one partner wants out. In a separation-based divorce, no matter how much the other insists on staying married, he can't force it. The same is true in most states in a no-fault divorce.

Although every state has either separation-based or no-fault divorce, over half the states still permit divorces based on traditional fault grounds as well, such as adultery, mental cruelty or abandonment. This is the reason we say that your sexual orientation *may not* be significant in obtaining a divorce. If you and your spouse are in one of those states and your spouse is so inclined, he or she could request a fault divorce—most likely asserting that you've treated him or her with mental cruelty or have committed adultery with a new lover.

Bear in mind one thing, however: No matter what type of divorce is obtained, "fault" (homosexuality or any other) may be raised in a child custody or visitation dispute.

Grounds for Divorce

The grounds for divorce are the legal reasons a spouse (or the couple) must give to request a divorce.

State	Fault Grounds	No-fault Grounds	Separation	Length of Separation
Alabama	•	•	•	2 years
Alaska	•	•		
Arizona		•		
Arkansas	•		•	18 months
California		•		
Colorado		•		
Connecticut	•	•	•	18 months
Delaware		•	•	6 months
District of Columbia	•		•	6 months
Florida		•		
Georgia	•	•		
Hawaii		•	•	2 years
Idaho	•	•	•	5 years
Illinois	•	•	•	2 years
Indiana		•		
Iowa		•		
Kansas	•	•		
Kentucky		•		
Louisiana	•		•	180 days
Maine	•	•		
Maryland	•		•	1 year
Massachusetts	•	•		
Michigan		•		
Minnesota		•		
Mississippi	•	•		
Missouri		•		
Montana		•	•	180 days
Nebraska	•			
Nevada		•	•	1 year
New Hampshire	•		•	
New Jersey	•		•	18 months
New Mexico	•	•		
New York	•		•	1 year
North Carolina	•		•	1 year
North Dakota	•	•	•	2 years
Ohio	•	•	•	1 year
Oklahoma	•	•		
Oregon	•			
Pennsylvania	•	•	•	2 years
Rhode Island	•	•	•	3 years
South Carolina	•		•	1 year
South Dakota	•	•		
Tennessee	•	•	•	2 years
Texas	•	•	•	3 years
Utah	•	•	•	3 years
Vermont	•		•	6 months
Virginia	•		•	1 year
Washington		•		
West Virginia	•	•	•	1 year
Wisconsin		•	•	1 year
Wyoming		•		

2. Dividing Your Property and Debts

If your marriage has lasted long enough for the wedding presents to tarnish or find their way to the back of the closet, you and your spouse have probably accumulated both property and debts. Property includes real estate, furniture, artwork, stereo equipment, cameras, jewelry, cars, RVs, savings, checking and money market accounts, CDs, patents, royalties, stocks, bonds, income tax refunds, money owed to you by other people, retirement funds and pensions, vacation pay, a business and everything else you can think of.

How a court would divide the property accumulated and allocate the debts incurred during your marriage depends on where you live. Arizona, California, Idaho, Louisiana, Nevada, New Mexico, Texas, Washington and Wisconsin follow community property rules. All other states follow equitable distribution principles. Under both systems, property acquired during marriage (except gifts and inheritances) is basically divided equally.

Regardless of your state's laws, you and your spouse may divide your property however you want. For help in dividing your property fairly and without incurring substantial professional fees—lawyers, accountants, appraisers and the like—we highly recommend *Divorce and Money: How to Make the Best Financial Decisions During Divorce*, by Violet Woodhouse, with Dale Fetherling (Nolo).

3. Paying or Receiving Alimony

Alimony is the money paid by one ex-spouse to the other for support following a divorce. Some states call alimony spousal support or maintenance.

Few divorced spouses pay or receive alimony. This is largely because both men and women routinely work. Indeed, when younger couples break up, and both work outside the home, alimony is rarely granted or requested.

This doesn't mean that alimony is dead. For many couples, where one spouse earned the money while the other raised the children, alimony is still necessary—at least until the children enter school full-time or the non-wage earner develops skills necessary to enter (or re-enter) the work force.

"Fault" Considerations When Dividing Property and Awarding Alimony

If a court finds you "at fault" in ending the marriage, you might be awarded less than your share of the marital property or be awarded less (or ordered to pay more) alimony. But this is not a universal rule.

And even if your state no longer permits fault divorces, fault might influence the marital property division or alimony award. Divorce statutes generally give courts discretion to consider "all factors," and as a practical matter, fault issues may influence judges' decisions.

If alimony is granted, it usually terminates after a set period of time, on the death of the recipient or on the remarriage of the recipient. The majority of states have extended this principal to cases of cohabitation—that is, when the alimony recipient begins living with someone. And a growing number of states have applied these cohabiting laws to same-sex relationships. The legislatures in Delaware, Georgia and North Carolina have modified their cohabiting statutes so that they now explicitly state that alimony will terminate if the person receiving alimony regularly resides with either a heterosexual or homosexual partner. Other states have not changed the wording of the law in the books, but judges have interpreted those heterosexual cohabiting laws to apply to alimony recipients in homosexual relationships.

4. Cooperating in Your Divorce

It's possible to cooperate with your spouse in obtaining a divorce, even if your state has fault divorces. Many people make decisions about children, support and property in a spirit of common sense and compromise rather than "who is more right." As the saying goes, "Being right is the consolation prize of life."

If your state considers "fault" in dividing property, and you've accumulated a lot of property and are having difficulty dividing it, reconcile yourself to a long court struggle and start saving money for lawyer's fees. And realize that if you're the higher—or only—wage earner during the marriage, you may be ordered to pay your spouse's lawyer's fees too. If, on the other hand, you've agreed on a plan for dividing your property, congratulate yourselves. Then put your agreement in writing. You will want to use *Divorce and Money* to finalize matters. Below is a sample temporary agreement to help you begin.

Separation Agreement

Herb and Carol Fitzroy agree as follows:

1. They have decided to separate and no longer plan to live together.

2. Their children, John age 7 and Phillip age 4, will live with Carol; Herb will visit and babysit as much as his job allows—at least two nights and one weekend day per week.

3. Herb will pay temporary child support to Carol in the amount of $600 per month. We will increase the amount, if necessary, to comply with our state's child support requirements. But if this amount exceeds the state's child support requirements, we will not decrease the amount. That is, Herb will pay at least $600 per month.

4. Neither Herb nor Carol plan to marry again immediately, and they clearly understand and accept that both will have friendships that may involve sexual relationships with people of the same or opposite sex.

5. Herb and Carol will cooperate in getting an amicable divorce, and neither will attempt to influence the court's decision by raising the point that the other is having a sexual relationship, or living, with a person of the same or opposite sex.

_____ _____
Date   Carol Fitzroy

_____ _____
Date   Herb Fitzroy

This agreement is valid to the extent Carol and Herb follow it. Parents generally are free to make custody arrangements as they see fit. And as long as the noncustodial parent pays child support in compliance with the state guidelines, usually a court won't interfere. But if either Carol or Herb no longer wants to follow its terms—particularly with respect to the custody arrangement—the agreement has little teeth. As we explain below, if a court is asked to make a custody decision, it must decide what's in the "best interests of the child." Still, an amicable agreement is a valuable reminder that you both want to avoid a court battle. And, if you find yourself in court with your spouse complaining that you are gay or lesbian, a judge might give the agreement considerable weight. She's likely to ask, "If you didn't object to her (or his) sexual orientation the day you signed the agreement, why are you objecting to it now?"

B. Child Custody

Child custody is the issue that presents the biggest problem or potential problem for a lesbian or gay person going through a divorce. If you and your spouse agree on custody, the court will almost certainly accept your arrangement with no questions asked. On the other hand, if you can't agree, and you leave the question to the judge, he must consider all factors and arrive at a decision that is in the "best interests of the child." This means that anything relating to your life, sexual identity and behavior can be raised in court.

Custody is generally of two types—physical and legal. Physical custody is the right to have the child live with you; legal custody is your right to make the important decisions about your child—such as where to make the home, what school to attend, what doctor to use and what medical treatment to seek. Visitation, discussed later in this chapter, is the right of the parent without physical custody to spend time with the child. Physical and legal custody may be sole or joint.

Joint physical custody works well when the parents get along amicably and are equally dedicated to raising their children. Joint doesn't necessarily mean 50-50; you can divide the time in any percentage that works for you. If you're a mother who doesn't want to share custody with your children's father, bear in mind that studies show that fathers are especially likely to support and maintain close relationships with their children when they see their children with frequency. A common criticism of joint custody, however, is that arguments between the parents can drag on.

Joint custody isn't for everyone. If you want help in exploring it and other possible custody arrangements, let us suggest mediation. In most states, courts can order parents to attend mediation sessions any time they can't agree on custody (or visitation). Even if a court doesn't order it, mediation is an excellent idea. Mediators work with parents to help them come to a mutually agreeable solution. Mediators, unlike judges, don't impose decisions on parents. To locate a mediator, contact your local family or domestic relations court or look in the Yellow Pages under "Mediators."

To learn more about child custody mediation, see Child Custody: Building Parenting Agreements That Work, *by Mimi E. Lyster (Nolo).*

While few courts refuse to grant joint legal custody so that both parents have a say in how their children are raised, we don't need to tell you that a lesbian or gay parent faces a difficult struggle trying to gain physical custody in many American courtrooms. And that battle is even more difficult if the parent lives with a lover. Indeed, many gay parents have remained in unfulfilling heterosexual marriages, or have lived secretive, guarded gay lives after separation, out of fear of losing their children.

Still, an increasing number of courts—and even a few state legislatures—have held that a parent's sexual orientation cannot, in and of itself, be grounds for automatic denial of custody. Today, most states require that the party opposing custody by the gay or lesbian parent demonstrate an "adverse effect" before a parent's sexual orientation or involvement in a non-marital relationship can be used to restrict custody (or visitation, discussed in Section C). Ideally, when judges apply this adverse effect test they focus on the individualized behavior of the parent and the effect of that conduct on the child, instead of drawing conclusions based on the parent's "status" as a homosexual. For example, a court in Iowa ignored a father's emphasis on the mother's lesbian relationship and awarded custody to the mother, noting that the father had been financially irresponsible and was prone to violence (*Hodson v. Moore*, 464 N.W.2d 699 (1990)).

In addition, the District of Columbia has a law which states that sexual orientation cannot be a factor in determining child custody.

But it is fair to say that many judges are ignorant about, prejudiced against or suspicious of gay and lesbian parents. In 1998, for example, the Supreme Courts of both Alabama and North Carolina denied a lesbian mother (Alabama) and a gay father (North Carolina) custody of their children for the sole reason that the parents were gay. Similarly, the Supreme Court of Missouri, while holding that "a homosexual parent is not ipso facto unfit for custody of his or her child," managed to deny a lesbian mother custody on the ground of her "misconduct" of living with another woman.

Let us reemphasize our earlier point: Only if you and your spouse cannot reach a compromise either working on your own or with a mediator should you bring a contested custody decision to court. And you may need to appeal your case to one or more appellate courts to obtain justice, if the local trial court is unsympathetic or homophobic.

Of course, a case can be brought to court against both parents' wishes. Consider the case of Sharon Bottoms, the lesbian mother from Virginia who lives with her lover. Sharon's own mother sued her for custody of Sharon's son Tyler. Sharon fought it—even her ex-husband testified on her behalf. Nevertheless, the trial court granted custody of Tyler to his grandmother, holding that a lesbian is presumed to be unfit to have custody of her child if she lives with her lover. National lesbian and gay organizations

helped prepare Sharon's appeal, and she briefly regained custody of her son. Sadly, the Virginia Supreme Court ruled that "active lesbianism practiced in the home" could stigmatize the child, and returned Sharon's son to the custody of her mother.

⚠ **When you first separate, stay with your children if at all possible.** *If you leave to "get your head together," you risk creating a situation where it's easy for a judge to give custody to the parent who's taking care of the kids. Courts don't like to disrupt the status quo, and often put a high value on keeping kids with whomever they've been living with. If you have to get away for a period of time, try to first reach an understanding with your spouse that when you return, the two of you will share custody—and put your agreement in writing.*

1. Contested Custody Cases

If you think there's a serious possibility that you and your spouse will fight in court over custody, it is imperative that you get a sympathetic and knowledgeable lawyer. Don't be shy about bringing your attorney the list of resources we provide below. Regarding yourself, the cautious legal advice is not to live with your lover, and to be very discreet, at least until the court has made a decision. Many judges have an easier time giving a lesbian or gay parent custody if she or he lives alone.

And remember, the standard a judge uses is "the best interest of the child." Contested custody cases are full of uncertainties, not just related to sexual orientation. All issues related to what is in a child's best interest can come up. Your spouse may try to raise all kinds of things—your conviction for possession of hashish in college, your religious differences, your sloppy housekeeping and practically anything else he or she can think of.

The judge will view each allegation with his own standards and prejudices. Some judges will frown on drug convictions no matter how old; others won't. Some judges will be concerned if a parent has unusual religious or political leanings. Many are biased against lesbians and gay men. Others are themselves lesbian or gay. Don't overgeneralize or jump to conclusions. Each judge is different and each case unique.

During the hearing, the judge may want to talk with the children. Each judge handles this differently. Many talk to children they believe are old enough to have a sensible opinion; others never consult kids. Most judges give little weight to the views of children under seven, and give considerable respect to the desires of teenagers. For children between seven and twelve, it usually depends on their maturity. In any event, most judges try to keep brothers and sisters under the same roof unless there's a strong reason not to.

Remember that custody disputes are never truly settled until the child reaches 18. As long as the child is a minor, the court retains power over child custody. Custody decisions can be reopened and changed, if a parent shows change of circumstances and that the status quo is not in the child's best interest. If you hide your sexual orientation during your divorce and your ex-spouse later figures it out, he or she may run back to court claiming a change in circumstance and requesting a change in custody.

2. Gay or Lesbian Parent's Role During the Case

The first step is to get yourself a good support system. Find people or groups concerned with gay or lesbian custody issues. A local lesbian mothers' or gay fathers' group is ideal. You will need a great deal of support if you are going to engage in a court struggle, and no one can give it to you better than folks who have been there. The National Gay and Lesbian Task Force in Washington, D.C., can help you find a local support group. The address and phone number is in Chapter 10, Section C.

Your next step is to get a sympathetic and knowledgeable lawyer—and you do need one. Although we favor people doing their own legal work whenever possible, and are convinced that our laws and procedures can be changed to make it easier for people to represent themselves, a custody battle is not the place to do it. You face an uphill struggle even with a lawyer, and you need someone who knows the local judges and custody laws. It's sad but true—some judges evaluate litigants by the quality of their attorneys.

How do you choose an attorney? If you find a support group, ask around for names of attorneys other gay parents have used. If that doesn't work, we've provided a list of lesbian and gay legal organizations in Chapter 10. Call one for referrals. Get the names of more than one lawyer; call and speak to them before making an appointment. You've got to feel comfortable with the one you hire. If you can't afford an attorney, don't give up. A lawyer might take the case "pro bono"—that is, for free. Also, some lesbian and gay organizations have helped raise funds to pay lawyers representing lesbian mothers and gay fathers in custody battles.

Once you pick a lawyer, work with that person in figuring out exactly what you want, and then to decide what you're willing to settle for. Your strategy is to pursue your wants, and be willing to compromise to obtain what you'll settle for. In court, you'll have to be prepared to persuade a judge why your "wants" are in your children's best interests.

Don't worry about legal technicalities or rules of evidence. That's your lawyer's job. In most custody cases, judges cut through the legal morass to learn the facts and decide what's in the child's best interest. Most judges flatter themselves that they try to be objective. While convincing a judge that your sexual orientation is irrelevant will be an uphill battle, it's possible. The most important point you want to make is that you having custody is in your child's best interest. Never, never, never let the judge think you are just trying to punish your spouse.

As your lawyer begins to do work, so must you. Don't give up day-to-day preparation and decision making. Also, by gathering the facts and doing other legwork, you'll be connected to the case and will save some lawyer's fees. Don't pay your lawyer $200 an hour to do background preparation you can do. What follows is a list of some things you can do to help prepare your case. Discuss these with your lawyer before doing any of them.

- Find stable, respectable people (religious officials are always good) who know your situation and will tell the judge why you should have custody.
- Have stable, respectable people send letters to your lawyer stating that you're a good parent. Your lawyer can try to get these into court.
- Prepare a list for your attorney of friends, relatives, children's teachers or day care workers, neighbors, clergy and anyone else willing to speak on your behalf. Outline what each is prepared to say and who is likely to impress the judge.

Below is a sample letter. It's included to give you an idea of what is needed, not to copy. The letters you get should be personal, focused on your situation and succinct. Judges have quite a bit of paperwork, and may not give much attention to anything more than a page or two.

Sample Letter

May 10, 20—

To Whom It May Concern:

I have been a neighbor of Sandra Welch for six years. I know her family intimately, including her children, Joy and Teresa.

Sandra is a warm, sensitive and dependable person and parent. She is wonderfully patient and loving with her children. Her husband, Frank, never seemed very interested in his children and did not spend much time with them.

Sandra has discussed with me the fact that she and Georgia Conrad are lovers. I have visited their home; it is my observation that they are a very stable and caring couple who provide a warm, loving, clean and nurturing home and environment for the children. The children seem comfortable with both women and in a way act as if they have two mothers. Knowing the family background as I do, I am convinced that they are happier with Sandra than they would be living with Frank.

I am a mother and I happen to be heterosexual. Like many others, I was somewhat surprised to learn that my friend Sandra is a lesbian. It took some getting used to, but I know that it in no way negatively affects her being a good parent. My two children, one boy and one girl, are about the same age as Sandra's. All the kids are in and out of both of our houses all the time and they are very fond of Sandra and Georgia. I have no hesitation about my children being with Sandra and Georgia, and I often leave my children with Sandra when I go out.

I can see no way in which Sandra's sexual identity has adversely affected her children. And I don't see any problem in the future. It's just not related to her being the children's mother.

I would be willing to testify to my observations and beliefs in court if this would be helpful.

Sincerely,

Joyce Johnson

3. Making Your Case a "Political" Statement

Some organizations have urged any lesbian or gay man involved in a custody fight to "politicize" it—that is, take a militant gay rights stand, focus media attention on their struggle and use it to advance lesbian and gay causes. This is a decision only you can make. But you're more likely to succeed by downplaying the political concerns of gay custody than by using them as a rallying cry. Winning custody seems enough of a political statement to us. Maybe we're being overly lawyerly, but in most courts, most of the time, you'll do better if your sexual orientation is not made into a political issue.

There are many arenas for fighting for lesbian and gay rights; a child custody case is usually legally difficult and emotionally traumatic enough without adding the risks that politicization brings. If you know your spouse will raise the issue of your sexual orientation, strategically it is wise for you to bring it up first to eliminate any shock value and to present yourself as open and honest. But that's not the same as holding a press conference.

4. Looking for a Nonhomophobic Court

Parents caught in custody battles often think of moving to a part of the country where judges are likely to have more liberal views. San Francisco can seem like paradise for someone who lives in Oklahoma. Although legally you can take a child to a new state unless a court order prohibits you, a law called the Uniform Child Custody Jurisdiction Act (UCCJA) limits a judge's power to make a custody decision. If you move to San Francisco from Oklahoma and eventually request custody, the San Francisco judge doesn't have the authority (called "jurisdiction") to hear your request, and will send you back to Oklahoma. One purpose of the law is to stop parents from moving about in a search for a court that will grant them custody. The mere presence of a child in a state does not necessarily mean that the state has the power to make a custody rul-

ing. Rather, the law provides that a court can make a custody ruling if (in this order):

- The state was the child's "home state," generally being the state where the child lived at least six months before the custody case was filed in court.
- It's in the best interests of the child that the court make a decision because the child and at least one parent have a significant connection with the state, and there is available in the state "substantial evidence concerning the child's present or future care, protection, training and personal relationships."
- The child is physically present in the state and has been abandoned or needs emergency protection from mistreatment or abuse.
- No other state has authority over the case.

The UCCJA disfavors giving custody to a parent who relocates just to create a home state or significant connections. If you've moved, you'd better be able to convince the judge it was for a better job and therefore a better life for your kids, not to find a more enlightened court.

If you and your spouse both begin custody proceedings but in different states, the court in the state with lower ranking jurisdiction under the UCCJA must stop all proceedings or dismiss the case. In other words, unless you can show a dire emergency, all you'd get for your trip from Tulsa to San Francisco would be a determination that Oklahoma had jurisdiction. You might even get fined. The act provides that a court can order the parent to pay the other's attorney's fees and travel expenses.

If a court in one state has already issued a child custody order, your chance of persuading a court in another state to modify that order is extremely slim. If you took the child out of state in violation of the order, you may be guilty of kidnapping. The UCCJA provides that a court, in declining to hear a custody case, can notify the prosecuting attorney of the original state that the child has been illegally removed. And a federal law called the Parental Kidnapping Prevention Act can be used to prosecute you for kidnapping.

The UCCJA can work for both parents. Although it greatly limits a gay or lesbian parent's power to move to a more favorable state, it also limits the nongay parent's power to take a child to a conservative jurisdiction, hoping to get a custody change because the other parent is gay.

5. Resources for Lesbian and Gay Parents Seeking Custody

If you're involved in a contested custody case, your lawyer will need help. Chapter 10 includes names and addresses of gay and lesbian legal rights groups; contact any one of them or visit their websites for updates to the law.

One particularly useful publication, called *Lesbians and Gay Men Seeking Custody and Visitation: An Overview of the State of the Law*, is available for download from the Lambda Legal Defense and Education Fund website, at http://www.lambdalegal.org.

6. Using Expert Witnesses

One key to winning your case will be the testimony of expert witnesses. Expert witnesses are psychiatrists, case workers, psychologists and other professionals who testify in order to educate judges and juries about issues that require specialized knowledge to decide. Experts are often used in custody cases, and are a must for a gay parent. An expert can evaluate your home environment and testify about your fitness as a parent, your child's health, welfare, relationship to you and relationship to the home environment.

But most important, an expert can educate the judge about lesbian and gay parents in general. Attorneys who regularly try custody cases for lesbian and gay parents say that overcoming myths and misconceptions about homosexuality—particularly that gay people are ill, perverted, abnormal and child molesters, and that their children will be harassed at best and become gay at worst—is the biggest obstacle to winning. Here's where the expert comes in.

However you personally feel about psychologists and the like, courts are frequently impressed by credentialed "experts." It takes the wisdom of Solomon to decide many custody cases, and although few judges publicly admit it, most welcome all the help they can get. An expert lets a judge pass the buck to another "professional" when having to make a difficult decision. Ideally, an expert should testify that:

- You are a well-adjusted, stable and fit parent.
- The children are, or will be, well-adjusted, healthy and happy with you.
- It is in the best interests of the children to live with you.
- Gay and lesbian parents are no less likely than heterosexuals to provide loving, stable homes, and that all studies show that children raised by gay or lesbian parents grow up to be happy, healthy and well-adjusted.
- The children won't be molested or seduced by the gay parent or the parent's friends.
- Gays and lesbians are not promiscuous or unstable.
- Gay people are as "adjusted" and happy as heterosexuals.

An expert should also be able to address issues concerning the children's relationships to their peers and anyone significant to you. In other words, the expert should explain away all the fears the judge may have about homosexuality. Your expert will want to review the extensive positive material published regarding gay and lesbian parents and their children.

Your expert might be countered by an opposing one. Lawyers know that you can find an expert who will support almost any position, provided you have the money. Cross-examining and discrediting an opposing expert is a job for your lawyer, which is another reason why you'll need someone knowledgeable about both custody and lesbian and gay issues.

C. Visitation of Children

Judges have hindered and obstructed gay parents' rights to visit their children with the same coldness and caprice that they have exhibited when denying custody. In general, the problems confronting a lesbian or gay parent in a custody proceeding are the same ones to address in a visitation case.

But there are significant differences too—legal precedent states that a parent may be denied custody simply when it's not in the child's best interest. To deny visitation, however, the court must find that visitation would be actually detrimental to the best interests of the child.

More specifically, before denying (or greatly restricting) a parent's right to see his or her child, the court must find extreme behavior—child abuse, violence, repeated drunkenness or sexual acts in front of the children. Once your spouse learns this, she or he should be much less inclined to fight over visitation; if she or he insists and takes the case to court, you should win.

Our advice to parents worried about visitation is the same that we gave in the custody section—compromise if you can. If you and your spouse agree that you should have visitation, the court will probably give you "reasonable visitation rights" and leave you and your spouse to work out the details. If, however, you're relating so poorly that you cannot agree on when, where and how the visitation will take place, a judge will specifically define visitation rights. For example, a court might make the following order:

> *Herb Fitzroy is awarded the right to visit with John and Phillip Fitzroy every weekend from 10:00 a.m. Saturday to 8:00 p.m. Sunday, plus six weeks during the school vacations, the weeks to be agreed upon by the parties.*

or

> *Carol Fitzroy is awarded the right to visit with her children on the first and third weekends of each month from 5:00 p.m. Friday to 8:00 p.m. Sunday, and for the children's entire summer vacation, on the condition that she pick up the children from, and deliver them to, the home of Herb Fitzroy.*

A judge can impose specific rules on visitation. A noncustodial parent may be required to give the custodial parent 48 hours notice before coming to visit. Or, a court may prohibit the visiting parent from removing the child from the county or the state, or, in rare situations, from the child's own home or the home of a third party. It's common for courts to require that parents with histories of drinking not use alcohol while visiting the children.

But can the court restrain Herb from visiting with his children in the presence of George (the man with whom he lives)? Can the court prohibit the children from spending the night with Herb if George is present? Some courts have said yes; others no. Can a court prohibit a gay father with AIDS from visiting with his children? Because the children are not at risk of contracting AIDS from their father, there's no medical ground for a prohibition. In most cases, visitation has been permitted. But some judges will prohibit visitation, supposedly to "protect" the children. In any of these situations, you will want an expert or two to testify on your behalf. If the court rules against you, especially in the case of a gay father with AIDS, consider appealing—but it's rarely wise to violate the court order.

Once a visitation order is entered, it's enforceable just like any other court order. Parents with custody have been known to refuse to comply with visitation orders, to spite their ex-spouse. Whatever the motive, it's not in the best interests of the children, and it's illegal. A parent violating a court order can be held in contempt of court, fined and even jailed.

D. Child Support

In every state, parents are required to support their children. It makes no difference whether the parent has custody or has been denied visitation, or whether the parents were married when the child was born. Although the amount of child support used to be set by the judge, every state has adopted a formula to establish support. You can certainly agree to an amount more than what the formula produces, but to go below it you will have to convince the judge your child will be adequately supported.

Only legal parents are obligated to support children. Your lover is welcome to pay the bills, but is not required to. Nevertheless, if your lover pays *your* bills, a court may decide that that frees up your money and you need less child support. Or, if you're the payor, the court might decide that your lover's generosity means you have more money to pay child support.

Here are a few examples showing how child support works.

EXAMPLE 1: Toni is a bank president and Mort, a bank guard. After a whirlwind courtship behind the vault, they marry. Before long they have twins. Everything is smooth until Toni goes to a series of bankers' conventions and carries on an affair with Keija, who is also in bank management. Toni finally informs Mort that she and Keija plan to live together. Mort, who has some new romantic notions of his own, is not terribly upset and agrees to Toni having custody, but feels he shouldn't have to pay child support because Toni makes more than he does. Too bad. All parents must support their kids. Toni will be fulfilling her obligation to pay support by virtue of having custody. Mort will be ordered to pay support, though less than he'd be required if Toni did not work outside the home.

EXAMPLE 2: Now Mort has custody. His salary is $20,000 per year and Toni's is $150,000. Toni will be ordered to pay considerable support. She has the ability to do so, and Mort will find it impossible to keep the twins clothed without Toni's help.

EXAMPLE 3: This time, custody is joint and the kids spend roughly half the year with Toni and half with Mort. Mort will have to pay a small amount of support when the kids are with Toni, and Toni will be required to pay a larger amount when the kids are with Mort.

EXAMPLE 4: Now Toni has custody. Keija commonly spends large chunks of her salary on the kids. When combined with Toni's income, the twins are lavishly taken care of. Mort wants his support obligation reduced because of Keija's behavior. But her contributions are voluntary—she has no legal obligation to spend as she does. If Mort asked a court to reduce his support obligation, the court won't unless Mort can convince it that because Keija contributes to the household expenses, Toni now has more disposable income to spend on the twins, and he can pay less.

EXAMPLE 5: Now assume that Mort starts living with Alex and Alex's two kids. Between raising the kids and doing his carpentry work, Alex can barely pay for groceries and Mort finds himself chipping in to help support the family. Before long, he's short of money to send Toni. He asks the court to reduce his child support obligation, explaining that he is helping support Alex's kids, who really need it. Will the judge reduce Mort's support obligation? No. Mort has no legal relationship with Alex's kids and no legal duty to support them.

⚠ **Failure to support is a crime.** *In all states, it is a crime to fail to support your kids, whether you were ever married or not. It also doesn't matter if you've separated, but not yet divorced.*

A parent sometimes tries to avoid paying child support by moving to a different part of the country. Hiding out is hard to do, however, because of laws that connect state and federal governments in their support enforcement efforts. In addition, federal laws make Social Security, IRS and other federal files available to child support enforcement officials. If someone with the ability to work refuses to do so (and therefore claims inability to pay child support), he'll be ordered to pay support anyway. Many judges define "ability to support" to mean "able-bodied," and demand that parents who aren't employed show up in court periodically with lists of potential employers they've contacted.

Must You Pay Child Support When You're Denied Visitation?

Suppose your ex-spouse refuses to comply with court-ordered visitation. Can you retaliate by refusing to pay child support? No. Support and visitation are not intertwined—you must pay support no matter what happens with visitation. A court may grant a reduction, but don't count on it. In addition, you probably can seek reimbursement from the custodial parent for costs incurred in trying to exercise visitation. You must go to court before actually reducing the payments; if you reduce them without court authorization, you may be held in contempt of court under the original support order.

E. After the Divorce

Finally, your marriage is over. You've settled custody, support, visitation and property division. You and your lover are settling down to enjoy your new life. It's nice to be able to forget about courts and lawyers. But bear in mind that questions of custody and child support are never finally settled until the children are adults. Either parent can request the judge to modify custody or child support if the circumstances have significantly changed since the previous order.

EXAMPLE 1: Remember Mort and Toni? Toni (the banker) has custody and Mort (the guard) was ordered to pay $400 a month in child support. After a year, Toni quit her job to go back to school. Can she ask the court to raise the amount of Mort's support? Of course she can ask. Will the court do so? Maybe. If a judge feels her new education will lead to an even better paying job and lifestyle for her kids, he

may increase Mort's support. If her schooling is to learn basket weaving, however, he won't. On the other hand, had Toni been fired and unable to get another high-paying job, the court would almost surely order Mort to pay more.

EXAMPLE 2: At the time of the divorce, Mort made $20,000 a year. He later quit his job and went into sales, eventually earning $100,000 a year. Can Toni ask the court to raise the child support? Yes. Does the court have the power to do so? Yes. Will it? Yes.

EXAMPLE 3: At the time of the divorce, Toni was living with Keija, but the judge never knew this. Later, they moved to a lesbian commune with the kids. Mort asks the court to change custody, claiming that living on the commune is not in the children's best interests. Will he win? Yes, if he can show that the commune is truly detrimental to the children and that he can offer them a good home—or if the judge is biased against lesbian mothers.

There is very little you can do to keep your former spouse from taking you back to court. The best way to avoid or minimize future court hassles is to maintain good communications with your ex. Go more than halfway in the small areas; you'll be in a good position to work out larger ones. If you are unkind and uncooperative, your ex will be too. Be flexible. As incomes go up and down, be ready to adjust, even if it means you pay more or receive less.

If you agree on a change, have the court approve it. It is not difficult to have an agreed-upon child support, visitation or custody change entered as part of a court record. It's especially wise to file your papers with the court if your ex has given you trouble or has a history of "forgetting" or ignoring agreements. If you don't have it approved by the court, at least write it down and sign it. This will give you some protection.

Sample Support Change Agreement

Herb Fitzroy of 27 Apian Way, Spokane, Washington, and Carol Fitzroy of 11 State Street, Yakima, Washington, make the following agreement concerning a change in the amount of child support for their children, John and Phillip:

1. Herb has suffered an attack of hepatitis making it impossible for him to work for nine months; his income has been reduced by 60% because of his inability to work.

2. Herb and Carol want to avoid a court fight and agree to change the amount of support to fit the new circumstances.

3. They agree that commencing July 1, 20__, and continuing until April 1, 20__, the amount of Herb's child support obligation shall be reduced from $600 per month to $240 per month.

4. They further agree that this agreement may be presented to a court with jurisdiction over John and Phillip's child support at any time.

_____ _____
Date   Carol Fitzroy

_____ _____
Date   Herb Fitzroy

Sample Support Change Agreement

Veronica May of 17 Leafy Lane, Palos Verdes, California, and Robert Lee, of 311 Hennepin Drive, Minneapolis, Minnesota, make the following agreement:

1. Because Veronica has received a promotion to chief buyer at Racafrax Department Store and now earns $4,000 per month, it is fair and equitable that she increase the child support she pays Robert for Ricky and Sharon.

2. Therefore they agree to raise child support from $600 per month to $1,000 per month to continue at this new rate indefinitely or until they make a subsequent modification.

3. This agreement may be presented by either party to a court having jurisdiction over this case at any time.

_____ _____
Date   Robert Lee

_____ _____
Date   Veronica May

Going Separate Ways

What if the romance begins to fade, or even worse, the relationship begins to disintegrate? You and your partner may find yourselves living out a drama which can be even more daunting than the recent political struggles for gay marriage: the gay divorce.

The anger and sense of loss which so often accompanies a separation cannot be overcome by *any* law or legal counsel—emotional crises are best addressed through the help of friends, family and therapists. And even though the break-up may, in time, emerge as the best thing that ever happened to you, along the way you will surely have to wade through a crushing morass of emotional and practical obstacles.

On the legal front, however, a dissolution does not have to be such a disaster. If you and your ex can work together rationally to divide up your property and sort through your financial affairs, it's possible to avoid the costs and the heartache of an ugly gay divorce. Because you are not legally married, you don't *have* to use the court system, as heterosexual married couples do. Same-sex couples are exempt from the complex rules of family law, and can break up in private—according to whatever arrangements the two soon-to-be-ex-partners can agree on.

But watch out: If you and your partner are unable to resolve your disputes in an amicable fashion, you may have to make use of the legal system to resolve your property disputes, and this can become a bloody mess. Contrary to most public opinion, there are laws that regulate the dissolutions of unmarried couples, and the court system will be quite willing to take on your problems. But the applicable law is not easy to master and it can be quite hard to implement. Moreover, the lack of codified divorce procedures can make moving on via the court system a very arduous undertaking for same-sex couples.

In order to make sense of the dissolution process and to minimize the likelihood of an ugly gay divorce, therefore, it is vital that you understand a few fundamental legal principles and have a good grasp—ahead of time—of how the legal system generally deals with same-sex dissolutions. Once you have a solid understanding of these underlying concepts, you will be far better equipped to tackle the business of breaking up.

This chapter is divided into three sections. The first section summarizes the relevant law both for married (legally) and for unmarried couples to help you make sense of what you are going through. Section two walks you through the basic stages of a break-up, explaining the procedures and chores you will need to handle to navigate the troubled times. The third section explains how the law applicable to unmarried couples generally deals with most types of property you are likely to fight over. The final section also outlines the delicate and ever-changing rules regarding disputes over your children.

A. Rules of the Game— Married and Unmarried

Even though legal marriage remains out of gay people's reach, it is helpful for couples breaking up to understand how the traditional marriage system works. Having a good grasp of these principles will help you understand how different same-sex dissolutions are, and may actually offer some insight regarding your own dissolution. If you register your civil union in Vermont, Vermont's rules for marital dissolution will apply to you when you split up. And, if same-sex marriage is ever allowed, understanding the rules of marriage and divorce will give you a very good sense of whether or not legal marriage is for you.

Every society has its own rules of marriage and divorce, and ours is no exception. The rules are an odd amalgam of anthropology, social history, economics and law, and no one is quite sure how our rules came to be. Most states in this country base their laws either on Mexican and Spanish law or on English law, depending on where the founders of that state happen to come from. Those laws, in turn, are based in many respects on Roman law, which is vaguely derived from social practices of the Biblical era. But along the way religious practices, social norms and hard economic realities have been intermingled with the legal doctrines. It's a complicated history, but fortunately only a few of the basic principles need to be mastered.

1. Marriage Rules

For most of the past two millennia, marriage has been an odd legal animal. It's a "contract" between two consenting adults—except that unlike most other contracts, neither party ever reads or approves of the contract provisions. These are established by the state, and once the couple says "I do" all the laws of marriage apply automatically. So do the laws of divorce.

The legal rules for married couples (and those in Vermont's registered civil union) can be summarized as follows:

- In most states, only a formal license issued by a state-approved judge or clergyperson can formally sanction a marriage. In addition, about a dozen states allow heterosexual couples to establish their marriage simply by living together for a long period of time and holding themselves out as married. In those "common law" states, the rules of divorce apply to any couple that meets the state's common law marriage standards.

- Once a couple is married, any debt or asset acquired by either spouse during the course of the marriage is likely to be treated as "marital" or "community" property. This means the items will be considered jointly owned in the event of a dissolution—unless the parties signed a pre-nuptial agreement modifying these rules. In most states, something called equitable distribution laws apply, and the judge generally can divide the marital property however he sees fit, though each party is supposed to get a fair share. Arizona, California, Idaho, Louisiana, Nevada, New Mexico, Texas, Washington and Wisconsin have adopted community property rules, which means any assets and debts (other than gifts and inheritances) are divided 50-50.

- If either partner wants to part ways, she or he has to apply to the local court system for a divorce decree. A local judge must grant the request—which is usually done routinely—unless the parties cannot agree on a distribution of their property. Then, the court will divide the property in accordance with the state's particular rules—either 50-50 or "equitably," as the case may be.

- If either party believes that he or she has become financially dependent on the other, or if one partner earns significantly more than the other, the judge can order the higher earner to pay alimony (also called spousal support or maintenance) to the other—sometimes just until the dependent partner can get a job, and in other instances, for as long as the recipient is alive and unmarried.

- If the couple has children, the judge will supervise who has custody, how visits by the noncustodial parent will be arranged, who will pay child support and how much. The courts are expected to make these decisions based upon what is in the best interest of the child.

2. Cohabitation Rules

The rules for unmarried couples who live together, or cohabit—which as of today includes by definition every lesbian or gay couple except those in registered civil unions in Vermont—are totally different from the marriage rules. Even if you have had a glorious celebration and uttered sacred vows of commitment, the state is *not* going to recognize you as a married couple. Only a state-approved marriage or civil union makes you a married couple, and until the laws prohibiting same-sex marriage are lifted, your marriage is in your eyes and your officiant's eyes only.

While the specific rules differ slightly, the basic legal principles which regulate the rights of same-sex couples are fairly consistent from state to state.

- In general, the laws governing married couples do not apply to same-sex couples, except under Vermont's civil union rules.

There is one notable exception. A Washington state appellate court ruled in a case involving the break-up of an unmarried heterosexual couple that because the couple had no written agreement, the trial court should apply the equitable principles set out in the Washington marriage and divorce laws. Local courts in Seattle are now applying this case to same-sex couple break-ups.

- Absent an agreement or an express decision to merge your assets and debts (such as opening a joint account or putting both names on the deed to your home), each partner solely owns his or her assets and debts. Your salary is yours alone, your credit card debts are yours alone and your savings account is yours alone. In some states, this presumption of sole ownership can be overcome only by a written agreement; in many other states, a court may enforce or find an oral or implied agreement to share assets. But proving that such an agreement existed can be very difficult in the absence of written proof.

- Similarly, if an account or asset is in both names, the presumption of joint ownership will be overturned only if one party can prove that an agreement superseded the written document. This is very difficult to do. In addition, joint accounts and assets are generally presumed to be owned 50-50 unless the title document or a separate agreement explicitly states otherwise.

- Unless one partner can prove a clear agreement that the other will provide post-separation support—and some states require a written agreement—neither partner is entitled to alimony. The fact that one of you supported the other one during your relationship or that you signed wills to provide for each other upon death is irrelevant. And even where courts will let you file this sort of claim, proving such a contract is very difficult.

- If you are raising children and you are both legal parents, the issues of custody, visitation and child support will be handled just as they are for straight couples—assuming you can avoid the ire of a homophobic judge. But if only one of you is the legal parent, in most states it is unlikely that the other partner will have any rights or obligations regarding the child.

- Unlike heterosexual divorces, your legal disputes will be handled by the "ordinary business" section of the civil courts in your county, not the family court of domestic relations division. You are likely to be assigned to a regular judge and required to follow standard court rules, as though you were dissolving a business partnership.

Remember: Court action is not mandatory for gay divorces, and court cases can be expensive, time consuming, emotionally draining and unpredictable. For these reasons, alternative dispute resolution methods such as mediation and arbitration can be especially appropriate for same-sex dissolutions. With mediation, you and your soon-to-be ex meet with a professional (such as a therapist or an attorney) to work out your differences in a mutually cooperative fashion. The mediator can suggest solutions, but cannot impose them. Arbitration is more like a trial, except that it is far more informal and generally there is no right to an appeal. The decision-maker is usually an attorney or a retired judge, and the parties can present their "case" without attorneys.

Try to be fair! *It's essential to remember that but for a ban on same-sex marriage, you probably would have gotten married and thus be subject to the family law rules. It's equally important to remind yourself that the person you are now fighting with is someone you once loved. Give some consideration to what the law would require of you if you had gotten married, be honest about the agreements you made (and didn't make) with each other, and please make every possible effort to reach compromises and resolve your dissolution conflicts in a fair and considerate manner. Fighting for every last dollar will only cost both of you more money and create more pain for you—and everyone else around you—and will only enrich lawyers.*

B. Stages of Separation

There are two different ways of analyzing the break-up process: by following the chronological course of a typical dissolution or by looking at how to make decisions concerning specific items of property. This section explains the timeline approach; the item-by-item discussion is covered in Section C, below.

1. Thinking About Breaking Up

If you are the one initiating the dissolution or you sense that the sky is growing cloudy, it is essential that you take some predissolution precautions. Here is a handy list of the tasks you should be attending to:

- Locate the critical documents of your joint financial lives; make copies and store them in a safe place. These documents include bank records, property deeds, business records, insurance policies and credit card account information. Don't be ignorant of the framework of your economic infrastructure.

- Give serious thought about how to secure particularly valuable items of personal property. If you own precious art or have acquired irreplaceable family heirlooms, store them with a friend or be prepared to remove them on a moment's notice.

- Start thinking about who is going to live where. For some couples, living apart for a while is essential for gaining peace of mind as you struggle to iron out the longer term conflicts. If you have a friend or close relative you can stay with for a while, make some preliminary arrangements.

- Learn about laws that might cover specific elements of your lives, particularly if you have children. (See Chapter 10 for information on researching the law.)

- Avoid putting large sums of money into your partner's or a joint account. Consider shutting down joint credit card accounts.

- If you are concerned about domestic violence or extreme antisocial behavior, set up a support system for yourself. You may want to talk with a therapist, trusted friend or family member, or seek the assistance of a gay community center. Whatever you do, make sure your partner isn't the last one to hear the impending bad news.

Your goal is to try to minimize disaster, understanding that it may be impossible to avoid all arenas of conflict. If your relationship is characterized by high-pitched emotions and strong impulsive actions, you may need to move very quickly if the conflicts suddenly explode into the open. Follow that boy (or girl) scout maxim: Be prepared.

2. Immediate Break-Up Tasks

Once the bad news has been declared, or even if you are undergoing an interim "trial" separation, each of you will face a few immediate challenges. While every dissolution presents its own particular hardships, here are a few simple guidelines that should help keep things under control.

- Immediately close any joint accounts and credit cards, and make sure that joint authority is needed to withdraw any joint funds. This may limit your access to some of your own money, but that is far better than having your ex abscond with everything.

- Figure out which bills are essential to pay, such as home insurance or the mortgage payment, and make arrangements to keep these bills current. If necessary, ask a trusted friend or an accountant to coordinate these payments, so you don't lose your house or find yourself uninsured in the midst of a relationship crisis.

- Try to make amicable arrangements for handling payment of the nonurgent bills, but don't get too bent out of shape if you are a few months behind on department store charges.

- Make some reasonable practical decisions about the furniture and personal possessions, but don't feel compelled to sort everything out the moment you break up. Valuable items should be handled with some thought, and it may be necessary to put them into a storage locker for a few months. Spending a few hundred dollars to store disputed valuables safely is far wiser than letting them be destroyed or stolen.

- Reach amicable and realistic decisions about the custody and care of your children, if you have any. Your children's needs should come first. If access to children or child support is at issue, you may need to consult an attorney right away. But try, try, try to work this out between the two of you.

- Try to assess what the longer-range disputes will be and acknowledge that it is okay to agree to disagree if necessary. If you can both acknowledge that certain conflicts remain un-

resolved, and can agree on a method of resolving them, you will both feel far more at ease—and less compelled to sort everything out the day you leave.

- Figure out who is going to live where, and try to put together a written agreement on how you are going to handle the costs and likely legal implications of your short-term housing decisions. If you own a home together, you will need to decide whether the temporarily absent one should pay any portion of the mortgage or insurance costs, and you'll want to make it clear that a temporary departure is not a permanent abandonment of the residence. If you are renters, you may need to decide who is going to stay on the lease and who is entitled to return of the security deposit.

Here's an agreement for handling housing issues:

Agreement Regarding Housing

Adrian Wallace and Chris Urban hereby agree as follows:

1. We have agreed to live apart, effective March 1, 20__.

2. Chris agrees to remain in our apartment, and Adrian agrees to move out no later than March 1, 20__. If Adrian elects to leave any of his personal belongings behind, he will remove them no later than April 1, 20__, at his expense, with three days' prior notice to Chris. Any of Adrian's personal belongings which he does not remove prior to April 1 may be retained by Chris, or may be disposed of by Chris, unless we jointly agree in writing otherwise.

3. Any household-related expenses incurred prior to March 1, 20__, will be split between Adrian and Chris, following the allocation generally followed by us prior to that date. Any household expenses incurred after March 1, 20__, will be the sole responsibility of Chris.

4. [If you are renters] Chris will be solely responsible for any and all rent due after March 1, 20__. The security deposit in the sum of $1,000 will be retained by Chris, in exchange for his agreeing to pay the utility bills, telephone bills and insurance after March 1, 20__.

4. [If you are homeowners] Effective March 1, 20__, Chris will pay all monthly bills for the residence, including the mortgage, the insurance and all utilities and related expenses, since he will be living in the residence. The property taxes and all necessary repairs will be split by Adrian and Chris equally. However, as long as Adrian continues to pay his share of these expenses, Adrian shall be entitled to half of any increase in property values between March 1, 20__, and the time it is sold. Adrian and Chris each agree to make a good faith effort to promptly resolve the issue of long-term ownership of the residence. Unless an agreement is reached by December 31, 20__, or we agree jointly in writing to extend this agreement, the property shall be listed for sale on January 2, 20__, and the proceeds of sale shall be split equally between us. Adrian's agreement to vacate the residence at this time shall not be interpreted as a waiver of his claim to an equal share of the equity, either through a buy-out or a market sale.

5. Any disputes arising out of this agreement shall be submitted first to mediation, with the parties agreeing to meet for no fewer than four meetings in a month's time, with expenses shared equally. If any disputes remain unresolved after the mediation, the disputes shall be submitted to binding arbitration, with the costs of the arbitration split equally between Adrian and Chris.

_____   _____
Date   Adrian Wallace

_____   _____
Date   Chris Urban

3. Stages of Resolving Disputes

If you can conceptualize the dissolution process as a series of tasks handled over time, you will feel far less overwhelmed by the ordeal. Each particular component may seem daunting, that's true, but if you have the sense that you are making progress along a fairly predictable path, you are less likely to feel defeated and discouraged. Here are the major steps and alternative paths you will need to follow to reach resolution:

1. Agree on what process you will use to resolve your disputes so you can move forward to actually tackle the problems themselves. You have several options to choose from. (These are covered in Section B4, below.) If you agree on a process for resolving your conflicts, write down your agreement so you can move on to tackling the substantive issues. (A sample agreement is at the end of Section B4.)

2. Figure out a realistic pace and timetable for resolving your conflicts. Don't feel compelled to resolve everything in a day, but don't let the process drag on for years. Commit to a schedule of meetings or phone calls, and then make a conscious effort to keep the ball rolling.

3. Make a clear list of what needs to be resolved. Anything that is on either partner's list is by definition a problem needing to be resolved. Be brave enough to face each other and admit that you've got a lot to deal with, and don't argue over what is appropriate to argue over.

4. Gather the facts you will need to resolve your conflicts. For house-related disputes, you may need to get an appraisal or learn how to transfer title. For automobile disputes, you may need to get the car's value (this can be done easily online at http://www.kbb.com, *Kelley Blue Book*'s site) and obtain a form from the state motor vehicles department for transferring ownership. If you have major investments, a visit to a tax consultant may be necessary.

5. Take stock of the likely emotional barriers that may prevent resolution, and work on trying to overcome them. For some couples, this may require counseling or finding a mutual friend who can work with the two of you to

calm your anger. You also may need to locate a "safe place" where you can discuss these problems without increasing the level of hysteria. In some instances, a letter from a lawyer may be needed to pressure a recalcitrant party into meeting from the outset.

6. Evaluate the likely outcomes for each area of dispute. Be realistic about what it could cost to mount a serious battle and compare that to the benefits of compromise. Know your own bottom line, but don't talk of ultimatums.

7. Once you have made significant inroads in your education and planning process, initiate the meetings or discussions. Try face-to-face meetings, telephone calls, letters, or perhaps best of all, email as a mode of communication. Start negotiating, resolve as many issues as you can each session and move on. Continually narrow the issues and eventually you will resolve everything.

8. Document each decision in writing and make sure both of you sign the agreement. A simple exchange of letters or a basic settlement agreement will be sufficient, as long as you itemize your agreement clearly. If a few issues remain unresolved, you can write up what you've agreed to thus far, but make it clear that you're not completely done yet.

9. Last but certainly not least, implement your agreement. For items such as furniture and art objects, it may simply be a matter of hiring a mover. For financial accounts a joint letter to the bank or the stock broker will usually be sufficient. For real estate a more formal set of tasks await you. You may need to work with a broker or an attorney to be sure you fill out the forms correctly. In some places, a hefty tax is charged on real estate transfers, so be sure you allocate who pays any such costs.

4. Methods of Resolving Disputes

As you work toward resolving various issues, you can choose from several different methods to help

Settlement Agreement

Arnie and Stefan agree as follows:

1. In consideration of the promises described in this agreement dated April 1, 20___, Arnie and Stefan have agreed to settle all their disputes arising out of their personal relationship and the co-ownership of their residence in Orlando, Florida.

2. Arnie shall purchase Stefan's interest in their residence for a payment of $40,000, which shall be paid by cashier's check no later than May 15, 20___, and shall assume the existing mortgage of $150,000. Within three days of the payment, Stefan shall sign a quitclaim deed for the property, which he shall deliver to Arnie. Arnie shall pay all costs of the deed transfer and its recordation. Arnie shall be solely responsible for any future loan payments under the existing mortgage, but he shall have no duty to refinance the existing mortgage. All costs relating to the residence incurred after April 1, 20___, shall be the sole responsibility of Arnie.

3. Stefan shall have possession of the Audi automobile currently registered in his name, and Arnie shall have the possession and ownership of the Jeep Cherokee currently in both parties' names. Stefan shall sign the required transfer document for the Jeep, which Arnie shall prepare.

4. All items of shared or co-owned personal property have been distributed by the parties, and any items left remaining in the residence as of the date of this agreement shall be the property of Arnie.

5. If at any time prior to December 31, 20___, Stefan is able to sell the parties' antique music box collection which is currently in his possession, one-half of the proceeds of sale shall be paid to Arnie. However, if Stefan is unable to sell the collection by that date despite his best efforts to do so, he shall pay the sum of $2,500 to Arnie and then Stefan shall be entitled to retain full ownership of the collection, without any further liability to Arnie.

6. Any disputes arising out of this agreement shall be resolved by arbitration, on the written demand of either party. Should this occur, the parties shall jointly select an arbitrator, and if they cannot agree on an arbitrator within one month of a written demand for arbitration, Judge William Bennett of the Superior Court will select the arbitrator.

7. The costs of the arbitration shall be split equally between the parties. If either party wishes to, he may bring an attorney to the hearing, but each party will be solely responsible for any attorneys' fees he incurs. Each party will provide the other one with copies of all documents relevant to this dispute and a list of any and all witnesses, no later than one week prior to the arbitration hearing.

8. The decision of the arbitrator shall be binding on both parties, and either party may enforce the decision through the local Superior Court if necessary. If an attorney is reasonably needed to enforce the decision, the prevailing party shall have the right to seek reimbursement of the attorneys' fees incurred specifically for the enforcement of the arbitrator's decision.

9. Contingent upon the implementation of the provisions of this agreement and the resolution of any disputes which arise in enforcing the terms of this agreement, both parties hereby agree to release each other from any and all claims arising out of or relating to their personal relationship, including any claim for financial compensation or property ownership.

_____   _____
Date   Arnie Cott

_____   _____
Date   Stefan Catahoula

you settle your conflicts. Most couples move among several options, depending on how amicable or how bitter their conflicts are. This section provides short explanation of each process, along with the benefits and burdens of each.

a. Direct Discussions

The easiest and most direct way to resolve your conflicts is to talk them out. Whether you select the face-to-face, written, telephonic or email method, this is likely to be the cheapest and the quickest approach—but only if you follow a few simple tips.

- Schedule your discussions ahead of time, and pick a location and method that ensures privacy, concentration and a calm interchange. Don't talk about heavy topics in the middle of the work day, if at all possible.
- Do your homework ahead of time, and don't be afraid to postpone a discussion if you aren't ready—but only for a few days.
- Keep good notes of your discussions, and memorialize any agreements you reach in letters to each other afterwards.
- Limit your discussions to the practical items, and focus on finding solutions, not allocating blame. Don't view your property disputes as opportunities for resolving the emotional rifts of your dissolution.

b. Third-Party Negotiations/Mediation

If you can't keep focused or can't avoid gut-wrenching psychodramas, you probably will need to ask a third party—or two such third parties—to moderate and structure your conversation. This can be done in several different ways. The major factors to consider in choosing the right approach are cost, time delays, the need for special expertise and available resources. Here are two practical options:

Advocacy negotiation. You each select an advocate or representative, and the two of them communicate with each other, without either of you around.

This kind of shuttle diplomacy is basically what a lawyer would do for you, and if you want to avoid hiring a lawyer, there is nothing wrong with having a trusted (and clear-headed) friend, real estate broker or accountant play this role. The advocates can exchange letters or phone calls, or meet personally, but without either of you present. They convey messages to each of you and eventually you hammer out an agreement. It's a slow process, and if you use attorneys it can get expensive, but it's a calm and rational method of dealing with extremely volatile situations.

Mediation. You meet face-to-face to talk about your disagreements with a neutral mediator working to help you find realistic solutions. You can come to mediation solo or you can each bring an advocate along—either a friend or an attorney, depending on how complex your disagreements are. Mediation can produce fabulous results, and it is far more speedy than a protracted exchanges of letters. The key is having a good mediator and allowing enough time to air the conflicts and find solutions. Most people find that a series of short sessions works best, although sessions as long as four to six hours can be very useful if you have the time and can handle the emotional strain of a day-long session. Select a safe place, be prepared to make decisions quickly and remember to document your settlement in a clear and legally binding written agreement.

While it isn't necessary to have a lawyer with you in a mediation session or to use a lawyer as your negotiator, it is often useful to meet with a lawyer for an hour or so before you commence the mediation or negotiation process. The lawyer can provide you with the basic rules of dissolution for your particular state, and can caution you about any particularly negative aspects of your situation. Choose an attorney who has worked with unmarried couples—gay or straight—so you don't have to pay to educate the lawyer, and come prepared with a detailed outline of the facts and issues about your personal drama.

c. Arbitration

Arbitration is a kind of trial, except it is more informal than courtroom litigation. You submit your dispute to a neutral decision-maker and agree to be bound by the decision. It rarely makes sense to allow either party the right to appeal such a decision. To make arbitration effective, you will need to reach several initial understandings.

- How will you select the arbitrator? You can delegate this to a friend or an attorney, use a local arbitration service that provides a list of arbitrators (with you each having the right to strike proposed arbitrators who seem unfair or unqualified) or jointly pick a person from the outset. The arbitrator doesn't have to be gay, but should be comfortable listening to your stories and rendering a fair decision. If you don't know much about the proposed arbitrator, try to get some references. The arbitrator's fee is split by you and your ex.

- Sign a written agreement stating that you will be bound by the arbitrator's decision, and agree to waive any rights of appeal. In most states, arbitration agreements are enforceable by the local courts, so you can enforce yours in court if your ex doesn't comply with the arbitrator's order.

- Will you give the arbitrator the authority to award attorneys' fees (which could get expensive) and costs to the prevailing party?

- Will you have the right to bring attorneys or advocates with you to the arbitration hearing?

- Will either of you bring any witnesses, and if so, how many?

- Will you have the right to conduct any investigation or obtain any documents before the hearing? If only one of you has access to the real estate or the financial documents, you may need to agree on a "discovery" process as part of your agreement to arbitrate.

- Agree on a rough timetable for bringing your disputes to a conclusion. Even though the precise date of the hearing can't be set until you select your arbitrator, try to get a sense of how many months you will need.

- If at all possible, make a list of the issues which have to be resolved. Acknowledge that some new issues may arise later on, but try to be as specific as you can about what it is you are fighting about. This will help you select your arbitrator and will provide you some assurance that in the end your conflicts will be resolved, one way or another.

Here's a sample agreement for your procedural decisions:

Agreement Re Mediation and Arbitration

Sandy and Erika hereby agree as follows:

1. We have agreed to submit the following disputes to mediation, and if mediation is unsuccessful, to arbitration:

   a. Ownership of our residence in Akron, Ohio, including the disposition of the residence and both our claims for reimbursement for contributions made to the purchase and upkeep of the residence.

   b. Ownership of our two automobiles, including disposition of the automobiles and both our claims for reimbursement for contributions made to the purchase and upkeep of the automobiles

   c. Erika's claim for reimbursement of moneys paid to Oberlin College in connection with Sandy's education there.

   d. Erika's claim for a partial ownership in Sandy's accounting business.

2. We agree to submit these disputes to mediation to a mediator jointly selected by the two of us; however, if no mediator is selected by April 1, 20__, each one of us will nominate one friend, and the two of them shall select the mediator. If no mediator is selected by May 1, 20__, Judge Marilyn Strauss of the Akron Superior Court shall select the mediator.

3. We shall meet no fewer than three times for mediation sessions of two hours' length, within one month of the appointment of the mediator, with all costs of mediation split equally between us. The mediator shall determine the time and place of the mediation.

4. Until such time as an agreement is reached, proposals made by us are nonbinding. If an agreement is reached, it shall be documented in writing and signed by both of us. The evidence and materials presented in mediation shall be confidential, and shall not be disclosed to anyone else or used in any subsequent arbitration.

5. If no settlement is reached and we elect not to schedule any more mediation sessions, either of us may demand arbitration of these disputes. Should this occur, we shall jointly select an arbitrator, and if we cannot agree on an arbitrator within one month of a written demand for arbitration, Judge Strauss will select the arbitrator.

6. The costs of the arbitration shall be split equally between the two of us. If either of us wishes to, she may bring an attorney to the hearing; however, each of us will be solely responsible for any attorneys' fees she incurs. Each one will provide the other one with copies of all documents relevant to this dispute and a list of any and all witnesses, no later than one week prior to the arbitration hearing.

7. The decision of the arbitrator shall be binding on both of us, and either one may enforce the decision through the local Superior Court if necessary. If an attorney is needed to enforce the decision, the prevailing party shall have the right to seek reimbursement of the attorneys' fees incurred specifically for the enforcement of the arbitrator's decision.

_____ _____
Date Sandy Stone

_____ _____
Date Erika Chavez

d. Litigation

If you absolutely can't agree on one or more issues, and can't agree to participate in mediation or arbitration, the courts will be your last resort. This is going to be expensive, ugly, time-consuming and very depressing, so use the courts only when nothing else will work. On the other hand, when nothing else will work, you at least can be assured that the courts *will* resolve your conflicts.

Here are a few basic guidelines.

- Decide whether you can handle the case yourself or whether you will need an attorney by your side. Some attorneys will assist pro per clients on an hourly basis, and others will only help you if they take on the entire case. If you need an attorney, make sure you go with someone whom you can afford and who has experience in this or similar areas of law. The sexual orientation of your attorney is far less important than his competence.

- Even if you will handle your case by yourself, consult for at least an hour with an attorney who has handled same-sex dissolutions to figure out if particular rules or procedures must be followed. Learn whether you need to file any papers immediately, especially if your name isn't on title to property you claim is part yours. Learn whether there are any legal deadlines (statutes of limitations) which apply to your case. And try to get a handle on whether you can afford the time and the likely costs of litigation.

- Try to evaluate how your ex is going to respond to litigation. In some instances, the mere mention of litigation will bring your ex to the bargaining table; in other situations, it will just make her more explosive.

- Be candid with yourself about the public nature of litigation. Bear in mind that by taking your dispute to court you are not only outing yourself and your ex, but you are also going to be laundering the messiest secrets of your lives.

- Learn how litigation works for your particular problems, such as dividing up real estate, allocating joint bank accounts or deciding claims for postseparation support. Try to evaluate how litigation will actually proceed for your particular case: how much pretrial discovery will there be; how will the trial be handled; will there be a jury? The more you know ahead of time the better your decision-making will be.

- Make it clear to your lawyer—and to yourself if you are acting on your own—that while you are initiating litigation out of desperation, you should always remain open to compromise. It is NEVER too late to schedule a mediation session, and you should always remain open to a settlement. A divorce should never become a battle of principles; rather, always look for the opportunity to make a deal and move on. If you are using an attorney and your attorney doesn't share this philosophy, find one who has a more conciliatory approach.

C. Particular Solutions for Particular Problems

Now that you have a solid grasp on the law and the procedures of breaking up, you are ready to survey the particular kinds of issues that most frequently arise in same-sex dissolutions—the distributiuon of assets, and, for some couples, the care of your children. Not surprisingly, these issues are the same as those which arise in most straight divorces. While the law for us may differ in certain respects, the things we fight over when we break up are pretty much the same.

1. Renting Your Home

Renters must decide who is staying and who is moving on (unless you are both leaving), how to deal with your landlord, who gets the security deposit and who will pay any debts that arise in the process. Unless you had an agreement beforehand or only one of you is on the lease, there is no general preference for who gets to keep the place. Therefore, you need to act fairly and rationally.

If one of you lived in the place first or has particular practical needs, you should be the one with the first right to stay where you are. But the departing one should receive some equitable compensation to cover moving costs and perhaps some portion of increased rent in a new location. If the departing person paid some or all of the security deposit, he should be reimbursed. Debts arising out of the lease should be equally split. Once the departing person has left, the remaining tenant should talk with the landlord and have the lease rewritten in his name.

2. Owning Your Home

Life is a bit more complex for those who own their home. If you never signed an agreement setting forth your dissolution process, you have two choices. You can leave it to the court to decide—meaning the court sells the property and divides up the proceeds—or you can reach a settlement.

To work toward a settlement, you will first need to resolve a basic issue—will you sell the place together or will one of you buy out the other? If there's interest on either or both sides to hold on to the place, consider the following

- If both of you want to keep the place, you can (1) flip a coin to see who get first dibs, (2) mediate the disagreement, (3) conduct an informal "auction"—the high bidder gets the house, or (4) submit the dispute to binding arbitration.

- If you agree on who will buy out whom but can't agree on a price, the best way to set the price is to get an appraisal. If you can't agree on an appraiser, you can each get an appraisal and then average the two values. Opinions by brokers are cheaper to come by than appraisals, but less accurate. Keep in mind that an appraised price usually assumes a brokerage fee will be incurred in selling the property; if you won't use a broker in the buy-out, you'll need to reduce the value by the amount of the commission.

- When setting the price, take into account whatever deferred maintenance may be needed to make the place marketable, and subtract those costs from the estimate of value. Then, subtract the remaining mortgage and any other liens—such as an equity loan—from the modified estimate of value, and you'll have the amount of equity. A buy-out generally involves paying the seller her percentage of the equity. Remember there may be other transfer costs as well, so make sure you decide how to allocate those amounts.

- If either of you is claiming reimbursement for excess contributions, binding arbitration is probably the quickest way to resolve the issue if you can't reach an agreement yourselves.

- Find out from a local broker or title company the procedures and costs for doing an internal buy-out. Some states impose hefty transfer taxes or recording fees; you must allocate these expenses between you.

- Get the proper forms and, if necessary, have a professional help you fill them out. Understand what transfer costs there may be, and do what you can to minimize them. You may not need to use a title company or buy title insurance if your transfer is a simple one.

- Even if the buy-out is amicable, write up a simple agreement affirming what you've agreed to. This way you will have a document memorializing your agreement, in case a dispute arises later on.

- Figure your options regarding the mortgage loan. In some states and with some banks, the buyer can retain the existing loan even after a buy-out, and with some loans you can even have the seller's name removed from any liability. In other situations, the buying person must get his own loan, unless the selling partner agrees to stay on the loan—with the buyer giving solid written assurance that the mortgage will get paid each month, so that the seller doesn't get a tarnished credit rating.

If you agree to sell the residence on the market, select a qualified broker who knows you are splitting up. The broker can then handle the delicate arrangements of fixing up and showing the home, knowing that things may be tense at times. You both have an interest in selling the property for the best possible price, so work cooperatively here.

Once you've sold the place, you will have to divide up the proceeds according to your ownership percentages, contributions, rights to reimbursement and the like.

Conflicts about reimbursement and unequal ownership can be very tricky to resolve. If one of you has put in more money up front or during the course of your relationship, or one of you has spent a lot of time renovating your home, you may feel you are entitled to a greater share of the proceeds or some amount of reimbursement. On the other hand, your partner may feel that he or she spent just as much money on other expenses or contributed to the partnership in different ways than you did but that were of equal value. The general rule in most states is that in the absence of a written agreement it's presumed that the property is owned equally, and the one seeking reimbursement or a greater share of the proceeds has the burden of proving an agreement to something other than equal ownership. In most states, contributions to a down payment and to improvements that raise the value of the property are more frequently reimbursed than are excess contributions to ongoing expenses such as mortgage interest or utilities.

Because the law in this area is often so vague and each partner's version of the relationship's history will be so different, reaching a compromise is often the best way to go. It makes no sense to spend a year and $25,000 in legal fees arguing over $30,000 in proceeds, especially if the house is sitting empty and unsold during the year-long fight.

A dispute about the division need not slow up a sale. You can put the sales proceeds into an escrow account with an agreement that the funds will be disbursed only when a settlement agreement signed by both of you or arbitration order resolving your dispute is given to the escrow agent.

3. Other Assets and Debts

If you own other real estate such as an investment property or vacation home, you'll need to go through the same resolution process as with your primary residence. Decide whether one of you will buy out the other or whether you will sell the place on the market. Then figure out the value and claims of reimbursement. You can keep co-owning the property as an investment, and if it's in your mutual best interest and you can agree on its management, by all means do so. But be sure to have a written management agreement for the property—you are business partners now, not lovers, so you need to act in a businesslike manner.

You must also divide up bank accounts, stock accounts and savings accounts. Remember—both names on an account creates a legal presumption that it's owned 50-50, and the one claiming a greater percentage has to prove an enforceable agreement. Try to reach a compromise, and if you can't, consider submitting the dispute to binding arbitration. In the meanwhile, make sure you instruct the bank or stockbroker to hold all the funds safely, to safeguard against either party absconding with all the funds.

If you have joint debts, try to pay them off sooner rather than later to minimize your liability. If the "joint" debts belong to only one of you, you will either need to pay them off or have the debtor obtain new credit in her name alone. Most banks and credit card companies will not remove one person's name just because you are breaking up. If you had an agreement to share assets, the implication is that you share debts as well.

4. Pets

Don't let your emotional turmoil put your pets' well-being at risk. Follow a "best interest of the pet" approach, and find a living arrangement that is really in the animal's best interest. If one of you is getting custody, consider making a financial adjustment (to allow the other party to buy an equivalent new pet) or allow regular visitation.

5. Children

It's sad but true; if you have children, you are likely to face some very difficult challenges. As any heterosexual couple can tell you, divorce is brutal on parents as well as children. One of the only decent features of straight divorces is that the law is fairly clear and quite vigorously enforced—at least regarding custody and visitation. Statutes cover nearly every variety of dispute.

On the other hand, the law can be very unfair to same-sex parents—both as it is written and how it is practiced. Making matters even messier, in many locales the law is changing nearly every year on these issues. Lesbian and gay parents are truly forging revolutionary territory—which is fine when you are in the mood to be a revolutionary, but not necessarily so when all you want to do is spend the day with your child. On top of all this uncertainty, same-sex parents occupy a harsh and highly visible fishbowl in society, watched as experimenters by observers who may not be sympathetic to your situation.

Because of all these pressures, it is vital that you try, try, try to reach a compromise on all child-related issues. Try to reach a resolution through talking together, in therapy or with the help of a mediator—but whatever you do, try to avoid a custody battle whenever possible. If you fail to do so, you will only harm your child in the process, as well as bring on mountains of agony for yourselves. If you can reach a compromise on the issues of legal custody (who makes decisions about the child), physical custody (where the child lives), visitation (how

often and under what conditions the noncustodial parent spends time with the child) and child support (the noncustodial parent's contribution to the costs of raising the child), you will save yourselves—and your kids—a great deal of pain.

And if you can't reach a resolution between yourselves? Then you will have to submit your disputes to the legal system. While the specific rules for child custody and visitation differ from state to state—and are in tremendous flux with regard to gay parents these days—this section provides a summary of the basic rules.

a. If Both of You Are Legal Parents

If both of you are legal parents of the child—either because the nonbiological or nonadoptive parent obtained a legally valid second-parent adoption or because the two of you jointly adopted—any and all child-related disputes should be handled just as they are for any straight divorce. The local family court judge has the power to make all decisions and is supposed to apply the "best interest of the child" standard to all disputes.

In most instances, both legal parents will retain legal custody, which means they each have equal authority over the central decisions in the child's life and each has full legal obligations to care for the child. The issue of physical custody usually will be shared over time, with the child spending some time with one parent and other times with the other parent. In some situations, one parent has primary physical custody and the child spends weekends and holidays with the other parent. In other situations, time is split fairly equally.

In either situation, any parent who doesn't have primary physical custody will be granted liberal visitation rights. Moreover, if incomes are unequal or if one parent is shouldering most of the costs of taking care of the child, the noncustodial parent will be ordered to pay child support. In most states, the family law court generally retains jurisdiction to resolve any future disputes about the child, and any orders or rulings can be revisited if circumstances change. Unfortunately, your property disputes generally won't be resolved by the same judge because you are still an unmarried couple.

b.   If Only One of You Is the Legal Parent

If only one of you is the legal parent, the situation is going to be handled completely differently. Generally speaking, it doesn't matter if the child was the child of one partner before the relationship began and the nonlegal parent never sought (or was never allowed) to obtain a second-parent adoption of the child, or if the couple reared the child since birth, but did not or could not obtain a second-parent adoption or a joint adoption.

Regardless of how the couple finds itself in this situation, the legal predicament can be truly horrific. In most states, the nonlegal parent cannot seek custody—either legal or physical. In some states, the nonlegal parent may be able to request visitation to some limited degree, but this isn't the case in most states. Indeed, by statutes in some states and by judicial practice in other states, nonlegal parents have no rights whatsoever. Nonlegal parents rarely have any financial obligations to their partners' children, although in most contested situations the nonlegal parent would be glad to help out financially, rather than be fenced out altogether.

More than any other area of same-sex family law, this is one arena where you must obtain advice from a skilled and knowledgeable attorney before making any decisions or taking any impulsive action. The law in this area is changing more than in any other area, and the outcome of any particular dispute can depend on which judge hears the case and how the case is disputed. Creative gay and lesbian attorneys are trying all sorts of new angles on this growing problem, and whether or not you choose to use an attorney to help you in your struggle, at a minimum you should be educated on where things stand in your particular state.

If you are facing exclusion from the child you have helped raise, the basic factors in framing your approach—from a legal perspective—are as follows:

- Does your state allow you to present a claim for visitation or partial custody if you are not a legal parent? If so, what procedures must you follow?
- If no such procedures have been established in your state, are you willing to be a "test case" and try to forge new law? Doing so will expose your most personal characteristics— positive and negative—to the brutal scrutiny of lawyers, judges and the public. Make sure you are ready to take this on before you open the door.
- If the law is definitively against you, consider whether you want to try to change the law. If not, you will have to explore more personal approaches, such as mediation or counseling, with your former partner.
- If you are the legal parent and you are facing a custody and visitation challenge from your former partner, make your child's emotional needs—not yours—your highest priority. If you truly believe that your partner was not a primary parent or would be seriously harmful to your child, then resist the claims. But if you are merely trying to avoid ongoing contact with your ex or you can't stand her anymore, these are not valid reasons to deny visitation on a regular basis.

Regardless of how the procedures are unfolding, keep the door open to reaching a resolution by compromise and agreement, rather than by legal decree. In some cases, you can craft an agreement but need to have it approved by a local judge; in other situations, the judge may not accept all the terms of your agreement. Once again, this is one place where a consultation with a local attorney would help enormously.

Here's an example of a typical agreement:

Parenting Agreement

This agreement is made on January 1, 20__, between Ellen Donato (referred to herein as "Ellen") and Charlotte Frieden (referred to herein as "Charlie") of Cincinnati, Ohio, regarding the parenting of the minor child Brenda Sue Donato (referred to herein as "Brenda").

The parties agree as follows:

1. This agreement concerns the parenting of Brenda, who was adopted legally by Ellen on July 15, 19__. Brenda has been raised equally in the home of Ellen and Charlie since her adoption and is equally bonded to both women in mother-child relationships. Even though Ellen is the sole legal parent of Brenda, the parties intend that Brenda shall continue to be raised by both Ellen and Charlie.

2. They shall continue to have Brenda in their physical custody for equal periods of time, and it is in their child's best interests that they continue this equal parenting arrangement. The parties will work cooperatively to make reasonable arrangements for the physical custody of Brenda.

3. Each shall contribute equally to the financial costs of raising Brenda.

4. They each will either maintain their current residences or will reside within twenty (20) miles of the other's current residence until such time as Brenda reaches the age of 18; if either party changes her residence outside of this distance without the other party's written consent, she will lose the right to have Brenda in her custody.

5. Charlie shall have the same rights and obligations to Brenda as if she were her legal parent. Should any dispute arise between the parties, Ellen may not at any time assert that Charlie is not a parent of Brenda or that she has a lesser parental status, by virtue of the lack of legal parentage. Moreover, the parties hereby affirm that it is in Brenda's best interests for her to maintain a parent-child relationship with both of the parties.

6. In the event of any dispute between the parties regarding the custody, care, financial support or upbringing of Brenda, the parties agree to attend mediation sessions in good faith to resolve the dispute. Each party shall willingly participate in at least four weekly mediation sessions, with the cost of the mediation to be shared equally.

7. The District Court of the State of Ohio shall have jurisdiction to resolve all matters regarding the custody, visitation and support of Brenda, and the enforcement of this agreement. Each party agrees to allow the participation of the other in any proceeding to determine the parentage, custody, visitation and/or support of Brenda, without any jurisdictional objection. Neither party will assert as a defense to a court action the lack of a legal parental status or rights of the other party.

8. If any attorney's fees or costs are incurred by either party in a court proceeding regarding the custody, visitation or support of Brenda, the court shall have jurisdiction to award attorney's fees and costs as provided by the relevant sections of this state's family code, even though the proceedings may be in a parentage or other action rather than in a dissolution or separation proceeding.

9. Charlie is hereby nominated by Ellen as the guardian for the person and estate of Brenda, in the event that Ellen becomes unable to care for Brenda, to serve without bond. If Charlie cannot serve as Brenda's guardian, then Ellen's mother Elaine Merritt shall be nominated to serve as guardian.

10. This agreement is the only agreement between the parties with respect to Brenda. It may be waived, altered or modified only with the written consent of both parties. In the event that any part of this agreement is held to be invalid, the remainder of the agreement shall be in full force and effect.

IN WITNESS THEREOF, the parties to this agreement have executed this agreement on the date and year first written above.

_____   _____
Date   Ellen Donato

_____   _____
Date   Charlotte Frieden

⚠ Don't perpetuate discrimination. *If the only reason your partner doesn't have any rights here is because the two of you couldn't get married, then it is wrong—morally if not legally—to deny your partner access to a jointly raised child. Being a flawed person isn't reason to be denied access to your child, and conflicts in your relationship certainly aren't grounds to cut off your ex's contact with your child. It is certainly appropriate to assert that you should be the primary parent, but try to make every effort to reach a compromise about visitation. Battles over the rights of nonlegal parents are destructive to the family and to our entire community, and rarely does anyone benefit from such a battle.*

D. A Few Final Words

Breaking up is hard to do, as everyone well knows. Straight couples have the tightly woven set of divorce rules and the imposing dominance of the family court judge to keep them from doing too much damage to each other. By contrast, our area of the law is much more nebulous. Unless we really insist on it we won't be dealing with courts and judges. Thus, even though legal procedures may be somewhat gray when resolving our disputes, we also have the power to resolve our conflicts between ourselves, without the need for court intervention.

Please accept some wisdom from those who have been through the dissolution process: Compromise, compromise and compromise again. You will only be the happier—and the richer—for it. Spending thousands of dollars on lawyers is rarely in your best interest, and a dissolution is rarely the time to assert yourself emotionally to your ex. Rather, it is the time to cut a deal and move on with your life. Be wary of your own overreactions, and fight the legal battles only if there is a great deal of money at stake or your ex is being truly outrageous. Remember that your ex-lover is someone you once loved and that things are only things. A battle over finances will generally enrich only your lawyers, and rarely will it bring you any degree of happiness or emotional satisfaction. ■

Help Beyond the Book

We hope you never need a lawyer. If you follow our urgings and create your own contracts, durable powers of attorney and wills, you may well escape the need for one. Still, there may come a time when you'll need one, especially if you and your lover want to become parents or co-parents, or have valuable assets and need complex estate planning. Other times, you won't need a lawyer, but you may want to look up a law yourself.

Here are some resources you can consult if you need more information or advice than this book provides.

A. Hiring a Lawyer

As a general rule, you should consider hiring an attorney if the amount at stake is high enough to justify the legal fees or if there is something the lawyer can do for you that you can't do or choose not to do yourself. There are many reasons you might want a hire a lawyer:

- to review the documents you've prepared using this book
- to complete more complex forms than we've provided
- to check your state laws on a particular subject
- to assist you in an adoption, or
- to represent you in a break-up or to obtain rights to a child you helped raise.

1. What Lawyers Can Do for You

There are three basic ways a lawyer can help you.

Consultation and advice. A lawyer can analyze your situation and advise you on your best plan of action. Ideally, the lawyer will explain all of your options so you can make the choice—for example, if you have a lot of assets and need a high-end estate plan. But keep on your toes. Some lawyers will subtly steer you in the direction they want you to go, often the one that nets them the largest fee.

Negotiation. The lawyer can help you negotiate —perhaps if you and your ex are in the midst of a nasty break-up. Some lawyers excel at negotiating— especially if they use that skill a lot in their practices.

Representation. For almost any situation involving children—adoption or a fight to see a child you've been co-raising—you may very well need a lawyer to represent you in court. You might also need representation in a property dispute if you've unsuccessfully tried every possibility to settle your break-up issues.

Bringing a Political Case

Whenever a lesbian or gay person is involved in a lawsuit because of her or his sexual orientation, it is possible to make the case a political forum for lesbian and gay legal rights. By treating your case as a "gay rights" case and seeking media coverage, you can turn an ordinary lawsuit into a political cause. This strategy can be seductive to you, and even more so to your attorney who can gain a great deal of publicity and notoriety from the case. But consider carefully whether making your case a political one is likely to achieve your goals or help other lesbians and gays. If your attorney raises the possibility, ask yourself if he's putting your interest, or his, first.

Making a discrimination case into a cause for civil rights can work—and the lesbian and gay community owes much of its legal advances to the brave men and women who have come out to fight.

In most "family" situations, however—especially those involving children—publicity and politicizing may be the worst possible strategy. Most cases granting joint or second-parent adoptions, and most cases where a lesbian or gay parent is awarded custody of or visitation with his or her child, have been done quietly, without stirring things up. This makes sense. To judges, the standard when dealing with kids is what is in their best interest, not what are the civil liberties of their parents specifically or gays in general. If your lawyer insists upon turning your petition for a joint adoption into the great gay case of the century, find a new lawyer.

And finally, keep in mind that political cases are often expensive and always exhausting. You run the risk of injuring your personal interests. We admire people who stand and fight injustice, but we urge you to avoid litigation if possible and, if not possible, to carefully consider before you embark on a political case. But if you do—more power to you!

2. How to Find a Lawyer

Finding a lawyer isn't a problem; the surplus is huge. But finding the right lawyer can be difficult. Make sure any lawyer you hire is familiar with the issues you bring to her—don't hire a bankruptcy lawyer to review your contract to buy a house. Also, any lawyer should be sympathetic to lesbians and gay men. In addition, many lawyers—gay or straight—have as their main goal living well, and you can guess who pays for the perks. So, check fees at the start. The lawyer you hire—female, male, gay, lesbian, straight, solo practitioner or member of a big firm—must fit your needs.

The best way to find an attorney is to ask your friends who they used and were pleased with for tasks similar to what you need. If that doesn't work, call a lesbian and gay legal referral line (often affiliated with a gay and lesbian community center or with the local legal bar association), or consult the resources listed in Section C, below.

3. What to Look for in a Lawyer

No matter what approach you take to finding a lawyer, here are several suggestions on how to make sure you have the best possible working relationship.

First, fight the urge to wholly surrender your problems to the "expert." You should be the one who decides what you feel comfortable doing about your legal affairs. Keep in mind that you're hiring the lawyer to perform a service for you; shop around if the price or personality aren't right.

Second, you must be as comfortable as possible with any lawyer you hire. A lawyer-client relationship should be one of trust and confidence. You should feel very comfortable coming out to your lawyer, and should do so at the outset. If your attorney doesn't meet your initial expectations, you have the absolute right to fire her and hire another lawyer.

When you talk with the lawyer, ask some specific questions. Do you get clear, concise answers? If not, try someone else. If the lawyer says little except to agree to take over your problem—with a substantial fee—watch out. You're talking with someone who doesn't know the answer and won't admit it, or someone who is likely to be paternalistic or pushy with you. If the lawyer admits he or she doesn't know an answer, that isn't necessarily bad. In most cases, the lawyer must do some research to find out how to best handle your specific situation.

Once you find a lawyer you like, make an appointment to discuss your situation fully. Most will agree to do this for a nominal cost. Your goal at this initial meeting is to find out what the lawyer recommends and how much it will cost. Go home and think about the lawyer's suggestions. If they don't make complete sense or if you have other reservations, call another lawyer and begin the search process anew.

4. How Much Lawyers Charge

The single most common area in which lawyers and clients have misunderstandings is over legal fees. Enter any relationship with a lawyer knowing that. You can help eliminate the chance of a fee dispute if you have a clear agreement in writing, signed by both of you. If the lawyer doesn't mention a written fee agreement, ask about one.

If all you want is a consultation with an attorney to find out your options, the lawyer should not charge more than $250 per hour. Some charge as little as $125 an hour, while others charge as much as $300 an hour or more.

If you want the lawyer to do some negotiating, the fee could pile up. A letter doesn't take that long to write, however, and as long as you are clear about what you want the lawyer to do and not do, you can keep the bill low.

If you hire a lawyer to represent you, the lawyer's fee will probably add up fast. A few lawyers might represent you for a flat fee, for example $1,000 to $1,500 for a routine adoption, but most

charge by the hour. If you enter into an hourly arrangement, it's best to add a cap beyond which the lawyer shouldn't work without your permission.

Hiring a lawyer solely to review your legal documents sounds like a good idea. It shouldn't cost much, and seems to offer a comforting security. Sadly though, it may be difficult, or even impossible, to find a lawyer who will accept the job. While this is unfortunate, we are not willing to excoriate lawyers who won't review a do-it-yourself document. From their point of view, they are being asked to accept what might turn into a significant responsibility for what they regard as inadequate compensation, given their usual fees. Any prudent lawyer sees every client as a potential occasion for a malpractice claim, or at least, serious later hassles —a phone call four years down the line that begins, "We talked to you about our living together contract and now ...." Many experienced lawyers want to avoid this kind of exposure and risk.

Also, many lawyers feel they simply don't get deeply enough into a situation to be sure of their opinions if they're only reviewing someone else's work. All you can do here is keep trying to find a sympathetic lawyer—or be prepared to pay more, enough so the lawyer can feel secure that she has been paid adequately to review your documents.

B. Doing Your Own Research

If you are not involved in contested litigation, you have an alternative to hiring a lawyer: Learn to do your own legal research. This book gives you a good start toward solving most of your legal problems, but many questions, especially peculiarities of state law, may not be answered. Why not research the subject yourself? It'll take time and diligence, and you may conclude it isn't worth the effort, but because lawyers charge $100 to $250 or more per hour, you might decide to give it a try. Often the work is not difficult.

1. Library Research

If you conclude that you need to visit a law library to answer your question, don't overlook librarians as valuable guides. Most law librarians in public libraries are very helpful, as long as you don't expect them to do the research for you. But they will be happy to help you locate the materials you need.

Here's what you should find in an average law library:

- the text of your state's laws
- published court opinions interpreting your state's laws, and
- legal articles containing explanations of laws.

Finding the Law

To do legal research, you need to find a law library that's open to the public. Public law libraries are often housed in county courthouses, state-funded law schools and state capitals. If you can't find one, ask a public library reference librarian, court clerk or lawyer. If there is no law library in your area open to the public, start your research at the largest nearby public library. Public libraries often have state codes and some major legal treatises.

Here are the basic steps to researching a legal question.

a. Statutes and Regulations

Once you get to the library, ask a librarian to help locate your state's statutes—called "codes," "laws" or "statutes," depending on the state. You'll want the annotated version, which contains the statutes, excerpts from relevant cases and cross-references to related articles.

Once you find the statutes, check the index for the subject of your concern. State statutes are often divided into sections. The major section is the Civil Code, which usually contains laws relating to contracts, living together, divorce, custody, adoption and credit. The Probate Code contains laws relating to wills and living trusts. There are other codes as well—insurance codes, real property codes, criminal codes and welfare codes. Each code is numbered sequentially, and once you get the code number from the index, it's easy to find the statute you need. If you have trouble, ask the law librarian for help.

Once you look at the statute in the hardcover volume, check the pocket part at the back of the book for any amendments. Then skim the summaries of recent court decisions contained in the Annotation section immediately following the statute itself. If the summary looks helpful, you'll want to read the entire case from which the summary was taken.

Legal Research: How to Find & Understand the Law, by Stephen Elias and Susan Levinkind (Nolo), can help you find your way around the law library.

b. Case Decisions

Judicial cases are printed in books called reporters. Interpreting a case citation is easy once you learn the abbreviations. For instance, the citation to the "Hawaii Marriage" case is *Baehr v. Miike*, 852 P.2d 44 (Hawaii 1993). What does this mean?

Baehr is the plaintiff—the person bringing the lawsuit—and Miike is the defendant—the state employee sued in his official capacity to defend the lawsuit. P.2d stands for Pacific Reporter—and 2d means the second series of these reporter volumes. The volume in which the case appears is the number before the name of the series; here you want Volume 852. The number after the reporter name is the page on which the case starts: here it's page 44. The parentheses contain the jurisdiction that decided the case and the year of the decision.

c. Other Resources

Another important library tool may be a legal encyclopedia, such as the ALR and Am. Jur. series. These are indexed by subject (such as custody, insurance, homosexuality, guardianship) and provide a synopsis of your state's law on the subject. Also, ask the law librarian to show you form books. These are collections of sample legal forms lawyers use in dealing with common legal tasks. Finally, ask if your state has any books designed to keep lawyers up-to-date. Most larger states have these practice manuals, which are fairly easy to use.

Unfortunately, however, the law for gay and lesbian couples is quite volatile and often hard to place into standard legal categories. For these reasons, doing legal research in this area can be particularly daunting.

2. Doing Research Online

Because much of the law dealing with gay and lesbians issues is new and changing fast, this area is particularly well suited to online research. In looking for information on your issue, you can check both general interest legal websites as well as sites that gather legal information of specific interest to gays and lesbians.

Below is a selection of general legal websites that can assist you in doing research.

- http://www.nolo.com. Nolo's website has a wide array of legal information for consumers, arranged by topics such as estate planning, family law and small business. You can also find links to state and federal statutes from the site.
- http://www.law.cornell.edu. The Legal Information Institute at Cornell Law School is one of the best organized and easiest to use general legal websites.
- http://www.findlaw.com. Findlaw's extensive database allows you to search for state and federal statutes and cases and provides links to many courts around the country.

In Section C, below, we list the contact information—including website addresses—for several national gay and lesbian organizations. The websites of these organizations often contain legal updates on issues covered in this book. In addition, here is a list of other websites that can guide you in your research.

- http://www.le-gal.org. This is a website sponsored by the Lesbian and Gay Lawyers Association of New York. This organization produces the *Lesbian and Gay Legal Notes*, which tracks national legislation and cases of interest to gays and lesbians. The Le-Gal site contains a link to archived editions of this publication.
- http://www.qrd.org/family. The family and parenting section of the Queer Resources Directory contains downloadable files and links on issues like same-sex marriage, domestic partnerships and gay and lesbian adoption and parenting.
- http://www.buddybuddy.com/toc.html. This is the site sponsored by the Partners Task Force for Gay & Lesbian Couples. The site contains information and links of interest to gay and lesbians partners, covering topics such as marriage, immigration and parenting.
- www.hrc.org This is the website of the Human Rights Campaign, a legislative advocacy group. The site contains news about legislation and court battles on the topics covered in this book, as well as on additional fights being waged in the gay and lesbian political community.

C. Lesbian, Gay and AIDS-Related Legal Referrals

Many national lesbian and gay legal organizations, local lesbian and gay bar associations and local lesbian and gay community centers make lawyer referrals. If there's no referral organization near you and you can't find a lawyer to help you with your problem, try calling one of the national organizations, or a local chapter of the American Civil Liberties Union (ACLU) or the National Lawyers Guild.

Someone on the other end of the phone may be able to give you the name of a local lawyer, or just offer a sympathetic ear. And if you have a lawyer, your lawyer may want to contact one of the national lesbian and gay legal groups to get some support. Many of the legal problems lesbians and gay men encounter have been faced before—a lawyer who fights for gay and lesbian rights full-time probably has helpful materials or suggestions.

1. National Lesbian and Gay Legal Organizations

American Civil Liberties Union (ACLU) National Gay and Lesbian Rights Project

132 West 43rd Street
New York, NY 10036
212-549-2500 (voice)
http://www.aclu.org

Gay and Lesbian Advocates and Defenders (GLAD)

294 Washington Street, Suite 740
Boston, MA 02108
617-426-1350 (voice)
http://www.glad.org

Lambda Legal Defense and Education Fund

National Office
120 Wall Street, Suite 1500
New York, NY 10005-3904
212-809-8585 (voice)
212-809-0055 (fax)
http://www.lambdalegal.org

Lambda Legal Defense and Education Fund

Midwestern Regional Office
11 East Adams Street, Suite 1008
Chicago, IL 60603-6303
312-663-4413 (voice)
312-663-4307 (fax)

Lambda Legal Defense and Education Fund

Southern Regional Office
1447 Peachtree Street, NE, Suite 1004
Atlanta, GA 30309-3027
404-897-1880 (voice)
404-897-1884 (fax)

Lambda Legal Defense and Education Fund

Western Regional Office
6030 Wilshire Blvd.
Los Angeles, CA 90036-3617
323-937-2728 (voice)
323-937-0601 (fax)

National Center for Lesbian Rights

870 Market Street, Suite 570
San Francisco, CA 94102
415-392-6257 (voice)
415-392-8442 (fax)
http://www.nclrights.org

National Gay and Lesbian Task Force

1700 Kalorama Rd., NW
Washington, DC 20009
202-332-6483 (voice)
202-332-0207 (fax)
202-332-6219 (TTY)
http://www.ngltf.org

2. Other Lesbian and Gay Organizations

The Lesbian and Gay Bar Association of Los Angeles (LHR)
P.O. Box 480318
Los Angeles, CA 90048
213-486-4443 (voice)

Bay Area Lawyers for Individual Freedom Gay/Lesbian Legal Referral Panel
P.O. Box 421983
San Francisco, CA 94142
415-956-5764 (voice)
http://www.balif.org

Gay and Lesbian Lawyers Association of South Florida (GALLA)
305-673-8988 (voice)
305-673-8668 (fax)

Gay and Lesbian Lawyers of Philadelphia (GALLOP)
P.O. Box 58279
Philadelphia, PA 19102
215-731-1447 (voice)

GAYLAW Attorney Referral
P.O. Box 76132
Washington, DC 20013-6132
202-842-7723 (voice)
http://www.gaylaw.org

Lesbian and Gay Bar Association of Chicago
3712 N. Broadway, Suite 415
Chicago, IL 60613
773-404-9574 (voice)
http://www.chilagbnc.org

Lesbian and Gay Law Association of Greater New York
799 Broadway, #340
New York, NY 10003
212-353-9118 (voice)
http://www.le-gal.org

Massachusetts Lesbian and Gay Bar Association
P.O. Box 9072
Boston, MA 02114
617-277-2101 (voice)
http://www.mlgba.org

Minnesota Gay and Lesbian Legal Assistance
P.O. Box 75224
St. Paul, MN 55175
612-879-1925 (voice)

New Mexico Lesbian and Gay Bar Association
P.O. Box 27438
Albuquerque, NM 87125-7438
505-243-6808 (voice)
505-247-4976 (fax)

3. AIDS Legal Referrals

If you need legal assistance and don't know where to turn, check your local telephone directory for an AIDS-specific legal organization, a Legal Aid or Legal Services office or your city or county's bar association. Many of those groups do AIDS legal referrals. You should also check with the national and regional gay and lesbian legal associations listed in the previous section. The American Bar Association maintains a clearinghouse for legal information about AIDS. Here is the contact information:

ABA AIDS Coordination Project
750 15th St., NW
Washington, DC 20005-1009
202-662-1025 (voice)
http://www.abanet.org/irr/aidsproject

Index